R.

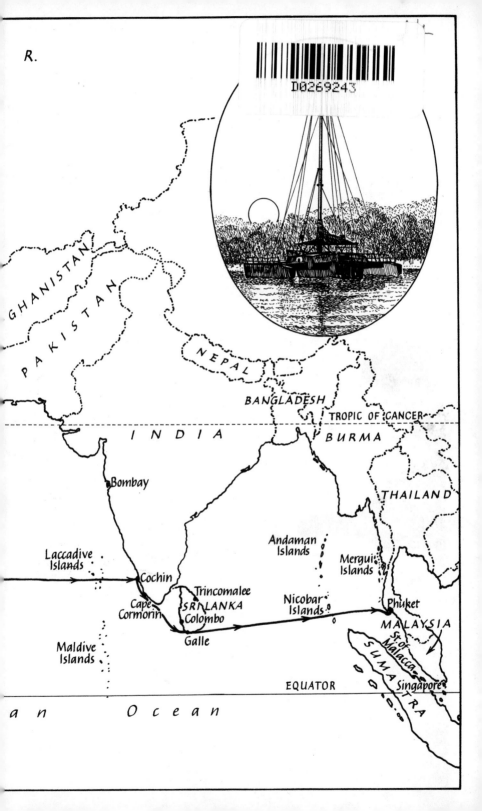

GHANISTAN

PAKISTAN

NEPAL

BANGLADESH

TROPIC OF CANCER

I N D I A

BURMA

THAILAND

Bombay

Laccadive
Islands

Andaman
Islands

Mergui
Islands

Cochin

Trincomalee

Nicobar
Islands

Phuket

Cape
Cormorin

SRI LANKA
Colombo

MALAYSIA

St. of
Malacca

Galle

S U M A T R A

Maldive
Islands

EQUATOR

Singapore

a   n   O c e a n

SOMEWHERES
EAST OF
SUEZ

SOMEWHERES EAST OF SUEZ

Tristan Jones

THE BODLEY HEAD

LONDON

British Library Cataloguing
in Publication Data
Jones, Tristan
Somewheres east of Suez.
1. Outward Leg (*Ship*)   2. Voyages and
travels——1951–
I. Title
910.4'5   G465

ISBN 0-370-31140-X

Printed in Great Britain for
The Bodley Head Ltd
32 Bedford Square, London WC1B 3EL
by Butler & Tanner Ltd,
Frome and London

First published 1988

To Henry Wagner of Sailor's Bookshelf,
his wife Joan, and his daughter
Sarah,
who
travelled a long way
to come and say farewell
to Outward Leg
when she left her native land
to cross an ocean

Foreword

In 1983, twenty-one months before this account commences, I set out from San Diego, California, in the thirty-eight-foot trimaran *Outward Leg*, on a voyage east-about the world north of the Equator, to the Far East. This, without doubt, is in the long run the most difficult of voyages, in every way. It was further complicated; my leg had been amputated due to an old wound, and I was setting off on a long sea voyage on one leg. In *Outward Leg* I sailed south to Panama, along the north coast of South America, north through the West Indies, and across the North Atlantic Ocean to England. That passage I describe in my book *Outward Leg*.

In October 1984 I hauled out of London, sailed for Holland, and up the Rhine to Nuremberg, where I was frozen in by the harshest winter Europe had known for fifty years. Thomas Ettenhuber joined me there as our mate. We hauled *Outward Leg* across to the Danube River and navigated that naturally and politically hazardous stream for seventeen hundred miles, down to the Black Sea. We then sailed our damaged craft to Istanbul, where this tale starts. That passage I described in *The Improbable Voyage*.

I had started the voyage to inspire other handicapped people, especially youngsters, to reach for their own star and achieve their own ambitions despite the obstacles, natural and man-made, placed before them.

By the time I fetched London I knew that this was presumptuous. I realize that much of my effort had been ineffective; my endeavors were being represented by the media (through whom in part I make my living and way forward) more as a marathon of my own achievement. This I did not need, and neither did the people for whom I was struggling. I concluded that the only way my dream could be realized was if I could discover and provide some way for the *handicapped themselves to participate in achievement.* In a small sailing craft, on a world voyage east-about, this was impossible. The only solution was to find some time and place where all the intricate, disparate skeins that would realize the dream might be brought together.

In every endeavor the two most vital elements in the equation of potential success are place and time. When I arrived in Turkey I knew the solution to the place element: where our Atlantis Society would set up its *home—western Thailand.* That left one other element to put in place: time. As this tale opens, there were only two members in the Atlantis Society—Thomas Ettenhuber and myself—and we had only thirty dollars between us in available cash. Why western Thailand? It was in the moderate, cyclone-free tropical climate of the west coast of Southeast Asia; it was stable, evidently; and it was reputedly *cheap.*

Our task, then, was to first find the place and means to refit our boat, write two books, sail *Outward Leg* for almost eight thousand miles, from Istanbul to western Thailand, and discover, obtain, and organize the means to bring the Atlantis Project to life. At Istanbul I set ourselves a year to do it. This story is about *why* we were, otherwise inexcusably, *tardy.*

Contents

Part Three: The Dawn Comes Up Like Thunder

Illustrations/Maps

Maps by Denys R. Baker based on drawings by Thomas
Andreas Nicolas Ettenhuber, 1987

List of illustrations

Photographs by Thomas Ettenhuber

Prologue

Ship me somewheres east of Suez, where the best is like the
  worst,
Where there aren't no Ten Commandments an' a man can raise
  a thirst;
For the temple-bells are callin' an' it's there that I would be—
By the old Moulmein Pagoda, looking lazy at the sea:
    On the road to Mandalay
    Where the old Flotilla lay,
    With our sick beneath the awnings when we went to Man-
    dalay!

    O the road to Mandalay,
    Where the flyin'-fishes play,
    An' the dawn comes up like thunder outer China 'crost the
    Bay!

                —Rudyard Kipling, "Mandalay"

A rannod, nef a gafas.
("Who has given, has seen heaven.")

The White Book of Ridderch,
Wales, A.D. twelfth century

There are four kinds of long-distance voyagers—
novices, retired, pessimistic—and dead!

—Tristan Jones,
On board *Outward Leg,*
Ao Chalong,
Phuket Island, Thailand,
February–April 1987

Part One

The Levant

The Levant

1

The Golden Horn

"How much?" I asked Thomas.

He was down in *Outward Leg*'s after cabin, leaning over the chart table, counting the few single-dollar notes in our cashbox.

"Thirty dollars."

"Any deutsche marks?"

"No . . . that's it."

"Mmm." I thought for a moment or two as I stared at the castle on the hill above the shore of the Bosporus. Then I shoved my head down the after companionway.

"Where's that Yankee embassy? Did you find the address?"

Thomas grinned up at me. His hair was streaked with white paint. He'd been painting the engine compartment. "It's not an embassy. I told you—it's a consulate. I don't have the address now. Dabney Chapman's coming down, anyway, at four o'clock."

"Who?"

"Dabney Chapman. He's the cultural attaché. His wife was here yesterday. They saw us arrive here from their house up on the hill. She was all excited. He's arranging a slide show for you at the consulate."

"Great. Roll up all our used charts, Thomas."

"?" He stared a question at me.

"Roll 'em up, me old son; and tie 'em up with a nice length of

blue tape. We'll take 'em with us and flog 'em." Then I remembered
Thomas was German. "Sell them, my son, sell them. Tomorrow
night at the United States Consulate the golden eagle's going to
shit all over *Outward Leg!*"

I supposed that for most travelers heading through Istanbul,
without much money, their main problems were finding a decent
hotel and cheap places to eat. Once those things were pinned
down, the rest must be fairly easy, apart from a few details like
navigating the crowded, noisy thoroughfares and winding alleys.

For we voyagers in *Outward Leg*, though, intent on somehow
reaching the Indian Ocean and the Orient, our problems in Istanbul
were of a different stamp: how to find a decent berth for the boat
where she wouldn't get bounced around by passing ferries and
merchant ships, where she wouldn't get covered in thick fuel oil,
where she wouldn't be invaded by hordes of Turks, young and
old, all eager to practice their scanty English, smoke our few cigarettes, and eat our meager food.

Not that there was much harm in most of our casual visitors,
but in every big city there's always the odd man out. Thomas and
I both kept one eye warily open the whole time we were in Istanbul.
In *Outward Leg* we paused in the Bosporus after our escape from
Rumania and worked as well as we could with our slim resources
to repair the ravages of our Danube passage, both natural and
man-caused.

We patched our damaged hulls and mast tabernacle sufficiently
well to enable us to get the boat to somewhere with the facilities
and the material to refit her properly, which wouldn't cost the
earth. That somewhere we reckoned, from all accounts, was
Cyprus.

Our main problem, then, was to reach Cyprus, but not before
I had gathered together enough money to pay for the refit. We
decided to do it under sail mainly (there would be little money for
diesel fuel), hopping along the coast of Turkey, where the cost of
living was lower than in Greece, and so we would do it in short
hops, taking our time.

We couldn't head out for the Far East through the Red Sea on
an eight-thousand-mile jaunt till we had *Outward Leg* and her gear
in a fit state. We had to have a refit, and we had to have the money
for it. Meanwhile, we would sail at a steady rate down the Turkish
coast, and I would set to writing and trying to earn our way forward.

Bebek, a resort on the shore of the Bosporus a few miles northeast of Istanbul city, where *Outward Leg* was first berthed, was crowded, mainly with Turkish xebecs. These are wooden craft, anything up to a hundred feet long, with usually a ketch or schooner gaff rig. During the time we were in Turkish waters we never saw one of them under sail, but always motoring, and very often with the stern gangway still swung out over the stern, no matter what the weather. The xebecs are the pleasure craft, mainly of rich Turks, their families, their friends, and their friends' families. It was a wonder to me, often, that the xebecs didn't sometimes capsize and sink under the weight of the crowds on board them. Some of the xebecs, belonging to the richest of the Turkish owners, had British skippers and crews to give them, at least in the eyes of the Turkish elite, extra prestige, if not panache.

Besides the xebecs in Bebek there were a few cruising yachts from afar—mainly British and German, although one or two Italian craft showed up, too, and, like *Outward Leg* and the xebecs, put out their main anchors into the Bosporus and tied up their sterns to the Bebek "seawall" so that the end result was a great variety of craft of all shapes, sizes, designs, and origins, all lined up cheek by jowl, in front of the seawall, jiggling and rolling in the wakes of passing ships.

Bebek was to us a friendly town, with plenty of little shops full of goodies and dozens of good, cheap restaurants. We found it a pleasant place, with fine scenic views over the Bosporus and the shipping, mainly Soviet, passing through the strait. We saw many interesting old castles and fortifications on the shores of the Bosporus near Bebek, but the port had three major drawbacks: It was crowded with craft, it was noisy from the highway which passed along the shorewall, and its waters were often inches thick in gooey black fuel oil.

At first we imagined that the fuel oil floating in the harbor came from passing ships, but later found that it was, in fact, pumped out of the tanks of a shoreside hotel right on the harbor, and that this was a regular occurrence.

The first money we earned for our onward passage was at the American consulate in Istanbul where we gave a slide show, courtesy of the cultural attaché, Dabney Chapman, of the voyage of *Sea Dart* down the west coast of South America twelve years before. That raised a hundred dollars, and the sale to various guests of some of *Outward Leg*'s used charts raised almost another hundred dollars. I hated to see the charts go: In the chart agent's, where they're all new, a chart is a chart is a chart; but in a voyaging vessel, when those charts have done their work, they represent intrinsically everything that happened, every emotion that was experienced, every reckoning calculated, every little incident that occurred on board during the time that the boat was sailing through the area depicted on the chart. Selling our used charts from the Caribbean, the Atlantic, and the Black Sea, to me, was like selling part of my very self, of my life.

But you can't eat used charts when you're broke on the coast of Turkey, so they had to go. Besides, every bit of weight counts in a cruising trimaran, and the charts weighed quite a few pounds. I felt bad about the charts going to hang on the walls of people who perhaps had little idea of exactly what they represented. But that was, I now realize, a better fate than what was to happen later to the rest of *Outward Leg*'s charts off the Zuquair Islands in the Red Sea.

The American officials in the consulate were kind and gave us sherry and cigarettes, and a new American ensign to take back on board with us. For these comforts we were indeed grateful.

Istanbul in mid-July was hot, and there was no fun in sweating it out every afternoon in an oily, crowded, noisy berth. We set out to find a more amenable anchorage, and after a couple of days' meandering up and down the Bosporus, we found a rare spot. This was just south of the railway station at Haydarpasa, on the Asian side of the Bosporus. It was lively with ferries coming and going day and night, but it was clean and safe, because the station landing steps were watched by Turkish soldiers. At first these were reluctant to let me land, but I regaled them with a joke or two and they let me pass freely after that.

Being on the "far" side of the Bosporus in Haydarpasa we had a panoramic view of the whole of the old city of Istanbul, with all the domes and minarets spread out before us; a lovely sight, and under the full moon a thing of dreams. And so *Outward Leg* arrived in Asia, her fourth continent on this voyage.

If I had been able-bodied, I suppose, I would have been chasing over to the city of Istanbul every day to see the sights. I did manage once to cross the Bosporus on a crowded ferry, but for me it was a difficult outing, and dangerous too, with the continual risk of being pushed over by the hurrying crowds on the swaying gangways, so after that one trip I stayed around Haydarpasa. I was quite happy to do this, for the railway station there is, I think, a marvel of a building, that certainly has the best views I have seen from a rail terminus. The meat pies were good, and cheap, too.

I could stand in the middle of the station and see the busy Bosporus all around, on three sides, through the massive doors. Then I could swing around and see steam trains limbering up for their journeys into and out of Asia. Then the platforms were crowded with peasants and merchants arriving loaded down with their goods. Now and again there would be a few European backpackers heading in and out for their great adventure. I used to watch them sometimes and reflect on how much easier their mode of travel was than ours, how much less complex; but at the same time, how much less rewarding it must be to be trundled around by other people, and have to sleep in someone else's bed every night. Then I would turn around and gaze through the station doors south toward Haydarpasa harbor, where *Outward Leg* waited at anchor, and know that my own home was there, only a few yards away, with my own bed and my own few belongings, but my home, and now my home was in the Bosporus. That's the main difference between voyaging in a sailing craft and any other form of travel, except, perhaps, Gypsy travel in a caravan. But even the Gypsies are, more often than not, on other people's land, whereas we, when we reach offshore soundings, are on nobody's water but our own.

Haydarpasa is not far from Scutari, where Florence Nightingale worked to nurse British soldiers during the Crimean War. I would have liked to visit the hospital where she worked, but it was beyond my range, without my risking a bad fall or being a burden on someone else, and that I won't be. There's enough people already being burdens on others. Besides, we couldn't afford to spend on frivolous outings.

It cost us nothing to sit sometimes in the park near the bus station and talk with the Turks: Outside of the upper-class people whom we met at the American consulate it was impossible to talk with Turkish women, unless they were whores, and we had neither the money nor the inclination to do that; so mostly our conversations were with men young and old, and for the greater proportion, "working class." We found that the few who knew some English had a good sense of humor, but were liable to exaggeration, and they generally approached a given point by the most oblique references. They were all past masters at simply idling away the time, talking about everything under the sun, or simply staying silent.

At the street stalls around the bus station we could eat good food, well cooked, and sufficient to keep us going, for a few cents. If we stuck to food made from local products, and native soft drinks, we could both live well enough on less than two dollars a day, and the anchorage cost nothing. Generally, we found this to be so all the way down the coast of Turkey, and we found the ordinary Turkish peasant and artisan to be good people, who treated us well and honestly. It was only to be in places south of Chesme, then, where "tourism" had seized onto everything around, and spoiled it, and brought opportunists, Turkish and non-Turkish, flocking like the vultures they are to the Aegean shores of Turkey, that we were to be dismayed or disappointed. But of this sad fact we were as yet unaware.

In Haydarpasa we made plans for repairing the three hulls, which had been damaged during *Outward Leg*'s besetting in the ice on the River Main, the previous winter, and again badly abraded when the Czech police in Bratislava had tried to sink her by setting her up for a collision in the River Danube. The gel coat had been cracked and even worn through in many places. Water had soaked into the sandwich filling of foam. This needed a specialized repair job with special materials. After weeks of inquiry in Istanbul it was obvious that these materials were not going to be available in Turkey.

By late July we were ready to set off down the Turkish coast. But of the $175 earned from the slide show at the consulate and the sale of charts, we had spent $45 in Haydarpasa, mainly on meals in the railway station and in the market in the thronged bus station nearby. This is how *Outward Leg* departed from Istanbul, on her way to the Far East, almost eight thousand miles away— still in need of a thorough refit of her hulls and rigging, but with a cargo of dreams, shining bright and steady, stowed below.

The bare facts of the matter were plain; we would have to stretch out our remaining $130, until my little naval pension was due, or until my earnings from some writing would catch up with me.

On the last day of July, after breakfast, I started up our Yanmar engine, and we weighed anchor, waved farewells to the lasses in the station restaurant (we were that close to them) and shoved off out of Haydarpasa harbor and south into the Sea of Marmara.

It was a hot day, and there was no wind. This was a foretaste of many days to come, it turned out. The Sea of Marmara was as flat as a billiard table. It was also filthy, oily and littered with rubbish. But we hardly noticed that, pleased as we were to be back at sea again and on our way. Astern of us the city of Istanbul faded dimly into the morning mists. Either side of us the far mountains showed low, Asia to port, Europe to starboard. Often, in the morning, narwhals played around the boat and reminded me of the dolphins, so far away in the North Atlantic. But these narwhals were not like the Atlantic sea-dogs; they had little of their flashing vibrancy; these Turkish narwhals were much more relaxed, and rolled over lazily, with a sigh, as if they were going to retire to a sofa and smoke a hookah. Thomas, with a grin, set a tape of "Bolero" on the player, and the music fitted the narwhals' movements, lethargic, rhythmic, *exactly*.

Mostly, we spent the morning identifying the mountains which loomed ahead of us, to the southeast, over Asia. This was good practice for Thomas as he studied inshore navigation. Some of the mountains, like Karadag and Adam Kaya Mutu, were very high, and reminded me of the Massif Central of Madagascar, far, far away, viewed from the Bay of Majunga. I didn't mention this to Thomas though, as he was too busy reckoning his bearings in the Sea of Marmara.

In the afternoon we sighted the island of Asmalikoy, and steered for it, so as to be able to enter the little port before dusk. The Strait of Gallipoli was no place to be in a small craft after dark. Shipping would be heavy, and the currents strong, although evidently there would be a good radio-beacon system. But Asmalikoy looked inviting, a tiny village set under the soft shoulders of the hills of its island, and our passage through the Sea of Marmara had been hot and tiring, so in we went.

It was almost suppertime when we tied up, again stern-first, against the little jetty, alongside a small fishing craft wearing a Turkish ensign. On board it was a prosperous-looking little old man who was sitting alone at a small table, being served his dinner by a middle-aged giant with a completely bald head, all dressed in white, even to his shoes. The old man hailed us in English and gave us quickly to know that his eldest son was living in California. He also insisted on pressing into our hands basins of what he assured us were iron pills and yogurt. Whatever it was, it was delicious. Soon Thomas and I were seated at the little old man's table on board his fishing craft, swapping fishing yarns. The old man was proud indeed of having reached the age of seventy-nine and I agreed that it was quite an achievement, especially as he lived in Istanbul, which is about one of the most hectic, hot, dirty, smoggy cities I'd ever been in. He laughed at this and said he liked me for my truthfulness.

As we returned to our own boat, the wonder of the full moon's rising over the sea off Asmalikoy was ruined by the loud racket blaring from a jukebox in the only café in the place, on the far side of the harbor.

I glanced over at the fishing boat and saw that the little old man was quietly playing patience, while his bald deckhand ate his supper at his own separate table. In their tiny craft—she was only twenty feet long—it was as if they lived on two separate planets.

The moaning, wailing, and banging from the café jukebox shook the night. My mind flew back a year or so, to my arrival in England at the end of the transatlantic passage. Then, at Falmouth, I had tried to telephone London to arrange for some money to be sent to me. It had been the same whining, whingeing voice blaring from a jukebox, back then, that had almost made the call impossible to make. I grunted, and set my mind again to getting east of Suez as soon as Christ would let me. Anything to get away from that moaning crap, that insult to anyone's ears who had a scrap of intelligence between them.

At midnight or so the noise from the café ceased, and I was left alone on deck with my thoughts, undisturbed at last, gazing at the moon sailing over the Dardanelles, and thanking the gods that I was not young enough to be fooled into thinking that crap was not crap.

We were to find that in the height of the tourist season in Turkey we would rarely be able to moor or anchor the boat out of earshot of dreary, mindless, neurotic, masturbatory, animalistic "Western" pop-junk issuing at the loudest volume imaginable from radios or jukeboxes. The farther south we went, and the more European holidaymakers were in evidence, the worse it was. We thanked God we could get away from it in the days at sea.

We sailed out of Asmalikoy the next morning and wound our way through the archipelago of islets off the northern entrance to the Dardanelles. There was a fair little breeze, from the northwest, and so we were able to clap on all working sail and the genniker and make a dead run against the current, which flows forever northward in those parts.

As we slowly pushed down the Strait of Dardanelles, I reflected on what Napoleon once said about it, that it was the most important stretch of water on earth. I told Thomas I didn't agree with Bonaparte, and especially where he was concerned. It was the English Channel that defeated him, not the Dardanelles. I also worked out that the name Dardanelles means "Gate of the Greeks" and that made sense, because holding the strait meant that the ancient Greeks, for centuries, were able to trade much more easily with northern and central Asia by sea rather than by the camel trails across Syria. As we pushed on slowly we talked of the Trojan War, in legend fought over Helen, which really had been a war to control this narrow channel between Europe and Asia, between the Mediterranean and the Black Sea, and about how Lord Byron had swum it, and of the adventures of Leander and the wonderful bridge built by Xerxes the Persian. We noticed how on the European side the scenery, of gentle green hills, was much like England, all green and tidy, so that it looked to be smiling, while on the Asian side it was like Wales, only even more wild and frowning. It was as if God, when he made these lands, had smoothed one side over with a trowel, looked at the clock, thrown the other side down onto the rocks of the earth, and gone off to lunch.

The boat was sailing well, even despite the weak breeze. So we ambled sedately south, keeping a wary eye on the many passing ships heading both ways, until we came off the entrance to the little port of Gelibolu, as Gallipoli is known to the Turks.

As we tied up at the jetty in Gelibolu, I noticed a small sloop lying already alongside. She looked a mite seaworn. Thomas and I took a closer look at her. The name on her transom gave out that she was *Yuki* and she hailed from Tel Aviv. This was interesting to me, because years before, when I had crossed over Israel in the yawl *Barbara*, there had been no sailing yachts capable of cruising abroad at all in the country. I recalled how *Barbara* had been the cynosure of every eye in Israel when she had moored in Haifa and crossed over to the Dead Sea.

I had just started to return on board *Outward Leg* when the owner of *Yuki* turned up. He was a man in his early thirties, and he introduced himself as Nino. He was accompanied by two companions, a young man and a woman. They had, he said, cruised from Haifa to Cyprus, across to Turkey, then coast-hopped all the way to the Dardanelles, but this was as far as they would go, before they turned back to head again home. They would leave the boat here and visit Istanbul overland, because of the sudden rough storms in the Sea of Marmara and the difficulty of finding a decent berth in Istanbul. Nino said that he had heard years before of the passage across of *Barbara* in 1970, and read of it later in *The Incredible Voyage*, which pleased me greatly. One of the greatest rewards for much hard labor is to know that your boat, and her voyages, are remembered. To me it is far more important than any other rewards, which anyway are mainly ephemeral.

No sooner had I left Nino on the jetty than I was accosted by two armed officials of the Turkish Immigration Police. Brusquely they requested my "Transit Log." This was a piece of paper which was issued, against payment of a fee, to every foreign yacht entering Turkish waters. This was fine if the yacht entered the usual way, on the west or south coasts of Turkey. But, amazingly enough, there had been no provision made at all for yachts entering Turkey from the Black Sea. To cut a long tale sideways, they said *Outward Leg* had been in Turkish waters illegally for almost two months! I showed the officials the crew list, which I'd had the foresight to have signed by the U.S. consul in Istanbul. Eventually, after much muttering by the Turkish officials, their chief, a short, fat man, sweating in the heat, arrived. He immediately confiscated our passports, despite my protests that this was illegal. I also showed him the written proof of our arrival in Istanbul from Customs in the Bosporus, and also our signed crew list, but all to no avail: Thomas and I were peremptorily ordered by the fat chief to the local police station, and marched there under armed escort through the town, the chief bringing up the rear of our procession, a smug look on his red face. The townspeople stared and glared at us, as if we were condemned murderers as we wended our way slowly through the crowded main square. We had to go slowly because of my hobble.

Inside the police station we were both told to sit on a hard bench and given a cup of strong coffee, while every official in the place helped himself to our cigarettes. Then we waited for the chief to decide on our fate, and everyone else sat around silently drinking strong coffee.

After a couple of hours in silence, apart from the whirring of fans and low coughing from the direction of the cells, everyone started at the noise of excited yelling outside in the roadway. Thomas and I stared at each other, not knowing what to expect. Shortly afterward a young man, waving a copy of an Istanbul newspaper, ran in, breathless, grinning and pointing at us.

Then he broke into English: "You are in the paper!" he shouted.

He was right. We were in the paper. We'd been interviewed in Istanbul by a young lady whom we'd met at the American consulate. She'd asked me what I thought of Istanbul and I told her about the oil and filth in Bebek harbor. I'd also asked that the newspaper publish this story about now, when we would be safely out of the Istanbul area!

But it did help. It soon brought the chief Customs officer out of his hidey-hole, apologizing, and shortly afterward a flunkey from the mayor's office with an invitation to tea with the town officials. The mayor issued us a safe-passage chit, so that we could reach Çanakkale, the next port along the Dardanelles, where Transit Logs were issued. Then he presented *Outward Leg* with a small plate, inscribed with the name of Gelibolu, as a memento of our visit, and I gave him one of our remaining used charts. His plate yet hangs in the main cabin of our boat. After the presentation the mayor, the Customs chief, the police chief and at least a dozen officials all paraded back to where *Outward Leg* was berthed, right through the town, all happy, smiling and triumphant.

Which goes to show, I suppose, the power of the press—at least in Turkey. The mayor was so effusive in his apologies to us for our reception in Gelibolu that he sent a Customs officer along to sail with us to Çanakkale, to make sure that we would be treated right.

That's the first and only occasion when I sailed with a Customs officer on board my boat. He was seasick in the Dardanelles—*in a trimaran!*

2

The Wine-Dark Sea

Çanakkale turned out to be, among other things, a Turkish naval base. It also had a tiny, but well appointed, yacht jetty. As we slowly pulled into the harbor, I spied a couple of British yachts. Two gunboats were tied up at the naval berth. When *Outward Leg* went alongside, a half-dozen young sailors rushed along cheerfully to help tie us up. We exchanged pleasantries with them and gave them a few cigarettes; then we trotted, or hobbled in my case, along the dust-blown waterfront with the Gelibolu Customs official, now recovered from the rigors of his three-hour passage across the Dardanelles, to the vast Immigration Hall. There we were treated civilly, although again the officials all helped themselves to our cigarettes in exchange for their coffee.

In an hour or so we had a proper, official, stamped and sealed Turkish government Yacht Transit Log, all green and new and inscribed with line after line of neatly penned handwriting, which, we were informed, told of our movements to date in Turkish waters.

One official, a lean, blond man who looked more Teutonic than Turkish, spoke with Thomas in excellent German. He said that *Outward Leg* was the first trimaran that had ever visited the Dardanelles. But the Turks, I had observed, are great dissemblers, so I doubted him. In retrospect, though, he might have been right; *Outward Leg* had been a curiosity all the way through the Bosporus and the Sea of Marmara. We would not, it turned out, encounter another trimaran until we were well into the Aegean Sea.

Back on board *Outward Leg* I went below to stow away our logbook, passports, and sacred Transit Log. I heard Thomas moving about on deck above my head. Suddenly the air was pierced by a woman's voice, demanding in a grating, tortured Oxford accent, so-called, "Ai sai, whai is youah skippah flaying the American fleg?" The voice screeched, obviously at Thomas. There was no "Hello" or "Good afternoon." I could hear her plainly even over the noise of the machinery on board the gunboats.

I grimaced to myself at the sound of the Voice that Lost the British Empire. For a heart-wrenching moment I thought that it might even belong to Maggie Thatcher, or even worse, Sissie St. John, the bishop's sister. Shaking, I peered through the cabin window. No, it was only, evidently, a regular British ex-colonial "lady" wearing knee-length shorts and a face like a hatchet—the kind that now calls itself "expat," instead of good old British.

Later we saw that she was from a British yacht close by, which was wearing a blue ensign, so we knew what that was all about. For those of us not familiar with British flag-practice, it meant that the owner of the yacht was either a serving or retired British armed forces officer, or that he belonged to a Yacht Club with a Royal Warrant to use the Blue Ensign. Among the British it's a status symbol.

My deckhand was down below in a flash. His English was far better now than it had been on the headwaters of the Danube, but still his accent was a mite thick. "Zere bin ein English voman and she vant to know vy you have der American flag?" he demanded. I won't try to write Thomas's way of speech, then, again. My ears ache to remember it.

I recalled San Diego and outfitting *Outward Leg* there, me only four months off the operating table, and running the gauntlet in Colombia, and how she was beset in the ice for a hundred days and nights in Germany, and how she'd worn her ensign through the Iron Curtain itself on May Day last, and how she'd been cheered all the way through much of Eastern Europe. But all I replied was: "Tell her *I'm* not *flying* it; *Outward Leg* is *wearing* it, and she's bloodywell *earned* it!"

Thomas clambered aloft again to do as he was bid, and typically repeated exactly what I'd said. That was the last of that particular biddy, or of anybody from her yacht, which suited us fine. The last thing a skipper needs is some "superiah," class-conscious, nationalistic, status-minded, narrow-visioned dabbler questioning his vessel's ensign. If the woman had looked at *Outward Leg*'s stern she would have seen her port of registry—SAN DIEGO, CALIFORNIA—not only in the Latin alphabet but in Cyrillic, too. Then, perhaps, we would have had a pleasant encounter, but I suspect not; she looked a real dragon.

Next day we slipped early for Bozcaada Island, which lies just outside of the southern mouth of the Dardanelles, in the Aegean Sea. It was a fine day, with a few clouds to moderate the heat and a stiff westerly breeze, so we crowded sail and let her fly. Now, even against the strong northerly current, we made a good eight knots, on a close reach. One advantage to being broke in a multihull is: The less stores you have on board, the less weight—and the faster you go. I think the weightiest thing on board then was the Atlantis dream; that weighed heavily on me all right.

Now to our starboard was a phallic World War I memorial, to commemorate the thousands of young men from the British Commonwealth, especially Australia, and their Turkish counterparts, who were slaughtered thereabouts so uselessly.

There was a Turkish gunboat anchored on the Asian side of the mouth of the Dardanelles, and she, with her crew running aft to lower her ensign, answered our own lowered flag. Courtesy costs nothing, so we could afford it.

At the very mouth of the Dardanelles there was a big, old dolphin swimming to and fro, a real sea dolphin, patrolling the waters, back and forth, back and forth, his back shimmering silver in the oily-calm water, probably watching for a ship to escort up the strait. . . .

Then the land, low, dropped away from either side of us, and the European continent with it, and we felt free, at last, at long, long, last, of the chains of the narrow waters that had fettered *Outward Leg* for most of the time since she had entered the Dutch canal system, twenty-two hundred miles and almost a year before. Now, to a much greater degree, the horizons of all the world opened up before us. Now we could choose our country of destination. Now we were again voyagers, and no longer mere travelers heading from one point to another along a fixed, immutable route. From here we could, should we desire, sail for a dozen different lands, and be at no one's behest. That is the significance of the Dardanelles. Now, indeed, we were sailing in Homer's "wine-dark sea," the waters of the home of the gods.

Bozcaada was inviting. A small island of low hills, it looked deceptively friendly. It lay a couple of miles off the Turkish coast, opposite the ruins of Troy. We entered the cozy haven, set among scrub-covered hills. There were two small fishing boats, but otherwise the port was empty. There was a well-built, obviously new, jetty. So we tied up to it, and were met by Turkish soldiers toting rifles.

Through sign language mainly, the Turks let us know that if we wanted to stay we must surrender our passports while we were on the island. I refused; unless we were suspected or accused of committing an offense, it was illegal, under international law, for anyone to keep our passports. Instead I offered them our Turkish Transit Log. They were adamant—no passport, no stay.

I was adamant, too. We'd been through this game so often behind the Iron Curtain I was damned if I would surrender our passports now. If I'd been right in Rumania, then I must also be right in Turkey.

The Turks told us that Bozcaada was a "military island," and that they were worried about Greek designs on the place. I looked around at the barren, sun-scorched hills overlooking the port, the few poor whitewashed cottages clinging to the hillside like shipwreck survivors, and a half-dozen skinny goats nibbling at what sparse scraps of vegetation were left, and concluded that any Greek who wanted to seize this place must be either blind or crazy.

We made ready to leave Bozcaada. I couldn't get angry with these Turks. They were a brave, manly-looking lot, even if a bit worn-down at the heels, and the whole argument had been good-natured. But I couldn't back down on a matter of principle which I'd maintained so much in Eastern Europe. It's a principle worth any island on earth.

We slipped our lines then, and *Outward Leg* headed off again down the Turkish coast, standing out about a mile to clear offlying hazards.

"They were very nervous, eh?" observed Thomas.

"Wait 'til the oil prospecting starts," I replied. We'd spied an oil rig under construction in Çanakkale. "Then the balloon'll go up all right. The Turks will have to do it in the wintertime, or the tourist trade will be ruined.

"You mean with the pollution?"

"No, I mean the Greeks will start shooting."

Now, in the mid-afternoon, the wind had freshened and was blowing at around twenty-five knots from the northwest. Our course was south, so we were on a quarter-run. This, for *Outward Leg*, was the first real, open-sea sailing, with a fair wind, that she'd had since we had been in the North Sea, almost a year before. We set the Aries wind-vane steerer and let her leap to the seas, while under our lee the gentle hills of the Turkish coast swept by.

Around early dusk we rounded Cape Baba and, in smooth water, went to anchor at Sivrice, off a moonlit fishermen's hamlet, in the northwestern corner of the bay. There we found good holding ground.

As we expected, the wind backed round to the east during the night, but it was very slight, and caused us no anxiety. We had caught a large fish in the late afternoon, with our trolling line, and no sooner were we anchored than Thomas had supper ready; fish-and-chips and cocoa, then we turned in. I slept well, fed sufficiently and knowing that our passports were on board, safe.

At dawn we pushed on down the coast of Anatolia, past the island of Lesbos, where cottages perch a thousand feet up the steep mountainside. We could not call there; that would have meant leaving Turkish waters, entering Greece, then later having to reenter Turkey, and spending money on another Turkish Transit Log, or getting yet more stamps impressed in the one we already had.

This manipulation of voyagers in transit was new; it wasn't mere registration anymore, nor even extortion for passage. Now it was full-blown manipulation of location and direction; attempts at enforcing where we could go and where we could not. Turkey was by no means the only culprit. Bureaucratic control of cruising craft was spreading all over the world. Worse still, it was being accepted without protest by people who should have known better. One of the reasons for it, so far as I could see, was that there had been so many novices and button pushers going to sea now, that everything, they imagined falsely, could be automated for them, as they had no idea of their rights and the proper, time-honored procedures between authority and seafarers. So the Turkish "tourist" coast, south of the Dardanelles, as well as many other coasts and sea-areas, and especially in the Third World, but worst around the Mediterranean, were little more than vast Dodg'em tracks for shuttle-service charter-boat "captains" who kowtowed to Authority, which, in many parts of the so-called developing world, was, in effect, managed by gangsters. In Turkey, the fact that the rules and regulations were posted on flashy signboards in every yacht-haven and quoted Turkish law didn't make them any less extortionate. Some of the "rules," by the standards of international maritime law, were illegal, too. For instance the "regulation" that made it an offense to anchor outside of Kusadashi harbor, *no matter for what reason*. That was a load of codswallop, invented by cash gougers.

By international law any vessel could shelter anywhere she could find safety, for twenty-four hours, without notifying Authority, if that was not possible—even in Soviet waters. That was the rule, and any nation which infringed it risked having its own vessels banned from navigating the waters of more civilized nations.

What a difference from the last time I was in Turkey, in *Barbara* in 1970. Then there were no rules or regulations posted up at all, and uniformed officials were hardly ever seen, and all the Turkish muggers and con men and thieves were in Istanbul and Ankara, where they belonged. And most of the charter-boat "expat" "captains" were at school, or on the dole.

We sailed on, and anchored or tied up every evening in a different port. A few havens, where the charter "flotillas" (!) and the "Mediterranean cowboys" had not yet reached, were peaceful, charming, and cheap, as they had always been, and some were loud, crowded, noisy, filthy and much more expensive.

In one little haven after another, once lovely, now raped and pillaged by the "tourist" interests, my reaction was mostly disapppointment, to compare the scene now to what it had been only a few short years before. I tried to find some exoneration for whoever had done this. After all, I told myself, the "tourists" had to have —were entitled to have—somewhere scenic to go to on their holidays; but surely to God, I asked myself, couldn't it all have been done better than this spreading, along a once-lovely coast, of lines of ugly concrete buildings surrounded by makeshift rural slums?

Soon, as we passed from one despoiled area to the next, my disappointment turned into despair, then rage, so that by the time we reached Rhodes I was so disgusted that I swore never again would I ever sail on the coasts of the Mediterranean. Rather, I would prefer to remember them as they once were, only two short decades before, peaceful, serene and majestic, before Mammon blighted them for all time. There was, except in a very few rare, precious places, which shall be nameless here, simply no joy in the havens of the Middle Sea south of Lesbos—only the continual, insistent, boring, and ultimately destructive chasing-after-the-tourist-dollar, not only ashore in the ports and all along the shore, but even, God help us, at sea as well.

With the advent and dissemination of push-button navigation, the hucksters had discovered "easy" money-making in the yacht-charter industry. Now they bent their cheap minds to persuade and con the urban West to "get away from it all"—and the urban West took "it all" right to what were very recently some of the most beautiful places on the face of the earth and committed irreversible ruin. I felt, and still do, that whoever was responsible should be arraigned for vile crime.

Many of the "expatriate" so-called charter captains on the west and south coast of Turkey were not fit to be in charge of a rowboat on the Serpentine. I have rarely, if ever, seen such a crew of incompetents and phonies. Very often it was obvious that some of them didn't know the sharp end from the blunt. Ashore, in the resorts, they were to be clearly recognized as they swaggered along with their earrings and tattoos—their uniforms, in some cases. They looked to me more like the cast of a musical comedy than people who were, after all, expected to be at times responsible for the lives of their guests. The generic name for these characters, among serious sailors, not only in Europe but the world over, was "Mediterranean cowboys." Use that phrase and every sailor from novices onward would know exactly the kind of person you were describing. But I thought the name "cowboy" bestowed on these specimens of detritus washed up on the shores of the Middle Sea in the wake of "tourism" was an insult to the good, kind, and gentle cattlemen I had met in Wyoming, Texas, and Colorado.

Thomas and I spoke with a few of these "Mediterranean cowboys." Most of their conversation, we found, consisted of accounts of how much they had ripped off from the last charterers or the owners of the yachts, or what woman they were offering a free ride in exchange for sexual favors, or where drugs could be obtained cheapest.

Among the professional charter-skippers that we encountered on the coasts of Turkey, Rhodes, and Cyprus, there were more than a few exceptions, good sailors and true, and they stood out like planets in the night sky. But very few of the "navigators," who on the Aegean coasts "led" the flotillas of "bare-boat" charter yachts, had any idea of navigation, coastal or otherwise, we found on talking with them; mostly they steered by guess and by God from one island to the next, using a series of photographs of the islands supplied to them by the Turkish agents for the owners. They "led" the flotillas—sometimes up to a dozen yachts, often wholly crewed by novices who, as they themselves told me, had never in their lives been in a boat under sail or otherwise. What would happen if a "levanter" blew up, as it sometimes does, without any warning, when these boats were being "led" from one island to another over a wider stretch of water by people who, as they themselves freely admitted, could hardly navigate around a bathtub, we could hardly imagine. As for the "leaders," in my view, they were mostly either starry-eyed "romantics" being themselves taken for a ride as cheap labor by the flotilla owners, who chose them for their "personalities," or they were nothing better than otherwise unemployed dead-legs, layabouts, moneygrubbers, and plain hustlers. I wouldn't have advised anyone to cross a duck pond with most of them, especially if their electronics didn't work.

Alibey, which was once a tranquil hamlet, was wholly given up to "tourism." Food tents and coffee stalls lined the waterfront; their jukeboxes blared all evening. The port's main saving grace was a lovely old teahouse, used by the fishermen, which was sedately but stoutly resisting the march of "progress," and an interesting old caïque-building yard.

In Alibey *Outward Leg* met up with her first fellow-American yacht since she departed the Azores, a year before. This was the sloop *Spirit of Pippin*. Thomas and I went to her in our dinghy, but no one was on board. We left a note and wished the crew well.

Next day we sailed forty miles to Ayvalik, through the Mytelini Channel. It was smooth, fast sailing. On every passage along the Turkish coast, Thomas practiced celestial navigation, in preparation for our coming voyage east.

Ayvalik made the last port of call seem positively peaceful. There was a fairground, in full noisy swing, spread out a mile along the waterfront. We shifted farther down the bay and anchored away from the row of the raucus crowds of Turkish "tourists" in the town.

At Badlemi, off the island of Garipa, about eighteen miles south of Ayvalik, we met our first trimaran since leaving Newport, Rhode Island. She was the ketch *Lady Jolliboy* out of Berwick-upon-Tweed,

in northeast England. The owner and his wife were on board and
most welcoming, and for the first time since leaving London we
had proper tea and cakes in the afternoon, before we all piled into
a dinghy and visited a hot spring nearby on the shore. There, in
lovely surroundings, we bathed in sulfurous water heated naturally
to around 100 degrees Fahrenheit. A Turkish Peeping Tom, an
elderly, erstwhile goatherd, spied at us from through a hole in the
flat roof of the bath house.

Badlemi and the next port, Saip, were the last places we found
on the Turkish coast that had not, then, been upturned, overhauled, capsized, and thoroughly spoiled by "tourism." In Saip,
one of the prettiest havens in the world, the people, especially the
young people, mainly Turks on holiday from the interior of the
country, were friendly, hospitable, and charming. Which is much
more than can be said for many places farther down the coast of
Turkey.

Day after day we made our way down the Turkish coast, now
spoiled beyond recognition from what it had been only a few years
before. Our only real enjoyment was to get out to sea, away from
the grind of mammon, which was so busy ashore it could be *heard*
a mile away at sea. But farther offshore, each day was as beautiful
as the one before, every view as scenically wonderful as the next.
Even yet, whenever we escaped from the money-chasing madness
ashore, we heard the songs of the sirens of the Sea of Ulysses,
unchanged and eternal; perhaps.

Through the Egri Liman channel *Outward Leg* flew, to Chesme,
there to shelter from a four-day northwesterly gale. We did not
idle. Besides regular maintenance chores, Thomas mastered *Taking
the Distance Off by Sextant Angle* by measuring the height of the
castle on the port and so reckoning our distance from it. He was
worried about slight discrepancies of a few feet or so in his results.
I explained they were caused by the swinging of *Outward Leg* at
anchor; each time she swung around, the distance between the
castle and his position on board would vary slightly.

After the gale cleared we sailed on, east now, to Sigasik, where
our anchor dragged several times; then to Kusadashi. This once
was a sleepy little fishing port. Now the harbor has been extended
by a mile or so of ugly concrete, fenced off, and called a "marina."
There the "expats," male, female, and everything else, were operating at full spate and in strident voice, and the place had been
changed into a garish, almost obscene-looking monstrosity. I went

for a stroll in the town, got as far as the "marina" gate, with its
armed guards, saw, heard and smelled the roaring traffic, and
returned on board. The noise of the traffic followed me into my
cabin, so I turned Beethoven's Fifth on at top volume, relaxed, and
let the music roll over me, to wear down, a little, my disappointment and my rage.

One night in Kusadashi was enough, but the "marina" insisted
on charging *Outward Leg* for a four-day stay. "That," stated an
aggressive young English lady "expat"—who seemed to have as
much idea of voyaging under sail as I have of making Caerphilly
cheese—"is the regulation."

On we sailed, pockets picked, chaste and chastened, through
the Samos Strait to Karakoyu, which once had been a green, deserted oasis, but was now lined with rows and rows of tawdry
sheds blasting out pop "music" day and night. Then to Gumusluk,
once a beautiful, remote, safe haven, now yet a safe haven, although half the harbor was roped off to make a great reserve for
roaring speedboats to haul water-skiers round and round, for hour
after noisy hour. Then on to Bodrum, crowded with charter yachts
in the harbor and "tourists" in the town, which was itself jammed
with hordes of holidaymakers and brigades of exhaust-spewing
trucks, cars and motorcycles day and night.

In the port of Bodrum the "expat" charter "captains," mostly
German and British, were within a fingernail of full command, so
Outward Leg shifted to anchor outside the port, to Gumbet. There,
next dawn, we surprised a thief stealing our dinghy. Thomas gave
chase, but the thief reached the shore very fast and shot off into
thorny scrub.

A Turkish doctor, in his xebec nearby, later told me that the
dinghy stealer was "probably a Communist trying to escape from
Turkey to Greece." But I thought that was more Turkish dissem-
bling. I thought the bastard who tried to steal our dinghy was a
plain, old-fashioned, dishonest, stealing, greedy *thief*. I thought he
was following, as best he could, the example set him by the "tourist" industry operators all around. The good doctor's excuses for
a Turk stealing might be good enough for some TV-fed "tourist,"
but not for ocean sailors. The ocean tells us, always, there's only
good or bad, right or wrong, and nothing in between.

Next day we pushed on, first to Knidos, a remote bay, which
was once tranquil but was now a den of Turkish charter xebecs.
These were positively a hazard when they went to anchor and

pushed in full speed anywhere regardless of who was already at anchor, or what damage they might have wreaked. One sight of their behavior and we were off again, this time to Kadirga Liman, a small fisherman's bay, well protected, close to Marmarice.

No sooner had we dropped our hook than a big French charter yacht motored in. Before long the scene was like the *Folies Bergères*, with naked people, men and women, all over her decks.

"That's all right in Paris, I suppose," I observed to Thomas, who was staring at the French, "but surely not in a Turkish anchorage, the home of devout Muslim fishermen and their families."

Thomas was grinning at me as my Welsh Nonconformism came out.

"I wonder what these buggers would feel if, when they were back home, a crowd of naked Turks suddenly appeared prancing around in their suburb?"

Thomas, who had been through quite a few French suburbs, said he thought it would be a real improvement, and sent me below, shaking my head, but he shut me up.

Marmarice was next; windy, crowded, noisy, expensive, unfriendly, and the anchorage choppy. We left after only an hour and found a quieter spot off Nimara, across the bay. There we slept the night before sailing the twenty-five miles south to Rhodes.

When we fetched Rhodes, we had sailed so far seven hundred miles from Istanbul, called at a dozen havens, and spent a hundred dollars in the thirty days of steady passage making. The biggest single chunk gouged out of our cash had been the four-nights-for-one "bargain" at the Kusadashi "marina." Apart from that, our food bill had come to twenty-eight dollars all the way from Istanbul. That was because we had used a lot of the older food stores on board, and had streamed the trolling lines out for fish at every opportunity. Of the seven hundred miles, we had motored only forty-five.

Rhodes, too, was crowded, noisy and the harbor water was filthy with oil, garbage and ullage (waste) from three hundred or so yachts tied up three or four deep, stern-to, in the harbor. But here there were mostly regular cruising sailors—a much better breed than the charter cowboys on the Turkish coast. Ashore, Rhodes seemed a madhouse of long crocodile-lines of "tourists" —northern Europeans, mostly, being led from one "tourist attraction" to the next by guides, many of whom, from what I could overhear, knew as much about the history of Rhodes as I did about Hardy Amies's dress designs.

But luck was ours in Rhodes. First, we squeezed *Outward Leg* into a berth only a few yards from the main post office (important on one leg); second, we had news waiting for us of income earned, the last payment of the British advance on the book *Outward Leg*; and third, we had friends there, who wined and dined us ashore. The temptation to stay awhile in Rhodes, visiting our friends' cottage, was great, but our minds were set on getting on our way. We now had enough money for the refit in Cyprus. I also had another book to write—*The Improbable Voyage*—the advance for which would help pay for our long voyage east from the Mediterranean to the Orient. Rhodes harbor was no place for me to write a book; but I knew of a place with a good harbor, and quiet, only a hundred miles away, which might yet not be spoiled—God willing.

With high hopes, and with most of the moored yachts in Rhodes harbor very kindly sounding their sirens and whistles for *Outward Leg*'s departure, we sailed a hundred miles east from Rhodes on 13 September, and found that we were again in luck. We fetched Kastellorizon Island on the fourteenth, and there, in a lovely, almost deserted harbor, surrounded by a grave-silent, long-ruined, ghost town, I wrote the book *The Improbable Voyage* in twenty-eight days. Within a week of receiving the typescript of the book, my British publishers, bless 'em, had paid into my bank account the advance due. So by October 31, 1985, *Outward Leg* was set to sail for Cyprus, at last to have her overdue refit, and I had the wherewithal—but only just—to head through Suez, and get ourselves that much closer to the realization of our dream of Atlantis.

3

Notice: Europe Starts Here

On the hundred-mile passage east from Rhodes to Kastellorizon we had little wind. All hot afternoon and all night long, *Outward Leg* was plagued by flies; hundreds of thousands of what seemed to us to be ordinary houseflies. Their cause mystified us, until the breeze sprang up next morning. Then the daylight showed us the Taurus Mountains marching north of us, and that we were over-hauling a small coaster, also heading east. She could have been making no more than a knot. As we approached her stern we saw her Greek ensign, and what looked like smoke belching out of her funnel.

It was only when we were within a cable's length of her that we saw—heard also—that she was carrying a deck cargo of sheep. Their bleating carried over the noise of her engine and her slowly thrashing propeller, and the cloud we saw, and swatted continually, were flies plaguing the sheep. The cloud of flies was thick enough to make the ship appear to us to be in darkness, even though the sun was shining broadly. The stink astern of the ship was enough, and more, to send us bowling south, five miles off our course, to get away from the stench.

We tried to imagine what life must have been like for that Greek coaster's crew, and pitied them, even though we ourselves were suffering badly. We must have been a good ten miles away from the ship before the buzzing of the host of flies eased off, and the horde diminished to the usual squadron of affectionate flies found anywhere on or around the Mediterranean Sea.

Kastellorizon, I thanked the gods, was much as I remembered it from the voyage of *Barbara* in those waters back in 1970. It was a small island, no more than a couple of miles around its rocky shores, which lay about two miles off the Turkish coast. On its north side a large bay, sheltered from the hard onshore winds in winter, faced the mountains of the coast of Anatolia, and the bay was almost surrounded by an old town, then almost completely in ruins, which was spread along the base of the steep hills which surrounded the bay.

Long ago, the Genovese colonized Kastellorizon for use as a port of call by their traders with the East. Windwise, before the days of steamships, it had been ideally placed for that; sailing coasters could use the onshore breezes during the day and the offshore wind at night, to reach it, and once in the harbor they were safe, not only weatherwise, but also from pirates and other predators, who, in the old days, infested those waters.

Around 1900, as an old photograph we saw on the island showed, hundreds of sailing ships made Kastellorizon their home port. Then steam muscled in and sail, within a few years, almost withered away. But Kastellorizon remained an Italian colony on and off, and between the world wars Mussolini had a seaplane base built there, mainly as an attempted counterweight to British and French power in the eastern Mediterranean.

When Italy surrendered to the Allies, in 1943, first the British Navy moved in and evacuated all the native islanders to Cyprus. Then the Germans took over again; only to clear out when the British invaded the western Dodecanese and the British Army moved in; the Luftwaffe bombed the place to bits, and some wayward British and their Greek irregular allies looted the remains. So it stood to that day, a far more poignant monument to the futility of war, it seemed to us, than any formal war memorial.

In 1985 there was yet no airport on the island, and so "tourism" had not yet reached it, apart from a few genuine land-travelers, who really were "touring," who stayed in the one small hotel, and a small number of cruising yachtspeople, who said they mainly kept to the central or eastern Mediterranean.

Before the main landing place in the bay, a large billboard proclaimed: *"Notice: Europe Starts Here!"*

I thought that was a bit presumptuous. There were any number of ports and havens all around the ten thousand miles of European coastline that could proclaim the same. As I read the sign, my mind went back to the westernmost part of Europe, the Azores Islands, where, a year and a month and five thousand miles before, *Outward Leg* had arrived from Rhode Island, at Horta, in Faial Island. What a voyage *Outward Leg* had made! Even then I found myself waking in the mornings to wonder if it had all been true. To voyage right across the whole extent of Europe, from west to east, from the Azores to the Dodecanese by way of Vienna and Budapest! It had been the stuff dreams were made of, and, in my state and at my age, I was fortunate indeed to have done it.

Another kind of regular visitor to Kastellorizon were the islanders, and their descendants, and their families, who had been evacuated during the war to Cyprus. Many of them had gone on to Egypt, but most had emigrated to Australia, rather than return to the poverty and ruins of the island.

Some even returned home to live when they retired, and all those spoke perfect English with a broad Australian accent. This made, sometimes, for very strange experiences, such as when I might greet an ancient goatherd complete with black beret and shepherd's crook, and he would reply, nasally, *"How's she goin', blue?"*

There were no cars or motorcycles on the island. At times there were a few cruising yachts berthed in the harbor, almost lost in the vastness of it, and now and again a really adventurous charter yacht from Rhodes might call for the night, then leave next day. There were a half-dozen little family restaurants around the water-front, and a shop or two amid the ruins that sold canned and dried foods. All the fresh food was hauled every day from Rhodes by a small ferry. There was also a minute post/telegraph office, where the operator had his own special brand of English, and a Greek Army outpost on the hill above the town, which sometimes made banging noises and bugle calls, and once while we were there, burned down almost all the already sparse vegetation while they were at mortar practice. Apart from that there was little besides a few olives and good fishing.

One of the yachts in Kastellorizon when *Outward Leg* arrived was *Quo Vadis*, another voyager. She was out of Australia. Her skipper was George Purkis, an Englishman, and his mate was his wife, Liz, who was one of the best sailmakers going. They had lingered awhile in Kastellorizon and were now to sail back to Cyprus, a couple of days' going to the south.

Here was an opportunity for Thomas. He could gain experience in a monohull sailing craft, collect our mail in Cyprus, take with him our shattered mast tabernacle for repair or replacement, and leave me in peace to write my book.

I was determined to take no more risks with a split tabernacle (the "boot" in which the foot of the mast was fixed to the deck). In a very heavy blow our mast foot could spring out, and cause tremendous havoc. We had taken this risk all the way from Rumania; we would have no more of it.

There were no cranes for lowering the mast in Kastellorizon, so we secured running blocks on the frames of bedroom windows in a gutted house on the waterfront, reeved long lines from the masthead through the blocks, and so lowered the mast safely. Next time you see the second-floor windows of an abandoned house, you'll know what they're for.

With our masthead lying on deck, it was off tabernacle, into Thomas's bag with it, and off Thomas to Cyprus in *Quo Vadis*.

We had moored the boat with two anchors over her stern, bows to the waterfront wall right in front of Jack's Cafe. That way I could pull the bows right up to the wall and clamber on and off shore whenever I needed to. Most of the time I was writing the book I didn't need to go ashore because Jack's family brought my breakfast and lunch on board and left it, silently, right outside my companionway, in the cockpit, without my hearing a thing. Then I had only to reach out of my cabin door when hunger struck, and there was my food, cooked and delicious. It was a sailing writer's dream come true. At eleven o'clock and again at three there would be coffee or tea, steaming, sitting on the cockpit seat. I don't think I walked more than ten yards from the boat the whole time I was writing *The Improbable Voyage*. I didn't need to; Jack, another Greek-Australian, made sure that everything I could need was brought to me.

I worked in a quiet frenzy in Kastellorizon, on board the boat, or relaxed, exhuasted, in between bouts of hard, concentrated effort, to get the book written in time to refit *Outward Leg* and be at the southern end of the Red Sea by the following April, when the change of monsoon would be due. Once I'd done that, and all else being fair, the voyage to the Orient was in the palms of our hands.

One morning—I don't know which; one day was welded into the next for me—the news came over the BBC that a terrorist attack had been launched against a yacht in Larnaca Marina, Cyprus, which was where Thomas had gone.

I've never been an enthusiastic ham radio operator. For the first time since we had been off the Azores, I switched on our set. It worked. I fiddled around with knobs to pick up the local networks, and within minutes I was in contact with hams both in Israel and in Lebanon, on different frequencies. They were monitoring events in Larnaca separately. The Lebanese operator was actually in telephone contact with the skipper of a Lebanese motor yacht moored in Larnaca Marina, even as I was listening to him pass on his news. I had a secondhand account of events even as they were happening, and a few moments later I could pass them on to my Israeli contact in Tel Aviv.

The Lebanese told me that two men and a woman had arrived in Larnaca a few days before in a small sailing yacht, and they had tied their boat up at the marina. Two other men had somehow made their way into the marina, boarded the Israeli yacht, shot the woman and held the two Israeli men hostages. There was a standoff; the marina was closed off by police and no one was allowed in or out.

All the day long I stayed hunched over the ham radio, with half the population of Kastellorizon on board the boat anxious for news—that made about twenty people, plus the priest, in his beard, robes, and tall black hat, although him I made wait on the jetty by the bows. (Bad luck, they are, in a sailing boat.) Eventually my Lebanese friend told me that the two Israeli men had been shot dead and the gunmen were giving themselves up to the police. A little while later he told me that they were being led out of the marina by the Cyprus police, and that one of them claimed that he was an Englishman. I passed the information, as it came to me, on to my friend 424DI in Israel in anger, for the outrage, and in sorrow for the victims and their families.

While Thomas was away in Cyprus, night storms, sudden and vicious, swept down off the high Taurus Mountains on the Turkish coast only two miles away. Six times I was forced to move the boat, alone, from one side of the harbor to the other. Unfortunately, Jack's Café was in a very exposed corner of the bay. It was not easy to do that, on one leg and bone-weary from hours of pouring myself out onto paper. Each time I would lose a few hours' sleep, yet each morning I was back to the grindstone just after dawn.

After ten days away from *Outward Leg* Thomas returned, hale and well, on the ferry from Rhodes, to where another ferry from Cyprus had taken him. He brought with him mail and in it good news of income earned and promised; but of the Larnaca attack he knew less than I. He and George had gone ashore and out of the marina to shop in Larnaca town. When they tried to get back into the marina they had been stopped by the police, heavily armed, and had to wait all day, until after the gunmen surrendered, before the policemen had allowed them back into the marina and so back on board *Quo Vadis*.

The spell in Kastellorizon gave me time and peace, not only to write the book, but also to catch up on all my correspondence, which had gone badly awry ever since we had hauled *Outward Leg* from the Rhine across Bavaria to the Danube six months before. I was always a stickler for replying to any letters sent to me, as soon as I possibly could.

One of the most difficult things about long-distance voyaging is trying to keep in contact with friends and relations, or, as in my case, editors and publishers, while on the move continually, and often not knowing precisely where I would be, or when, or for how long.

Keeping track of my delivered writings was almost impossible. One of the first things that Thomas handed me when he came on board was a package from my London publisher. In it was a copy of my newly published book, *Outward Leg*. I was, of course, pleased indeed to see the book in print, but I was shattered to see that none of the many photographs or documents, and no maps at all, that I had sent them with the script had been included in the publication. The last time I had seen the work had been in Varna, Bulgaria, where the proofs had somehow miraculously arrived from London, for my last changes before it went into print. Then I had been under strong pressure, from lack of money and the cold shoulders of the commissars, to get on my way to Istanbul. In six hours flat in Varna harbor, on board *Outward Leg*, I had worked on the proofs; then I had hobbled ashore, limped three kilometers, shouldered my way through mobs of Soviet sailors, and had the proofs back in the mails before nightfall—together with a letter reminding my editor to include the maps and photographs, and especially the maps. As I had told him in the letter, a book about voyaging without maps is like a pianist with no arms. Now this!

A more cheering thing that Thomas brought back from Cyprus was a new stainless-steel mast tabernacle. He had not found any-one to reweld the old aluminium one. The stainless unit had cost the earth—about a hundred dollars—but I considered that much cheaper than the cost of a whole new rig if we should lose the mast in the Red Sea, or in the middle of the Indian Ocean, or even on the short hop to Cyprus from Kastellorizon.

As soon as we had the mast erect again, and the rigging shipped in place, and the hull bottoms cleaned, and the sails rigged, we were off. It was late October. There was still some time to linger on the coast of Turkey and live comparatively cheap. We headed the two miles across a narrow strait, over the frontier, and so into Kas, in Turkey.

Now that the "tourist" season was over, Kas was quiet, except for one evening, when the town held a big shindig for Kemal Atatürk's birthday, even though he'd been dead for decades. All hell was let loose on that evening, with a half-dozen local bands and orchestras competing with each other, all playing at the same time. For the rest of the people, apart from the musicians, it was all very formal and sedate. The men and boys all sat, stood, or wandered around, chatting and ogling the girls, to one side of Atatürk's statue, while the women and girls, whispering quietly among themselves, sat on the other.

Kas had some good little restaurants and the harbor was safe even when katabatic winds swept down from the mountains at night. Outside the town mosque, an old navigation buoy was used as a street ornament, in the middle of the road. I thought that would be very effective in reminding worshipers of their own mor-tality. It also reminded us that it was time to leave Kas and get to Cyprus.

Outward Leg, bound for Paphos, on the western tip of Cyprus, didn't get much breeze until she was well offshore; but then around noon a stiff northeaster sprang up. Soon she was lifting her skirts and tripping along on a broad reach, so fast that she continually put the wind ahead of her, and we were forced to close-haul her, then to roll up the stay sail to slow her down. That we did to keep the apparent wind more than forty-two degrees from her bow. Otherwise she would accelerate faster and faster until the wind was dead ahead, and then stopped dead in the water, until the wind backed round again toward her stern, from where it was really blowing, and started to move her forward again.

During that night the wind eased off, and the sea with it, so that at false dawn it was almost calm. We were about twenty miles to the northwest of Paphos. I was keeping an eye out on deck when suddenly a loud noise came from somewhere over the eastern horizon. It was, I imagined, something like the sound of ten thousand one-cylinder outboard engines, with a knock in every cylinder, but much louder. I stared and stared toward the murky-gray east, but could see nothing, until all at once a black line, low on the horizon, transformed itself swiftly into a solid black block, miles and miles in area, which then turned into—first a gray, then a silver, *cloud* of wild geese heading, helter-skelter, southwest, as fast as they could fly. The cacophony of their cries and the drum of their wings beating, as for minutes they passed overhead, was so loud that even over the purr of our Yanmar engine below, it woke Thomas. The row brought him scrambling up into the cockpit, sleepily rubbing his eyes, then staring in awakened wonder at the majestic sight that was passing overhead. There were so many birds in that flock that the air stirred by their wings beating in the morning calm actually made our mainsail shake. I stopped the engine to await full daylight and a breeze. As suddenly as it had arrived, the cloud of geese was gone. Then all we could see, besides our boat, were the mountains of Cyprus, far away, the sea and the empty sky, and we were alone again, in the silence and peace of the biblical sea at daybreak.

We had a weak wind that day, but we sailed all the way into Paphos because the engine hull-seal alarm had warned us that one of the rubber seals that kept the sea out where the drive shaft protruded through the hull was defective. It had served its purpose over its allotted time, so we thought it a good omen that the seal had the good sense and courtesy to wait until we were within sight of Cyprus before it finally gave up the ghost. We trusted our Yanmar engine so much that it had developed almost its own personality for us, its own kind of wisdom. Staunchly it had held out until we were within sniffing distance of the only good place for us to refit for hundreds of miles, before showing any symptoms of all the rough usage it had been made to sustain during our voyage through Europe.

Gently we eased *Outward Leg*'s bow to the quay at Paphos,

where several other yachts were anchored stern-to. Soon, with surprisingly little fuss, we were entered into Cyprus by a personable young Immigration officer. But here, for the first time since we had departed Eastern Europe, we were told that we might not call anywhere we wanted, but must go only to prescribed ports along the coast. Of these there were three—Paphos itself, Limassol, and Larnaca. It seemed that the Greek Cypriots, who occupied the south of the island, were nervous about attacks and skullduggery by Turkish Cypriots, who, with the help of the Turkish Army, had seized the northern part of the island some years before, and declared their own republic.

I would have stayed in Paphos for a few days, if we had been able, to visit thereabouts the sites storied in ancient Greek legends, but it was dusty and windy, and the place around the port had a dry, worn-down, desert look to it, so we sailed anyway. I was anxious to get to Larnaca and haul the boat. So we slept a good night in Paphos and sailed next day.

With an engine hull-seal threatening to give way at any moment, we could not use our engine for propulsion, so we forged for twenty-four hours, at first in light airs, then in stiff winds, around the south coast of Cyprus, and a hard beat it was. We couldn't press *Outward Leg* too hard on the wind; twice our worn-out headsail blocks gave way, and I was concerned in case any heavy pounding of the hull should perhaps rupture the one remaining good engine-seawater seal.

By midnight on Friday, 2 November, we were off Cape Aspro, off Cape Zeygari by dawn; and rounding Cape Gata we found a flatter sea, so we hauled into Limassol Commercial Harbor, to see if we might spend the night there.

We hove to inside the port, without tying up, and waited for whoever might appear. After about an hour a young uniformed official, who spoke good English, turned up. In reply to my inquiry, he told us that we could stay in the far inner end of the harbor, at anchor, miles away from the town, and the charge would be $5.25 a day, but we would have to pay a *seven days' fee minimum*. His attitude was that we could take it or leave.

I reckoned up in my head. That made a total of almost thirty-seven dollars we would have to pay if we were to anchor in Limassol harbor until nightfall. I looked around, and then I stared at the anchorage the young man had indicated. It was far away, among mud flats, and surrounded by dozens of factories. Thirty-seven dollars for the privilege of dropping our anchor into six inches of their mud for a few hours! It was obvious to me that "marina-itis" had reached even this far.

I told the official what I thought of their charges—that they were close to robbery. The young officer glared at me. A policeman, wearing a very British-colonial-police-looking rig, complete with shiny boots and Sam Browne belt, marched smartly up to our young port official's side. He gave us his best rendering of a British bobby's *Hello-hello-hello-what's-all-this-'ere?* frown.

At my silent nod Thomas hoisted the jib and we shoved off out of Limassol harbor for Larnaca. Then we beat another forty-four miles along the coast until evening. We tacked our way behind the same seawall that, only two weeks before, the terrorists had scrambled over, into the entrance to the Larnaca Marina, and as dusk dropped so did our hook. Then we tied a long line to the seawall, ate a can of Hungarian ham with potatoes, and turned in.

The next day was Sunday. There was no breeze early in the morning and we could not use the engine. While we waited for a breeze to spring up so that we could negotiate our way through the marina entrance and so alongside, Thomas went ashore to the marina office, to inform them of our arrival and to see if any mail was awaiting us.

In a few minutes he was back on board. He had, he said, been stopped by a policeman: "Hey, you, where you going?"

Thomas had explained where he was headed.

"Who gave you permission to land?"

"We cleared in Cyprus," explained our mate, "at Paphos, and we have not been ashore anywhere since. That was two days ago."

"Well, it's Sunday now," observed the rozzer.

"So?" Thomas could put a lot of Teutonic thoroughness into that one word.

The policeman had stiffened at this. As he told me the tale, Thomas, too, had stiffened. "So you must enter Cyprus again. You must reenter Cyprus every time you go out to sea—every time you leave any port, even if you come back there. And this is Sunday, so if your captain wants the Customs and Immigration officials to come down to your boat and enter you, tell him he must pay ten dollars for their overtime!"

"So what shall we do?" Thomas asked me, after he'd finished his tale.

"Nothing. Sod 'em. Let 'em wait. I've lived all this time and only been to Larnaca once before, and that was over twenty years ago. It won't kill me to wait here at anchor for another twenty-four hours. Then we can reenter Cyprus without paying their bloody overtime!" Which we did, and while we lay at anchor I caught a big fat fish, which made a fit lunch.

Once *Outward Leg* was inside the marina things became friendlier in Cyprus. We already had some old friends there, and among the cruising people we soon made some new ones.

There were a dozen or so yachts in Larnaca that had made passages from afar, mainly from Australia, west across the Indian Ocean and then north through the Red Sea. But the vast majority of the craft there were of northern European origin. Many of the British yachts were inhabited by retired service officers, living cheaply on their pensions.

The retired army officers looked strange as they marched, ramrod straight, up and down the marina boardwalks, with their towels under one arm and the other arm swinging in true "Colonel Bogey" style, as they headed for the marina showers. Some, with clipped moustaches, and short haircuts, looked completely out of place, and they didn't seem to have wandered far afloat, but they did keep their craft in "first-class order" as they put it—meaning shipshape. Also they never seemed to be idle, and neither did they gossip, unlike many of the other "yachties" in Larnaca Marina. The retired officers, who tended to keep very much to themselves, were almost priggish in their ways and speech, but I reckoned they would be the ones to be with in a tight corner, all the same.

We were eager at this point to inspect the toll the Danube had taken on the hull of *Outward Leg*. The yacht-haulage facilities in Larnaca were two: a "travel lift," a sort of mobile crane that straddled a boat and lifted her between its legs up an incline and onto the shore, and a good old-fashioned concrete slipway which boats were dragged up. The space between the "legs" of the travel lift was nowhere near wide enough for *Outward Leg*, with her twenty-six-foot beam, so the concrete slipway it had to be.

Our main problem was that where the slipway ran down into the harbor there was very little depth, and *Outward Leg*, with her keel, needed at least four and a half feet depth over the seaward end of the slipway, so that she could sit on the slipway and then be hauled up to the hard ground at the top.

What followed was a small saga of ingenuity, endeavor, frustration, determination, defeat, resurgence, dismay, diplomacy, persuasion, faith, hope, and charity until, assisted in the end by a big British Army truck and a dozen friends, *Outward Leg*, canted over onto her port ama, was dragged, reluctant to the last, onto dry land.

Now, almost a year later, and thousands of miles from the scene, let me get the facts of what followed a few hours later as clear as I can. What happened was so quick, so unforeseen, so potentially fatal, that it left, at the time, only hazy impressions in my mind.

That same evening, while the boat, canting to port, was temporarily supported on one oil drum under her port ama, as well as by part of her main keel, I had clambered down the stern (we had yet no ladder) and I was poking around, under the boat, alone. Thomas was in the galley, making supper at an angle of twenty degrees (an unusual thing in a trimaran).

I was inspecting the damage to the cooltubes (a patented capsize-prevention system), which had been caused when *Outward Leg* had hit rocks on the bottom of the fast-flowing River Danube earlier that year.

I was sitting on the wet, slimy concrete slipway, under the boat, in the darkness of early dusk, with my good leg under the after end of the keel and my false leg stuck out at right angles to my body (amazing, the contortions we peggies can perform), and I was shoving my left arm into the portside cooltube, trying to drag out the ruined old copper lining.

Suddenly the whole bulk of *Outward Leg* moved sideways and down, toward me, all five tons of her, in the darkness. . . .

4

Limbering Up

I hardly remember shifting myself from under the hull. I must have swung my good (right) leg from under the keel, thrown my upper body down into the slime, and rolled over and over on the slipway, away from the keel as it crashed down and sideways onto the concrete. Even so it barely missed slamming down the full five tons of the boat's weight onto my good leg. I don't at all remember the ground heaving.

What I do recall was pulling myself out from under the boat, smothered in dirt, grease and slime, hauling myself up onto my foot, and hearing Thomas's voice from up on deck, calling "What happened?"

I was shaking. "It's all right," I told him, "it was my fault—I should have waited until the morning, when we got the boat better supported. Seems she slipped sideways. No harm done . . . I'm okay." And with that I took off for the marine showers to clean up.

It wasn't until I was returning to the boat from the showers that someone told me there had been an earth tremor that had shaken all of Cyprus.

So we were reminded that we were, after all, despite the superficial "Britishness" of the place, in the East, where it was nearly always futile, often foolish, and sometimes downright dangerous to force the pace of any enterprise.

The two weeks that followed were busy in the extreme. We worked day and night, from before dawn until after dusk, to refit *Outward Leg*. We were greatly helped in this by Alexander Puhfahl, a young German we had met back in Bamberg while we were beset in the iced-up Main River, now "holidaying" with us, and John Parry, a fellow Welshman, wintering in Cyprus along with his wife on board their *Snowgoose* catamaran. Nothing ever got John Parry down; everything always got Alexander down, but we were all the best of friends, and they freely gave us of their strength and time, until the refit was completed.

Many other yachtspeople stopped by to gossip. At first they got polite but short shrift. When the boat was first dragged up the slipway, many of them opined that we should need at least two months to make *Outward Leg* ocean-fit again, but we were to do it in fourteen days and nights.

First we straightened the boat so that she was horizontal and supported her on pallets, just as we had done for the haul from the Main to the Danube in Germany. Then we sanded off, mechanically and manually, the damaged gel-coating on all three hulls, tore off, and rebuilt, the cooltubes, and repainted everything. We also took the engine out of the boat and sent it to Hadjikyrios, the main Yanmar agent in Cyprus, for a complete overhaul.

All the while this was going on I was also busy writing, sending off articles, short stories, and telex messages to England, France, Holland, Sweden, Japan and Australia, left, right and center, to tie up my loose business ends. We had quite a few invitations to go and join the "yachtties" hanging out at the tiny marina bar, drinking, but we had far too much to do if we were to be ready to head for the Orient in the early spring, and it was now late November.

There were several interesting craft in Larnaca Marina, including one that had been, I was told, many years before, Lady Astor's pleasure craft. She was a neat-looking, shipshape little powerboat, complete with funnel, although she couldn't have been more than sixty feet long. Her name was *Golden Era*, and I thought it suited her very well indeed. Her time *had* been a golden era for some people.

Another craft was the Israeli sloop in which the terrorist raid had taken place. She was still tied up alongside, and there were wreaths around her mast step all the time we stayed in Larnaca.

There various tales were told of the terrorist episode by people who had been, they said, eyewitnesses. One was of an elderly crew member from a French yacht who had walked over to the jetty by the boat while she was being held by the gunmen, while the body of the dead woman yet hung head down over the pulpit, and shouted that they were cowardly murderers. The old man, said my informant, even offered to fight them, but the PLO men waved him away, and ignored him. The teller of this tale, himself English, observed that the old Frenchman had been lucky to get away with his audacity. "But then," he added, "one of the PLO blokes was an Englishman, and *we* don't shoot *old* people, do we?"

In between grinding away at the boat refit, we managed to get out of the marina a few times. The town of Larnaca was disappointing. It seemed to be full of policemen, dust, and half-empty or half-built concrete edifices which looked as if the architects had learned their trade designing public toilets for the 1950 Festival of Britain. Many of the sidewalks were all broken up and dangerous to anyone who was not an Olympic-class hurdler. Along them navigated a continuous trickle of elderly British "tourists," many showing off their National Health spectacles and false teeth. Many of the dads wore braces as well as belt and most of the mums had their white hair frizzled. These couples were as often as not accompanied by an insistent lout of a Cypriot tout, edging them, like as not, toward "souvenir" shops to be ripped off for rubbish.

The heat in Larnaca, away from the sea breeze, the glare and traffic noise rebounding off dirty-white concrete walls, were almost unsufferable. The food in the cafés was as fifties-British as the architecture and the policemen's uniforms. On the one occasion when we ate in Larnaca town we found the fried egg and chips (the *pièce de résistance* of the establishment) the same as the attitude of the townspeople to anyone not of "Greek"-Cypriot origin: cold and greasy.

I found it hard to believe that the people of Larnaca were, as they harped on so often and emphatically at every opportunity, related in any way by race, culture, customs, or manners to the people of Greece. To me, they seemed to have the same relationship to Greek-Greeks as Atilla the Hun had to Socrates.

This was one time in my life that I thanked the gods that be that there was a marina to stay in. What Cyprus would have been like without the company, even though on rare occasions, of fellow yachtspeople there, was too depressing to contemplate. Even that customary escape-hatch, the local cinema, was a grubby fleapit.

It was empty, apart from a seat attendant, who cadged cigarettes off us, on the evening Thomas and I went. The film we saw, a Hollywood thing of sex and gore, was scratched and flickery. After the first solution-of-problem-by-gun I left. Even the real world of Larnaca, deserted, dusty streets and all, was preferable to that. Thomas stayed. He said later that the film wasn't too bad. I made allowances for his age, when he told me that, and the fact that he is a bit nearsighted. That was our big night out in Larnaca. On the way back to the boat a Cyprus Communist party procession had wended its truculent way along the seafront. I wasn't overimpressed. If the NATO or UN forces in Cyprus had been red Indians, the Cypriots would have been parading as cowboys, or vice versa. If they ever did get a repressive Communist regime, they would, in the main, be one of the few peoples that deserved it.

The United Nations contingent in Cyprus was there to keep the peace between the "Greek" Cypriots in the south of the island and the Cypriots of Turkish descent, in the north. Their commanding officer, Major Robin Duchesne, who was himself a keen ocean sailor of repute in racing circles, sent us an invitation to visit the UN headquarters in Nicosia. So we borrowed a car and, Thomas at the wheel, took off for the drive of sixty miles or so.

Once out of Larnaca, and seeing the land at much closer range than we had from the sea, it was soon obvious that Cyprus had a different nature from the other islands that we had cruised among, Greek or Turkish; it was *Asian*. We stopped now and then to look around. As the afternoon onshore breeze picked up, it heated over the land to a hot blast that blew clouds of dust before it so that we squinted our eyes, and looked Asian, too.

The earth was bleached by the hot sun almost a silver color. Here and there a patch of green vines or a flock of tawny or black goats, or a small, half-finished concrete building, or a shabby army post were all that relieved the arid solitude. Casuarina and cypress trees had been planted along the roadsides, but they looked windblown, wretched, and defeated. On the outskirts of the villages and towns, urban sprawl in the shape of laundry-bedecked minihigh-rises, with asses braying about the ground-floor windows, ended abruptly in the reflected heat of the glaring sun from thin, parched earth and glistening rock.

In the distance, as we drove, there were always mountains to the north of us, across the vast white-silver plain. At one of our stops I asked a young Cypriot what they were. In broken English he replied that "Turks" lived there; and he spoke the word "Turks" as if he were naming the unmentionable. The mountains were, as we knew from our navigational charts, the Troodos range.

If anything made Cyprus beautiful, though, it must have been the light. It hung over the whole scene, the plain and the mountains, as though it was filtered through a steely-pink lens. It brought into clearer focus, somehow, everything I looked at—the few scrubby trees, the dirty-brown rocks on the plain, the currant-black, sultana-tawny goats, the scruffy, sunburnt Cypriot soldiers, the shimmering blue mountains—and made them stand out from the earth as though I was looking through a pair of large, heavy, and very expensive binoculars.

The lunch at the United Nations headquarters was one bright interlude during an otherwise hot, dreary day. The UN base was right in the no-man's-land between the two sworn enemies, "Greek" and "Turk," who had torn the island into two chunks, with the "Greeks" getting the bigger chunk.

We met soldiers, officers and men, from Canada, Britain (including Ulster, of course), Sweden, and the Republic of Ireland. We swapped yarns in the Irish contingents' bar and Major Duchesne presented *Outward Leg* with a huge United Nations flag.

A few days later, when *Outward Leg* was relaunched in Larnaca, a kilted, bonneted bagpiper, from the Royal Ulster Rifles was in attendance, courtesy of Major Duchesne, and he did us the honor of being with us, together with his staff. The piper, a good lad, at my request played airs both from Ulster and the Irish Republic. We wanted none of our Irish friends to feel at all left out of our joy; the joy of relief and contentment, as *Outward Leg* once again floated, her hulls refurbished, her engine overhauled, and all her gear checked and made good for the long voyage to the Orient.

The total cost of the refit, including a crane to relaunch *Outward Leg* safely and gently was $720. The engine overhaul was made without charge, courtesy of the Yanmar Diesel Engine Company of Japan.

To some $720 might seem a paltry sum for such extensive work, but to us it was a small fortune. To be able to afford it we had scrimped on meals for months, and forgone a drink for weeks, ever since the last of our cheap Rumanian wine had been finished off in Rhodes. But at the relaunching, Irish whiskey flowed like Niagara, thanks to the UN forces, and so we made up for lost occasions, but not before pouring out a drop into the harbor waters for the gods of the sea, so that they would smile kindly upon us in the coming months of voyaging and look with favor upon our enterprise.

During the preceding month a good friend in the U.S.A. had invited Thomas and me to visit some boat shows in that country. There I could sign my books and meet my readers. I do that on every occasion I can; I feel that as an author it is my duty to my readers to meet as many of them as possible. If they can spare the time, effort, and money to buy and read my books, that is the least I can do in return, apart from writing more books. Besides, to meet my readers is like meeting members of my own family.

It would be four months ahead before the northeast monsoon stopped howling its head off in the Indian Ocean and the Gulf of Aden, and the best time to be in the Red Sea, heading south, would be April. This was December, so we were in no rush—we couldn't be, unless we wanted the wind right on our nose all the way across the Indian Ocean. A couple of weeks in the United States would be a good way to pass the time until February, when we would head through Suez.

There were other reasons for us to accept the invitation to visit the U.S.A. First, it might give us the opportunity to place our *Small Craft Pilot for the Danube* into the right hands. This was now completed: eighty full, foolscap pages of it, giving a total length of the drawing of the river, when it was laid out, of over *thirty-six yards*. It showed all the features on, in, under, and beside the Danube, on both banks for over *twenty-five hundred kilometers*, through seven different countries, and five of those behind the Iron Curtain. We knew that one day, perhaps even before the Rhine-Main-Danube canal is completed in 1992, our *Danube Pilot* would be the key to safe small-craft navigation of the whole navigable length of the river from Bavaria to the Black Sea.

The third reason for our accepting the invitation to visit America was that it would be a chance for us to tell our friends about our dream of the Atlantis training project. If we could do that, we knew, they would help us to make the dream come true. I know, from living in their country for some years on and off, that if anyone in this world can make "impossible" dreams come true, it's the Americans. Once they have seized on the value of an idea, a project, they will move heaven and earth to help make it a reality.

The question then was: Should we leave *Outward Leg* alone in

Larnaca Marina while we were in the States? There would be no problem in having a friend keep his eye on her while we were away, but was there a risk of another terrorist attack? From the lax state of security around the marina—the seawall was still unguarded at most hours—it looked not only possible, but also probable.

We all know that in a hurricane or typhoon, the safest place to be is in the eye of the storm. Following that principle I decided to sail for Israel, the eye of the Middle Eastern political storm. There we would leave the boat while we were away in America. In Israel any terrorist trying to harm her would have his work cut out, I concluded.

Before we sailed we gave the kids from the cruising boats, and their friends, a day out at sea in *Outward Leg*. It's a poor vessel that can't be enjoyed by children. There were all nationalities of kids on board: British, French, American, Canadian, Australian, and a few little Cypriots, too, the offspring of the marina workers. They enjoyed being able to scamper about wherever they wanted to, and climb the mast and bounce in the trampoline-like netting between the bows.

The last thing we did before we left Cyprus for Israel was to have a stainless-steel "devil's-claw" welded onto the bow-roller fitting, to hold the anchor chain in between hauls. I knew, from long before, how exhausting it can be to try alone, to haul in an anchor chain in a strong blow. This simple contrivance, like two fingers sticking out from the bow-roller fitting, into which the anchor chain links could be slid and held, would ease the work a great deal.

The devil's-claw had been the last item on a long list of work to be done in Larnaca. We departed from Cyprus about one hour after the welding was completed, with small sorrow and few regrets, except for leaving our boatpeople friends, and especially the kids. So on December 10 we cleared and hauled out for Israel, to spend Christmas, my third, in the Holy Land. We both agreed, later that day at sea, that if we ever were to find ourselves in Cyprus again, we hoped it would be on the "Turkish" side of the island.

All the time we had been refitting in Larnaca the wind had either blown strong during the day from the northeast, or died at night. That would have been good for a broad reach all the way to Haifa. But east-about nothing comes easy. Now we found the wind blowing strong, at about thirty knots, from the *southeast,* which, of course, was the direction we wanted to go. We could still go southeast, but to do it we had to make tacks to the south and the east, hard on the wind, and we beat like that all the next twenty-four hours, at around twelve knots in a lumpy sea.

On the southing tacks we were all right; there was nothing in the way until Egypt; but on the easting we had to be careful not to wander too close to the coast of Lebanon. We did not fancy an encounter with probing Israeli gunboats or PLO raiders in marauding rubber raiding-craft during the night—or the day either.

Early next day the wind diminished to about sixteen knots and veered around to the southwest. By daybreak it was down to ten knots, and had swung right round to the usual quarter of northeast again. On our eastern horizon, about thirty miles away, we could see Mount Hebron, a tiny hazy-gray lump, where the coast of Lebanon meets the shore of Israel. We headed in for the coast, on a close reach, port tack, making around five knots in a bouncy, confused sea. By lunchtime we were about five miles off Ras En Nagura, where a long, wide, white, livid scar had been gouged out of the uplands right down to the shore, and we knew that was the frontier line between Israel and Lebanon.

We had just finished our lunch—boiled beef and carrots—and Thomas had slid below to clean up the galley. *Outward Leg* was plodding along nicely, when suddenly an ear-splitting voice rent the air around my head: "STOP YOUR VESSEL AND IDENTIFY YOURSELVES!" I came up into the wind and hove to, almost before I could see the gunboat, which had been hiding in the glare of the reflection of sunlight on the sea, in direct azimuth-line from the sun relative to us. Quickly I called Thomas topside to show himself and to douse the flogging headsail. Then we could clearly see that the gunboat was Israeli all right, and that all her crew were on deck at action stations, either on the bridge, manning the forward gun, or stationed around the upperworks, their submachine guns trained on our boat.

Over our hand-held VHF radio (which I had not used since *Outward Leg* had been in the Atlantic Ocean—it had been defective and I couldn't afford to have it repaired until Cyprus) I told the gunboat skipper who we were and where we'd come from. "Oh, yes, Captain," he replied, "We've heard about you. Carry on into Haifa, good luck and *bon voyage*!"

By teatime we were off the port of Haifa, so to enjoy the view of Mount Carmel and the city that flows over its shoulders, as well as our Darjeeling tea, bought in Cyprus, we hove to for a half hour. How were we to know that hundreds of Israelis were waiting to welcome us to the Carmel Yacht Club?

Outward Leg was given a welcome she had never experienced anywhere else. There were only a half-dozen yachts tied up, obviously wintering, but there must have been five hundred people, men, women and kids, waiting to welcome us, waving and cheering as if we were returning heroes. Nino of the sloop *Yuki* (whom, you'll recall, we had met in Gallipoli) had rounded up all of his friends and many others, and they had been waiting for us all the time we had been sitting out in the bay, innocently sipping our Darjeeling tea, and me telling Thomas about how much Haifa had grown since I'd seen it last fifteen years before.

It took two Immigration officials, who had traveled down from the main port, only a few minutes to clear us into Israel. I was interested, but not surprised, to see that one of them had a computer-printout list of unwanted visitors that was all of three inches thick.

Many of the crowd of welcomers remembered how I'd hauled *Barbara* across Israel from Haifa to the Dead Sea and the Gulf of Aqaba in 1970, and one chubby old man, with red cheeks and sidewhiskers, told the wondering kids around us that I had introduced modern ocean-sailing craft to Israel, while his friend, even older, who later turned out to be a Viennese, exclaimed to the kids around that I was "the father of Israeli cruising."

This embarrassed me so that I muttered, "More like a son of a bitch." That amused the red-cheeked old man, who had been a New Yorker, and he almost broke up laughing.

Soon we were in the Youth Boat clubhouse, crowded with youngsters who learn boatmanship, rowing, and dinghy sailing around Haifa Bay. I told one of the instructors that if the kids, aged from six to twenty, would like to look around *Outward Leg* we'd be more than happy to have them on board. "Only," I stressed to her, as the youngsters' eyes lit up like fireworks, "don't let them on board more than six at a time, or they'll crowd the boat, and won't be able to move around or see very much."

They came on board all right—*all 160 of them at once.* There were so many, eagerly packing through the boat, that I was trapped for a full two hours in the after cabin, unable to move against the mob. One young professorial-looking type, aged about eleven, with thick pebble-lenses on his spectacles, held forth on the further development of satellite navigational systems on a continual-position-reporting basis. It was obvious, very soon, that he knew far more about the subject than I ever would, so I let him expound on the matter, and merely nodded my head, trying to look as if I really did understand what he was talking about. As he departed up the ladder, after shaking my hand (they *all* did that) he promised to send to me, if I liked, a copy of a treatise he'd written on the possibilities of the future transmission of matter by means of laser-like rays. . . . dizzily I assured him there was nothing that I could think of that I would like better, as he disappeared into the heaving mass of youngsters in our cockpit. They were all trying to get down into the forward cabin through the galley companionway hatch, for yet another tour around the innards of *Outward Leg*. And so it went on for more than four hours, until, leaving both Thomas and me exhausted, the last of the young Israelis, after gravely shaking our hands, jumped ashore and wandered off along the jetty, still chattering away.

The youngsters, all Jewish, were of all kinds of coloring, from fair-skinned blond to fuzzy-haired black. The latter, I was told, had immigrated to Israel from Ethiopia, where their ancestors, who counted themselves one of the Lost Tribes, had maintained the Jewish religion for centuries, completely isolated from all the rest of Jewry until last century, when their presence had been revealed to the outside world by Christian missionaries.

Carmel Yacht Club offered us a berth for *Outward Leg* for as long as we wanted, at a much-reduced rate, but we had to turn down this kind offer. The club moorings were remote from the town shops and transport system, tucked in front of the city power plant. The area was both smoky and noisy from the machinery of the plant. Even if I could have reached them, the public transport buses stopped work at six in the evening. The nearest taxi stand was more than three kilometers' distance, even if we could afford to ride in taxis, which we couldn't. The shopping for fresh food and other necessities while we lived on board (the money for a refrigerator would be better saved for Atlantis) would demand three or four hours of Thomas's time every day. Either that or we would have to depend on someone else's time and effort to look after our needs, and that, if there was any alternative at all, we would never do. There's enough of that already in the world without us putting our pennyworth in.

There had been vague rumors, in the cruisingman's bush-telegraph system, of a newly built small port for yachts at 'Akko, which is the Israeli name for the ancient town of Acre, one of the oldest ports in the world. I had been there before, in *Barbara*, in 1970, but then the haven had been a mere open anchorage off the town, with no protection at all in gales from the west or south.

We made shift to 'Akko, about twelve miles north of Haifa across the bay. When we fetched it, we found several pleasant surprises. The old anchorage had been almost completely surrounded by a new seawall, and inside it there were now floating pontoons for yachts to berth alongside, all with electric points for power supplies, and water at the turn of the taps at each berth. Besides this, the surroundings of the yacht haven were as scenic as anyone could desire. On one side was the seawall, with beautiful views across Haifa Bay, and on the other the old Arab town of 'Akko, with its walls, sunlit or moonlit, mosques and ancient buildings. These were fronted by a small but busy fishing port, where fishermen mended their nets on the quay in the mornings, before the sun became too fierce. There was a market in the kasbah, only two or three minutes' walk even for me, a post office at the top of the hill on which the lovely old town is crowded, a small American-owned bar right opposite, where the coffee was good, little family-restaurants aplenty, Arab and Christian, and a telephone in the port office. The Arabs of the town and the fishermen, too, were warm toward us, or at the least, civil. The marina staff, Arab and Jewish, were friendly, efficient and helpful, and the charges, at around four dollars a day, were reasonable for what was provided. What more could wandering voyagers ask for?

Another surprise for us when we fetched 'Akko was to see *Quo Vadis*, from our Kastellorizon days, sitting at the end of one of the pontoons; she was the only other non-Israeli yacht to winter there. We could hardly have had better company. Liz made us all a tasty Christmas dinner, and George promised to keep his eye on the boat while we were away. We all four held a New Year's Eve gathering at Dick's Shamrock Inn, a tiny hole in the wall (of the mosque) at the top of the old town. There we celebrated the coming year, but two days early, and not too deep, knowing that as the old year died Thomas and I would be headed for America, by air, to gather the means to ensure the long passage of *Outward Leg* to Thailand, and to bring closer to reality, God willing and the weather permitting, our dream of a base for the Atlantis Project.

1 Tristan Jones and *Outward Leg* at Kas, Turkey

2 Kas, Turkey. The Fishermen's Monument

3 Sailing through the Bosphorus

5

Magnificent Munificence

Our swift visit to the U.S.A. was to be like stepping off a stage between acts, or perhaps more like a quick return-trip to another, richer planet, with more rarefied air than poor old Earth.

We traveled overland from 'Akko to Tel Aviv, where one of Nino Schmueli's vast network of friends, Al Bresler, a self-exiled (or perhaps returned-home) American, put us up for the night. Al's wife, brought up in Austria was fascinated as we regaled her with tales from the Danube valley. Al had been a boat owner, cruising out locally, but the thoughts of nights at sea had discouraged his wife. When I told her that I'd arrived in Israel from London, all the way, with only three nights at sea her eyes brightened. I hoped that I'd helped Al to persuade his wife that they should have another boat, and range farther afield.

Those three nights at sea, and all that distance safely covered, showed them the importance of what we were carrying to the world at large, our *Danube Pilot*. The completion of the Rhine-Main-Danube canal would mean that it would become possible for a vessel to navigate safely from northern Europe to the Middle East, avoiding the stormy areas off northwestern Europe. Thousands of pleasure craft would be able to use that passage, but there had been, until we drafted our *Pilot*, no real information in the West about it; merely vague rumors.

On the road from 'Akko to Tel Aviv it was obvious that Israel's
continual state of siege for the past four decades had taken its toll,
at least since I had last traveled that way with *Barbara* in 1970.
Roads were in worse repair; buildings in the inner cities looked
worn and tatty; and many of the older people, of my generation
and even younger, looked weary and tired, compared to their
liveliness fourteen years previous. But all the youngsters had the
same brightness and energy about them that I had always remembered. It was obvious that there had been great changes in the
population of Israel; far less people we encountered spoke English
to any clear degree, and there were many more people from non-
European backgrounds and of the European-looking folk, many
more spoke Russian.

At Tel Aviv airport Thomas almost brought everything to a
grinding halt. In the foyer, while I waited for him to book seats,
he left his bag, containing his camera and photographs, in a nearby
plant pot. Before I knew it, I was surrounded by about a dozen
armed security guards, and stayed that way for half an hour, while
the bag was gingerly removed from the plant pot, taken away,
and, evidently, inspected by remote sensors. At the same time
Thomas himself was pounced upon and thoroughly frisked down.
Then, as the young lady security guard returned the bag to us, all
was sweetness, light, and charm. I can't say that I blame them,
and Thomas learned a good lesson.

Again, as we flew across the Atlantic at six hundred miles an
hour, I found it almost impossible to express, even to myself, the
difference between air travel and small-craft voyaging, they were
so utterly different. In the El Al plane we were not, it seemed,
traveling so much as being conveyed from one point to another.
It seemed to me that no one on board the plane, not even the pilot,
unless he might be a suicide case, was master of his own fate. I
found it inconceivable, as we purred and dozed our way over the
mid-Atlantic, that all those vast reaches of solitary ocean could be
overcome in that manner, so easy; and so ineffably *dull*. Who has
ever heard anyone, at the end of a long airline flight, not happy
that it was over and done with?

In the U.S.A. we visited New York and Houston boat shows.
We were so busy; everything, every sight and everybody so welcoming, Thomas was so overwhelmed by his first-ever experience
of the pace of American life, that the whole episode passed like a
speeded-up filmshow. I must have spoken with two or three thou-

sand people, and signed many hundreds of my books. Every day was so exhausting that by late evening about all we were fit to do was collapse in a hotel room. The strangest episode was on the last day of the New York Boat Show, a dear old lady, who thought she was in the New York *Cat* Show (which was to start next day) cornered me and for a full hour gave me the life story of her Siamese pet. Another old lady gave me a detailed rundown of the Soviet naval forces in their base at Da Nang, in Vietnam. Everyone thought she was loopy, then.

Our presentation to the American boating public, at these shows, of our ambitions for the Atlantis Project, was received with every interest, kindness, and many offers of support. We wrote down the details of everyone who showed interest and promised to keep them informed of our progress. This would not be easy while on the move on a long voyage, but, as we shall see, we did our best.

We tried to leave the original draft of our *Danube Pilot* with what seemed to us to be the appropriate establishment in New York City. As we'd had no time or opportunity to telephone the place beforehand, we stepped into the luxurious foyer, from the rain, unexpectedly. We were met with, first, blank stares from the night office staff, and then suspicious, alarmed looks from several gentlemen attending a meeting. I tried to explain what it was that we were offering to leave with them, but we might as well have tried to present Tierra del Fuego Indians with the original Magna Carta. The members gaped at us, standing there wetly dripping, as if we were escaped lunatics, and told us to come back after we'd made an appointment to see the right committee. We, without further ado, picked up our thick volume of the very first really detailed account of the Danube River in decades, if not ever, to reach the West, and made for the door. Then we sloped off into the bright lights of Manhattan's midtown to wend our weary way back to Greenwich Village and flop down, tired out, in our cheap hotel room.

Next day we left the original of our *Danube Pilot* in the safekeeping of my literary agent, on Sixty-fourth Street. There, in his office safe, we calculated, it would not get lost. It wouldn't move far, but it wouldn't get lost, and that was the main thing, for the time being. We hadn't the time to try to interest a publisher in it, but at least it was in the Western Hemisphere.

The start of our journey back from New York to Tel Aviv was memorable. Our friend drove us to JFK Airport through Coney

Island; we felt quite at home among the high-rises surrounded, for a great part, by high fencing and barbed wire, as a defense, our friend told us, from street hooligans, rapists, and murderers. Many of the inhabitants of the flats, we were told, were recent immigrants from Eastern Europe. I thought they, too, must feel quite at home in Coney Island; it looked for all the world like some frontier district immediately behind the Iron Curtain. The winter garb of the people, too, reinforced the impression that we were somewhere by the Danube, in mid-winter Bulgaria or Czechoslovakia.

But Thomas and I were content that our visit and all the long hours and wearisome work had been worth the effort. Besides having met a lot of good people we were over two thousand dollars richer than when we had arrived in the U.S.A. That would be enough, and more, to keep *Outward Leg* fettled for the next six months, with some over as a contingency fund, in case of catastrophe. In only twenty days in America I had garnered more than I had earned in the previous year, from the boat on the move: *For the first time since I left San Diego, over two years previously, I was able to count on food and supplies for longer than six weeks.* This was a blessing; welcome and hardly hoped for, and much of it due to the magnificent munificence of our American friends. Now, nothing but irrevocable disaster could stop *Outward Leg* reaching for the East.

A sleepy, restful flight back to Tel Aviv was enlivened, even as our aircraft started its descent, and as the SEAT BELTS signs lit up, by the sight of more than a score of portly, elderly gentlemen, seated scattered around the plane, all rising from their seats, and donning their praying mantles. They all moved aft in the plane, one after the other. As we, tied down securely by our seat belts, curiously craned our heads to watch them, they turned to the "wall" of the plane, and, swaying and humming, praised Jehovah evidently, and thanked Him for their return to Israel. As the plane alighted on the runway with a thorough bump, I begged my own gods myself that the Jewish men were praying for a safe landing. With all their own weights, a good two tons and more excess in the rear of the plane, we might be in dire need of the direct intervention of whoever or whatever watched the shop. But there must have been a consensus of agreement among the Leaders in the Celestial Trade Union: All our prayers, Jewish and Druidical, it seems, were answered, and we arrived back in Israel to find *Outward Leg* patiently and faithfully awaiting us, safe and sound.

Back on board, now with cash in the kitty, we set to making *Outward Leg* fit for the hard weather, at times, and tropical heat, at all times, ahead of her.

First, Liz Purkis measured up and fitted for us a new cockpit-dodger top and windows. The old ones were badly deteriorated after the hard usage since San Diego. There's nothing more de-moralizing, on a long passage to windward, than being continually doused with seawater, no matter how warm the water, and this, in a fast trimaran, would always be the case unless we made pro-vision to prevent it. Liz also made and fitted three sail-covers. In the heat of the tropics these are absolute necessities, to protect the Dacron from swift deterioration. I'd never been able to afford them before. When the boat had last been in the tropics, in the Caribbean, we'd had to stow our sails every time we hauled them down, to save them from damage by harmful sun's rays. Now we had covers for the main, the roller staysail, and the roller jib. This was luxury indeed, and Thomas and I felt like millionaires whenever we no-ticed, henceforth, our new, bright blue sail covers in place. The three sail-covers cost three hundred dollars in all, but they would save the ruin, within a few months, of six thousand dollars worth of sails.

Next we insulated the after end of the after cabin, and the deckhead (or "roof") of the forward cabin with Styrofoam. This new insulation cost us a total of thirty dollars; we used loose Styro-foam padding from old electronics-equipment containers, given to us by a friend in a factory near 'Akko. It turned out to be the best value a sailor ever had for thirty dollars.

We resewed the whole length of the leech seam of the mainsail, where the flogging had tattered the stitching, a long, wearisome chore on twelve-ounce Dacron, in between rainstorms from the Golan Heights, northwest of us.

Every day I clambered to the post office, up the roughly paved, uneven, crowded passage through the kasbah, through the jostling groups of Arabs and Jews, dodging the kids, big and small, who ran helter-skelter down the cobblestoned street. The first time I had managed it had been a great achievement to me, and even though it became an everyday routine, I always held a quiet little celebration inside myself whenever I made it safely to the top of the hill. Soon I was even climbing up the steep approaches to the old Crusader-built ramparts, there to stand and look out over the sea, communing with my thoughts and the view. I always felt, in

'Akko, as though I had been there before, in some other life. I seemed to *know*, before I turned every corner in the narrow little alleys, what was ahead. There was always, all the time I was there, from the first day until the last, that sense of *déjà vu*. Yet I had never been to 'Akko, that I could recall, in my navy days, when our ship had called, once or twice, at Haifa. In fact, I recalled as I gazed out across Haifa Bay from the 'Akko walls, I'd never been ashore in Israel in those days, in 1946, when it was Palestine. On the first occasion my ship had arrived, there had been Arab anti-British riots in the town; none of our ship's crew had been allowed ashore. On the second, and last, occasion I'd been under punishment for something or other; probably some offense against stupid uniform-dress regulations, and I myself had not been allowed to go ashore.

When *Barbara* had called there in 1970, to anchor in the offing, I know I didn't go ashore; I'd had a bad cut on one foot in Haifa harbor, and couldn't walk well at all. I had sent my then-mate, Conrad Jelinek, into town shopping. The next day we'd had to shift because of a gale blowing straight in on our anchorage. There was simply no way I could have been in 'Akko before in this life. But I *knew* every house, every window, every turn of even the tiniest, longest, most twisting alleys. Then if I had not been ashore in 'Akko in this life, when had I? It was the strangest feeling. The only other times I'd ever experienced it when I first arrived at places were on the tiny island of Sark in the British Channel Islands, and, strangely enough, in Buenos Aires.

In 'Akko we went for coffee to the Shamrock Inn, a tiny bar opposite the post office. There Dick Lambert held court. He was American, ex-employee of the Grumman Corporation, who made airplanes and space vehicles. Dick, a laughing, rotund man of fifty-five or so, with a shock of white hair over Irish blue eyes, who had worked with NASA too, told some good stories. My favorite was the one (he swore it was true) of the night before a moonbound spacecraft was all ready and waiting to lift off its pad into orbit. The night guard on the launch pad espied a cockroach entering the crew pod, and duly entered the event in his notepad. Next morning the officials in charge inspected the guard's notepad and, almost out of their minds, raised the alarm. "And every telephone line in the U.S. of A. was buzzing all day, all night and the next day, while a couple of thousand technicians and scientists, all talking at once, tried to figure out how to get the cockroach out of the

pod alive. And it cost NASA," Dick went on, "millions of dollars
to stop the countdown and delay everything while they took everything apart and inspected every minutest part of the whole god-
damn shebang, in case the cockroach had laid any eggs, which
might hatch, see, and the cockroaches get everywhere, and mess
up all the electronics and everything."

Dick had been sent by the Grumman Corporation to Haifa to
help build a fast hydrofoil patrol craft for the Israeli Navy. He had
married an Israeli, and was now retired, and whiled his time running his bar, which was staffed by friendly and helpful young
Arabs. The food served was excellent and the company lively.

Thomas and I made friends with many Arabs in 'Akko. Most
of these were Muslim, although we knew a few Christians, too,
but not so well, as the Christians tended to keep more to themselves. Our Arab friends told us that the Israeli government wanted
them to move out of the Old Town, so they could "develop" 'Akko
Old Town as a "tourist attraction." Many of the Arabs had ancestral
homes in 'Akko going back over centuries, they said, and they did
not want to move to a newly built Arab settlement farther up the
coast, even though many of their homes were little better than
slums. Without any sentimentality because they were our friends,
we thought the Arabs were right. Without them, and their colorful
presence, 'Akko would become just another soulless "Disney World,"
like the old city of San Juan, Puerto Rico, or Dubrovnik, in Yu-
goslavia. It might spin money, but there would be no beat in its
heart. We thought that the best alternative, if 'Akko has to be
"developed" at all from the outside, would be to extend the yacht-
haven and make it a duty-free port. That would attract fleets of
yachts from all over the eastern and central Mediterranean, who
would come to winter there. It would save building big hotels, the
crews would spend money in the town for their needs, and em-
ployment would be provided for many locals. The eastern Mediterranean certainly needed more, safe, havens, as those that exist
now, in Larnaca, Rhodes, and Tel Aviv, are all vastly overcrowded.

One of the Arabs I met in 'Akko was a representative in the
Israeli Knesset. I asked him what, if we headed north to Lebanon,
wearing our American ensign, we could expect. He told me he
would make inquiries. When I next met him, he said that if we
went to Jounea, about ten miles north of Beirut, which was in the
hands of the Christian militia, as long as we paid our dues we
would be safe. Jounea was a cheap place, he said, and we could

buy booze there duty-free. In fact, he went on, there was a busy trade between Jounea and the Red Sea in booze carried by yachts, sail and power, to the oil rigs off the Saudi Arabian coast, where the booze, he said, was offloaded at great profit to the yacht crews.

In early February we found a new crewman to help Thomas in his onboard chores and to help us steer *Outward Leg* should the wind fail. One of the worst things about tropical voyaging is having to spend long hours in the heat of the day at the wheel. While we had wind, the Aries vane would steer us well enough, even in a full gale. But when the boat would be running free, with the wind anywhere abaft the beam except dead aft, *Outward Leg*'s forward speed would continually tend to shift the apparent wind ahead. Then we would need a helmsman by the wheel all the time, to make fine adjustments to the Aries gear. A good, strong, electric autopilot is the best answer for shorter passages, but they continually drain the batteries, and anyway there was no chance of locating one in the Middle East, and even if we could, at this stage we couldn't afford one. So an extra crewman it had to be. He was Svante Wagnerius, a stocky young Swede of twenty years, who had been wandering through the Middle East and previous to meeting us had done a stint in a kibbutz. He was anxious to reach India. He was, at home, a post office worker, and knew nothing about sailing. I told him it was about time that I learned something of the inner workings of the postal systems, which I used so much; I took him on. He turned out to be a cheerful, willing hand, and not a bad cook, too.

Many people have asked me about how to find good crewmen. It is a difficult and complex question to answer. No two people are the same, thank God. Finding good companions is never easy. In a small craft, for a long passage, it is even more difficult to find another person with whom to be cooped up, and yet remain at ease. That side of the matter is for everyone to solve for themselves. But one thing is clear: Before taking off for any length of voyage with a stranger, he or she must be quietly observed for several days; and that goes not only for crews, but skippers also. They must be watched for any idiosyncrasies which would be hard to live with, and especially any tendency to overindulge in booze, or any suspicion of addiction to, or even attraction toward, drugs. I am not moralizing; I am not against copious booze, or drugs per se, but I know the awkward, often tragic, and sometimes mortally dangerous situations the presence of either can bring about, and especially in small vessels. As regards hard drugs, I view anyone who indulges in them as first a fool (as is anyone who tries to gain heaven in an "easy" way), then a victim of greedy bastards who should be hanged from the nearest lamppost. But, I am not at all willing to have to pay for other people's foolishness by placing myself or my vessel in jeopardy, whether it be from the addicts' own lack of rational judgment or from the—justifiable—attentions of Authority. We get quite enough of that as it is, and too much of it unjustifiable.

In the case of Svante Wagnerius, we were lucky; he was a good lad, slow, steady, not too quick to learn new things, but sensible in every way. Both Thomas and I liked him and we never had a serious disagreement the whole three months he was with us.

In mid-February we ate our last falafel in the little square at the bottom of 'Akko market, drank our last *saha*—a strange, sweet blancmangelike concoction, and in the false dawn next day, pulled out of the port, bound first to bid good-bye to our friends at the Carmel Yacht Club in Haifa, then to Tel Aviv, about eighty miles down the coast from 'Akko.

We stayed the night in Haifa for old times' sake, then made our way out into the bay at dawn next day. The wind piped up in the early morning, fresh, southeast, and we sailed close-hauled, about a mile offshore, south. We fetched the marina entrance at Tel Aviv—a poky entrance, hard to see (it lies in 32° 05′ north, 34° 16′ east). It was even more difficult to enter, as we had to make two dogleg turns close to a shallow sandbank on which the sea beat furiously, then, right inside the narrow entrance, we very nearly ran into a wire strung across the port entrance. It was just high enough, if I had not brought the boat up all standing, in three seconds flat, to have taken Thomas's head right off. We waited, twenty minutes, heaving up and down with the swell, missing the stone walls by only inches with each heave, in a strong tide and a stiff swell, in the narrow confines of the entrance, for the wire to be removed, before we could get into the marina itself. In the marina office they explained to me that the wire was a new power cable being laid across the entrance. I thought that was baloney; there had been a few small barnacles clinging onto it. It's not easy to be happy and innocent, while at the same time possessed of very good eyesight. If they'd told me the truth, that they kept the wire rigged there to keep unwanted intruders out, I would have understood perfectly. But they knew I'd spoken with them on the

VHF radio before reaching the entrance; they'd given me permission to enter, and not told me about the wire.

Apart from that incident, they were good to us in Tel Aviv Marina, and gave me a berth close to the gate, so I could get ashore and out of the place easily. But we intended to stay only long enough to find and buy, next morning, two burners for our kerosene stove—they had been impossible to find anywhere else since Istanbul—then leave.

Tel Aviv Marina was backed by a busy highway, over which had been constructed a huge complex of raw-concrete buildings. It seemed also to be a sort of summertime promenade, but this was still winter, so there were few promenaders about, mainly UN soldiers from Holland and Sweden, if my memory serves me right. There were a few shops and restaurants, and good views of the sea, although at the outside café where we ate hamburgers, only Svante gazed out to sea. Thomas and I sat with our backs to it, and watched the people.

If you ever wish to know who are the newcomers in a boat's crew, watch the way they sit on the shore. Nine times out of ten the newcomer will sit facing the sea. If their boat is in a yacht anchorage, and they are ashore on the beach, in a bar or restaurant, and you wonder who is the skipper, watch for the one sitting where he can see his boat *if he moves his head around, or leans over a little*. He's usually the one that pays, too, unless theirs is a charter yacht. Then he's the one that laughs on cue. The charterer is the man, or woman, who pays.

We departed Tel Aviv on the twenty-seventh of February. In the offing we were hailed by an Israeli gunboat, whose skipper wished us *bon voyage*, again, after he had viewed us closely through his huge fixed binoculars. Another two miles out, right on the territorial-waters line, we passed and hailed the anchored ship *Peace*. She, we knew from stories about her, had been anchored out at sea, off Israel, for years, broadcasting messages of peace and pop-music to the whole Middle East. Years before the Western show-business opportunists had jumped onto the Ethiopian-relief bandwagon, *Peace*'s owner and crew had raised millions of dollars for the cause of feeding starving kids in East Africa. We hailed the crew, and one or two of them waved back at us. Thomas jumped into our dinghy and zoomed over to them with a bottle of whiskey, but he was told that they were all teetotallers, so when Thomas returned alongside we each, all three of us, drank a dram to *Peace's* health and long life, waved them good-bye, and hoisted the dinghy on board. Then it was up jib, and off for Port Said and the Suez Canal, 160 miles to the southwest.

At last we were heading out of the Levant, on our way to the Orient. There were almost another seven thousand miles of sailing ahead of us; six months had passed since I had set our deadline of eighteen months for organizing Atlantis, in Thailand. As the tall towers of Tel Aviv dropped below our eastern horizon, and we clapped on all sail for Suez, we had $2,250 on board and one year to keep our promise to ourselves; but we were healthy (making allowances for my missing leg), well stocked, and the boat was in first-class state.

The passage from Israel to Port Said was made mostly on a close reach, with a moderate breeze freshening to strong in the afternoon. We took care to keep a good lookout; the shore of Egypt was low and not easy to see, because off the coast the sea was the same color, almost, as the desert, a sort of very light khaki.

The night passed, with a lightening breeze until dawn, when the wind piped up again. We sighted no craft of any kind until we were closing Port Said, when ships canalbound hove into view over our western horizon.Then, as we drew closer and closer to the canal entrance, we could see dozens, scores of big ships laying to anchor or slowly cruising round and round, waiting for their turn to leave the Mediterranean and head for the Red Sea.

Svante acquitted himself well on his first night out at sea under sail, even though he suffered seasickness. Being the new lad, he kept the middle watch, from midnight until four A.M., which was also when the wind was weakest, so that the boat was sailing only at a mere five knots or so.

Outward Leg was well within sight of the Port Said lighthouse when the news came over the BBC; *"Units of the Egyptian Army are rioting in Luxor and other towns. It is believed that a revolution, led by Muslim extremists, might be underway throughout Egypt."*

Thomas was on watch. I switched off the radio and clambered up the companionway ladder to join him in the cockpit. He'd heard the news broadcast. "?" He looked the old question at me.

"I don't know. Shit, here we go again!" I replied. I looked over the side at the very light khaki-colored water, and glanced swiftly at the depth-sounder. It showed 18 feet. More than enough.

I repeated, "Here we go again, Thomas!"

Even as I said it there was a crunching, rumbling sound from below; with a shuddering judder, the boat stopped dead in the water, all standing. Just like that, right in the middle of the fairway to the Suez Canal, with a big steamer bearing right down on us only a mile away.

6

"Madam, You Have It"

It didn't take long for us to realize what had happened—in fact no longer than it took for Thomas and Svante to rush up to the bows and douse the yankee jib even as I, back in the cockpit, sprang the jib halyard from its cleat, and let go of the headsail sheet. Down the yankee clattered with a swoosh. A great number of fishing craft were milling about, setting and hauling their nets very close to the narrow southbound shipping lane. It was obvious that we had run into one of the nets, which were set just below the surface of the sand-colored sea. There were no buoys or markers of any sort to show anybody where the nets were. Now, no doubt, we had a net wrapped around our propeller.

I caught sight of the big merchant ship—a tanker—she was still bearing down on us at speed, now only a half mile away, blowing her siren stentoriously. No wonder, with *Outward Leg* almost dead in the water, lying directly in her path.

As I stared at the ship for a second or two, I also realized that the tide and the stiffish breeze were even yet moving us slowly through the water. We couldn't stay put; I couldn't start the engine, with a fishing net probably draped around the propeller. The only alternative was to try to keep moving, so that we could get out of the ship's way.

I hollered to Svante to get back aft and help hoist the yankee

again, which he did, while Thomas peered over the side to confirm
that it was, indeed, a fishing net we had in tow. With Svante
grinding on the halyard winch, then on the sheet, and me heaving
the wheel over, *Outward Leg* started to move again—slowly—no
more than a knot perhaps, but enough to get us to safety on the
inner side of the shipping channel. Even so the tanker barely managed to miss us. Over my shoulder I stared, fascinated, at the sight
of her bow passing by, as high as a six-story building, only five
yards off our stern. She was so close she took the wind off us
completely, so that we rolled and wallowed all the time her huge
bulk slid noisily past. Then we picked up the breeze again and
with the fishing net—"a bloody long one," Thomas shouted—in
tow underwater, and a dozen bumboats chasing us, touting for
business, we dragged our way the remaining mile or so, through
Port Said town and into the yacht mooring at Port Fuad, on the
east bank of the Suez Canal. There we brought *Outward Leg*, with
a gentle bump, alongside the police pontoon. So we brought her
to Africa, her fifth continent.

No sooner was the boat tied up than several bumboats all tried
to come alongside her, but I ordered them away smartly, so that
they stood off, a few feet away, with the "runners" shouting at us
the whole time. The way the agents' runners operated, as they had
for a century and more, was that the first one to board a vessel
was the one that got the business, for his boss, of representing the
captain of the vessel before Authority and traders. The bosses of
the shipping agencies were what most Levanters dream of being:
recognized, authorized "middlemen" who never soiled their hands,
but skimmed as much as the traffic would bear off every transac-
tion. The rule in the Suez Canal was: No agent, no permits. It was
as barefaced and simple as that. As the bumboats danced around
in the choppy canal, one man on each solicited for our business.
We had already contacted an agent of our own—Ibrahim—rec-
ommended by friends, and I told them this. Still they waved pam-
phlets, business cards, hats, umbrellas, spectacles, and even
briefcases at us as they all shouted in their own brand of English,
all demanding to be allowed on board *Outward Leg*. One of them,
a man of about sixty, dressed in a djellaba and a homburg hat,
claimed to be the port medical officer, come to give us health
clearance. I told him I was Haile Selassie out for a jaunt.

The man claiming to be a doctor then said that his name was
Shahawi, and that Ibrahim had phoned him, asking him to meet

us and fix us up with all clearances, which he would do for "only $250"!

I told him I could get Mrs. Thatcher to do it for less.

The "doctor" laughed, then shouted, "Hey, you no American! American no joke! You English!"

"Chinese!" I called back to him. "Queen Victoria very good man!" It had been the old jeer of the bumboat men; the old cheer of the sailors in response, long ago, when both the "doctor" and I had been young, and both he and I knew it, and so did several of the other bumboat touts.

They all grinned wisely as I shouted that, and shook their heads, while the "doctor" spoke to his befezzed helmsman, who grabbed at the boat controls, and they roared away, quickly followed by their competitors, to solicit other vessels arriving at the Gateway to the Orient.

We were not left in peace. No sooner had the bumboats taken off than several policemen shouted to us to move away from the pontoon and anchor stern-to the canalside wall. By this time the afternoon breeze was half a gale. We couldn't use the engine because we hadn't had time to remove the fishing net from the propeller. We tried to explain this to the policemen, but they were adamant. Bearing in mind the news we had heard only a couple of hours previously—about the army riots, I decided to do as we were bid. So, using the dinghy and long lines, we warped the boat over and anchored her stern-to. Then, as we waited for Ibrahim to arrive and obtain clearance for *Outward Leg* to transit the canal, I looked around me.

Across the main shipping canal the town of Port Said, lines of warehouses, a few domes and minarets, lay indistinct behind veils of sand dust blowing in the wind. Past it, at steady intervals of ten minutes or so, oceangoing steamers paraded, all headed south. At Port Said there were two canals, one going either way, north or south. The northbound canal branch was a mile or two east of us. All around the southbound steamers that I was looking at, dozens of small craft charged at what seemed a reckless rate, on what looked like heedless courses, all this way and that, without any obvious pattern. On our eastern side of the canal were huddles of half-finished or half-ruined—it was impossible to tell which— buildings, white-gray sunbleached and black-dead. Only close by us, immediately to our south, was there any sign of modernity, comfort, and even opulence.

This was the Police Club, which, surrounded by acres of im-
maculately tended, bright green grass and waving palms, gleamed
in the sun like a Beverly Hills mansion. Under its awnings could
be seen groups of people, men for the most part, relaxing in arm-
chairs, while waiters, all smartly dressed in white jackets done up
at the collar, stood by to serve them. Many of the loungers were
in light khaki uniform, but in uniform or not, all the men wore
dark glasses. I thought of the army riots, and nodded at the
loungers.

"It doesn't look there's any panic on," I said to my crew. "Not
if that lot is anything to go by."

Our crew were now stripped to bathing gear to go over the
side, knives in their belts, into the murky water and clear the net
from the propeller.

While I kept an eye on our crew from the deck of the ama, I
noticed a signboard right by our stern. It said:

> *Port Fuad Marina*
> *Yachts Welcome: No landing Witout prermit: Moring Chart $5.00*
> *Evry Twenty-Four Hours. Catamarans $10.00: Trimarans $20.00.*
> *Chandlers Stors and Enginers At Yor Srevice.*

I reflected that "marina-itis" had certainly infected Egypt, at
least here on the canal: Usually multihulls were gouged a mere
double the charge for monohulls; here we were being screwed for
four times the rate! "Port Fuad . . ." I ruminated to myself. "They
left the *r* out."

Even as our lads declared the propeller free, our appointed
agent, Ibrahim, a little chubby man of about forty, with thinning
hair and a wart on his nose, arrived with a briefcase full of forms
and declarations. There were eight forms, which Ibrahim had already filled in, for me to sign, and six crew-lists to compile. All
the while I copied details from our passports, in the hot after cabin,
Ibrahim recited a litany of stores, services, and other items available
to us, should we require them. One of his services was to obtain
landing permits for us to go ashore in Egypt. To get them we would
have to change $150 each! We decided we would forgo that priv-
ilege, and stick to the boat while we were in Egypt. "They've done
without you for five thousand years," I observed as Thomas's face
dropped, "so another year or two without you won't hurt Egypt;

anyway, it'll still be here when you come this way again, so there's no rush."

Another service provided by Ibrahim was to arrange for our canal pilot to turn up at nine o'clock the next day, to accompany us through the canal, as required by the regulations. Ibrahim would also arrange for the transport back to Port Said, by taxi no less, of the first pilot from Ismailia, about halfway along the canal. He would also arrange a relief at Ismailia for the first pilot, and the relief's taxi fare from Suez. . . . As it was, I changed forty dollars into Egyptian piasters, gave them to Ibrahim to buy fresh stores for our canal passage, and advanced him half his charge for arranging everything: seventy-five dollars in American currency.

"And tomorrow you feed the pilot, eh, Captain?" Ibrahim reminded me for the tenth time, as he took off, out of my steaming cabin, with one of his runners, to reappear in an hour with the fresh food we had ordered. To give him his due the food was fresh and it was good.

Guarded by Egyptian soldiers (!) *Outward Leg* was as safe from solicitations, exhortations, extractions, or depredations as could be expected that first night in Africa, but I slept, even so, the sleep of the wary.

Our Suez Canal pilot, appointed by Authority (and Allah, by his attitude) to guide *Outward Leg* halfway through what must be the straightest, most regular-width, most uniformly bottomed, *easily negotiated* stretch of water on the face of this earth, was Ali Wahad. He had a rakish face, and was dressed in a gray djellaba and sandals. Underneath the djellaba he wore a frayed business suit and tie. His first words, as soon as he stepped on board our boat at the appointed time, as I offered him *"M'haba"* were "Captain, you give me present, yes?"

Later, when Thomas showed him a photograph, he had to use binoculars to inspect it, so poor was Ali's eyesight. Even then Ali held the binoculars the wrong way around.

For the whole of that first day's transit, from Port Said to Ismailia, past the canal-rail-desert stations of Ras el Ish, El Tina, El Cap, El Qantara, and El Firdan, little concrete huts standing on the edge of a desert that seemed to stretch over the curvature of the earth, with only scrubby little bushes to break the monotony, Ali Wahad repeated that one, single, monotonous refrain. At every station we passed, he demanded two packets of cigarettes—"for-the-staff-see-they-no-make-problem-yes?"—then he threw one packet ashore, into the waiting, cupped hands of one of a dozen supplicants, and palmed one packet for himself, into his briefcase, which lay always ready to hand on the cockpit seat.

A man of about forty, Ali Wahad lived, he said, in Port Said with his wife and fourteen children, if we could believe him, which I didn't. One of the few things Ali Wahad said that I did believe was that he preferred American vessels to Russian, because the Americans always gave him "presents-much-presents-Captain-you-give-me-present-yes?" while the Soviets were stingy.

As *Outward Leg*, in the rising heat of an Egyptian forenoon, chugged away on and on along the dead-straight ditch, bordered on both sides by monotonous mile after mile of sand dunes, with me at the wheel, Ali Wahad luxuriated on the long seat in the cockpit, drinking copious drafts of tea, which kept Svante busy, and eating plate after plate of sandwiches. Anything between two pieces of bread Ali Wahad would scoff down voraciously, as though he had not been fed for a month. Anything except pork, that is; every time we offered him meat he demanded to first see the can label. Luckily we had some cans of Hungarian corned beef which had a picture of a smiling cow on the labels, and this satisfied Ali Wahad. Even so, Svante had to open the can and make the sandwiches right before the pilot's eyes. Thomas told me later that Ali Wahad had consumed six cans of corned beef, in the nine hours it took *Outward Leg*, at an average speed of five knots under our Yanmar engine, to make the passage from Port Said to Ismailia.

Apart from watching big ships passing northbound, their up-perworks showing over the tops of the sand dunes, there was little to break the monotony of motoring in heat, and sand dunes, sand dunes, but wince at the sight of our carefully hoarded stock of Hungarian beef, our hard-gained Earl Grey tea, and three whole packs of Jacob's cream crackers, along with most of our fresh bread, disappear down Ali Wahad's gullet.

But Allah be praised, nothing lasts forever; at six o'clock we fetched Ismailia and dropped Ali Wahad, along with "You-give-me-present-Captain-yes?" to the tune of thirty dollars, three more cans of corned beef—"for-my-starving-children-yes?"—a carton of cigarettes, a loaf of bread—"I-get-hungry-in-taxi-yes?"—and a pair of Thomas's cast-off shoes, into a waiting Canal Authority launch. Anyone who had ever seen the state of old shoes which Thomas can still wear might well have imagined the condition of those which Ali Wahad swiftly clutched and shoved into the maw of his ever-waiting briefcase before he took off back to Port Said.

We were peeling potatoes on deck as the boat lay at anchor in front of what had once been King Farouk's summer palace, and was now used by the president of Egypt. Svante, who was thoroughly a young Swede in his knee-jerk sentimental attitude toward "third-worlders," whether they deserved it or not, was amazed that Ali Wahad was so poor as to want Thomas's old shoes.

"He'll probably eat *them* in the taxi, too," I told Svante, "or get one of his kids to clean 'em up and sell 'em to some tourist as part of King Tut's jogging outfit!"

"Do you really think so?" Svante asked. He always took my remarks seriously. His sense of humor was dim.

"Or he'll use them himself when he bums for Egypt at the next Olympics," observed Thomas.

"He'll win a gold medal, if he does that," I added.

"He'll sell that to some fat tourist, too," added Thomas.

Our Swedish crewman stared us both for a full five seconds, his blue eyes open wide, then "Do you really think so?" he murmured, as he finished peeling his potato. Svante was turning out to be a good lad, naïve in some ways, but always cheerful, and never slow to have a go, even if, like most novices in sailing craft, he'd little idea, at first, what was happening. At first he might give the impression of slow-wittedness, but after a few days we had realized that this was mainly a language problem. Not only English, but sailing English; and they are like two distinct languages, as anyone who has ever tried to write about sailing knows full well.

At Ismailia the Suez Canal opens up into a big stretch of water—the Bitter Lakes. The town fronts one of the lakes, and the view from our boat that evening, after dark, was of a cool calmness. There was no sign, nor had we seen any, of the rioting soldiers, or revolutionary Muslim extremists which were being reported hourly over the radio on the BBC overseas service. It now appeared that the rioting was confined to the towns south of Cairo, and at Luxor a tourist hotel had been attacked, looted, and gutted. But nowhere within sight of the Suez Canal had there been any sign that things in Egypt were not as normal and corrupt as ever. On the canal the Egyptians we had met respected national symbols of many kinds, any kind but flags—cigarettes, cans of food, old shoes—but the national symbols that gained the Egyptians' deepest respect were made of paper; they were partly green in color, and on them was depicted, according to their stated value, printed on their face, pictures of different American gentlemen, unfortunately long departed.

But that night, anchored off Ismailia, we were left alone, except for the attentions of two fellaheen in a small rowboat, who silently, except for one telltale creak of an oarlock, nosed around *Outward Leg* in the dead hours of the night. They were sharply warned off by Thomas, whose watch it was, and disappeared, muttering imprecations of vengeance dire no doubt, into a misty gloom.

Shortly after that, at 4:15 A.M., a pilot boat bumped into us, as they usually did on the Suez Canal when they were coming alongside. It landed on board *Outward Leg* our second pilot, who was to take us the rest of the way, to the southern end of the canal, at Suez. With visions of Ali Wahad still fresh in our minds, I mentally cringed as the new pilot flung himself down into our cockpit.

The new pilot turned out, at first, to be the very reverse of Ali Wahad. He was friendly, polite, informative, begged nothing—yet, and, as he told me as soon as we met, he liked to steer himself. Willingly, I handed over the wheel to him. His name was Abdullah Hamid. He was about the same age as Ali Wahad, forty or so, and lived in Suez. When I told him about the inquisitive rowboat of only an hour previously, Abdullah dismissed my fears of theft. "No t'eef in Ismailia," he expostulated. "Police chief ver' strong. One fish'man he steal, all fish'man go jail—one week, maybe six week. Police chief ver' strong. He keep all fish'man in jail until t'eef say he t'eef. Police chief no take money from t'eef. T'eef go jail sure. Police chief rich man now—already—he take money from t'eef in Suez before. But now he no take money. He no need money now. What for he take money now? He have big house, car, he no want money sure now—ver' strong, ver' honest, ver' good chief."

Abdullah, true to his word, did like to steer, and steer he did, all the way to Suez. Despite my frequent offers to relieve him at the wheel, he would have none of it. Which suited me fine. Holding a steering wheel and turning it this way and that has never been one of my favorite pasttimes, at least not under power. I can enjoy it under sail, when there's a fresh breeze and the boat is lifting to the breeze, and I can feel the rudder's argument with all the forces about it, but not when the boat is under power in flat water and the rudder feels, if it feels at all, like a meek, flaccid thing, merely following orders.

The distance from Ismailia to Suez was forty-five miles. At the maximum speed allowed us in the Suez Canal, five knots, our Yanmar engine pushed us to Suez by early afternoon, so that in the hottest part of the day we were already at a mooring buoy off the Suez Yacht Club in the South Basin.

Abdullah, to my surprise, for he had seemed a quiet soul, had started to beg as soon as the boat was in sight of Suez, and the more our arrival was imminent, the more urgent, the more insistent, was his tone of begging. It started as a mere whisper—"Abdullah like American cigarettes, Captain,"—then went on, in a more urgent, more strident voice, as Thomas readied the anchor, to "Captain give Abdullah money, yes?"; then, in a loud shout, compelling and imperative, as the anchor chain rattled over the bow: "Abdullah ver' poor man-manee children, small-small food . . . maybe baby die. . . ." I gave Abdullah several packets of Edwards' dried foods, a carton of cigarettes, an old jacket, and pair of boots left on board by a previous crew. Unlike Ali Wahad, back in Ismailia, Abdullah Hamid placed his palms together and thanked me as he left *Outward Leg* and stepped on board the pilot boat sent to meet him.

As *Outward Leg* had neared Suez, so the scenery had changed. Gradually, like a reluctant promise emerging slowly, as we had chugged along, the tops of distant mountains had peeked above the everlasting sand dunes. Now, at Suez, we could plainly see mountains, blue and gray and misty, with a few clouds forming over their peaks, all around our western and northern horizons. Between us in the port and the mountains, far beyond the port, was a desert plain shimmering in the heat, dotted with clumps of quivering vegetation, which stretched as far as the eye could see. I knew I was back by the Red Sea, and the memories of *Barbara*'s voyage in these parts fifteen years before flooded back to me. Then the Suez Canal had been blocked by the wreckage of war. Then the east bank of the canal had been in the hands of Israeli forces. There had been no chance of such an easy passage as we had now had (despite the *baksheesh*); in those days, I'd had to haul *Barbara* the whole way across Israel, from the Mediterranean Sea to the Gulf of Aqaba. Then there had been no shipping at all in the Red Sea, the whole way, all the twenty-two hundred miles from Suez to Cape Gardafui, except, I recalled, one rusty Indian tramp steamer

loaded down with pilgrims bound for Mecca, off the shores of
Ethiopia.

Now, in 1986, as our crew gazed about, I reflected that everything was new to them, and wonderful, and I tried to imagine
seeing it through their eyes, instead of in the memory of the boy
who had first passed this way in a British troopship, back in 1944.
I had been as close to this modern world, then, as I had been to
the world at the turn of the century, 1902! I had known men who
were on board the first-ever ships to pass through the Suez Canal,
back in the 1880s.

The thought of that was staggering. Then I grinned to myself
as I remembered one old sweat in the trooper who had told me
the story of how Benjamin Disraeli, the British premier at the time,
after much financial juggling, had at last managed to buy for Britain
the majority shares in the Suez Canal Company, and of his laconic
message to Queen Victoria: "Madam, you have it." The old sweat,
who must have been in the British Army since the Boer War, had
waved his khaki-clad arm over the side of the crowded ship, at the
sand dunes and palm trees passing, and muttered to me, "I would
have said to 'er, 'Madam, you 'ave it, 'cos I don't bloodywell want
it!' "

It was now a world completely different; in many ways better;
in a few ways worse. I looked at both our crewmen and wondered
if they could ever realize how much the world had changed since
I had been young. But then I reflected that probably every older
man that ever lived had wondered the same about young people,
all throughout history. I watched my crew stare at a lone passing
zhambuk under power, scruffy and unpainted, or paint peeled off;
I wondered what they would have thought in the old days, when
hundreds and hundreds of them could be seen in Suez, all gaily
painted, all under sail and not one engine between the lot of them?
But I decided to say nothing. There were few things worse in a
small craft than an elder rambling on and on about the past, when
there were so many interesting things happening right then and
there. But all the time we were in the Red Sea my mind went back
continually to my younger days, for some reason. I suspected it
was because there were so few distractions on the shores of the
desert, especially for anyone who was not highly mobile, that I
was forced back into myself and my own memories. I'd been lucky
anyway; I had an interesting youth; in the archives in my head

there was no shortage of good entertainment. I could cry or laugh whenever I needed to.

In Suez we met up with a New Zealand sloop which had arrived from Port Sudan. With the family on board—I lost my note on her and don't recall her name—a middle-aged couple and their two teenage sons, both strapping lads, we swapped some charts, and, over supper on board their handsome vessel, plenty of yarns. We gave them a bottle of our Israeli wine, which delighted them. Anxious to be in the fabled Mediterranean (about which I did not disillusion them), they'd been beating, on this last passage, against the north wind, for six weeks continually and had seen no booze since they'd left the Seychelles six months before.

We all turned in early that night to be ready for weighing the hook at dawn, and setting off into the Red Sea. We were fifteen hundred miles on our passage from Istanbul. There was plenty of time for us to be at the southern end of the Red Sea, the Bab el Mandeb, fourteen hundred sailing miles to the south of Suez, by April. That was when the monsoon was due to change from an easterly wind to a westerly in the Gulf of Aden and Indian Ocean.

Even despite the baksheesh rendered to our two erstwhile pilots, *Outward Leg* was still well stocked. We had enough canned and dried food on board to reach Mombasa, India, or the Seychelles, given normal winds, as long as we ate as much fresh food as we needed, obtained ashore, when we were not sailing.

As for the wind, here in the Gulf of Suez it blew eternally from the north-northwest, as it had in the days of the Queen of Sheba. It blew hard every day at this time of year, but for *Outward Leg* it was the fairest wind even a soldier could ask for. Farther south, in the Strait of Gubal, where the Gulf of Suez narrows before it widens into the Red Sea, the wind we could expect would be a roaring ripsnorter, but it would yet be northwesterly, I knew, and fair for us. We would hang on to its coattails and with it ride south to Sudan, about seven hundred miles away, where we would be able safely to go ashore without having to exchange a small fortune in dollars, as we were supposed to do in Egypt. If we found a haven of some kind on the Egyptian shore, where it would be safe to spend a night without being shot at by the notoriously trigger-happy (outside of the Suez Canal Zone) Egyptian Army, rioting or not, we would do so, but we'd be damned careful. We had no visas for landing in Egypt because getting them would have meant having to change our valuable dollars for a wad of Egyptian pounds, and those we didn't use would be unrechangeable, or take reams of paper and weeks to change back into dollars. With those thoughts in my mind I fell asleep as, far away, a ship's siren hooted as she made in or out of the southern mouth of Disraeli's Ditch.

Part Two

Rerunning the Gauntlet

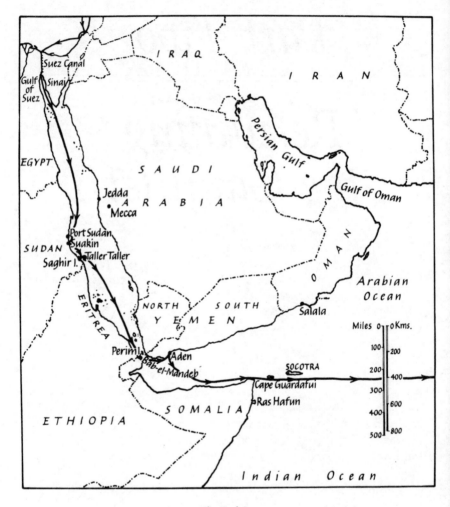

The Red Sea

7

Where the Best Is Like the Worst

Next day, after we'd paid Ibrahim and worked *Outward Leg*'s way off the rusty, expensive mooring buoy at the Suez "Yacht Club" (which seemed to consist, so far as I could see from the boat, of a rusty iron gate and a concrete roadway), we pushed off under our Yanmar engine for the offing.

From what we had seen of Suez, it had little going for it, except for fresh water on tap at the club pontoon, and of course, the canal. We wondered, as we motored out, what it must be like to live in a country where the foremost sign of progress, the most valuable asset, had been designed, constructed, and operated until it was a perfect work, for many decades, by others. To be conscious that our own people had only taken over a fully finished, going concern; merely grabbed it.

"But the Egyptians could say they built the Pyramids," piped up Svante, "and the world's first lighthouse at Alexandria, too."

I riposted, "Then a Welshman, looking at the motorways system in England could say his ancestors built Stonehenge and the first navigational line of position was discovered off the Welsh coast . . . and a fat lot of good that would do for his sense of national achievement when it comes to solving the world's problems. How many starving Ethiopians are fed by the Pyramids, and how many ships loaded with European food passing through this European-built canal?"

But Svante had seen the light and had moved forward to stow away our fenders.

It was a glorious day; the horizon to the south, and the mountains to the north and west were defined as clearly as if they'd been freshly laundered.

We left early, before the wind piped up. The shipping lanes and holding grounds off the canal entrance were always busy; there was little sense in sailing out in a stiff breeze among a score of closely packed, swift-maneuvering ships. That might be all right for sailing show-offs at Cowes or on the East River, but not here, in the Gulf of Suez, with thousands of miles to go before the next dependable boat-repair facility.

In the offing, clear of Suez and the ship-holding grounds to the south, the mountains of Sinai now showing on our southeastern horizon, we found that the wind—the fickle, treacherous, *bitch* of a bloody wind—for the first time since the days of the Queen of Sheba, had decided to blow not from the north-northwest, but from the south-southeast.

I know that the Hollywood heroes, the macho men of the Riviera races, and, had they been able to, the "Mediterranean cowboys" too, would have beat their brains, what they had, against that south-southeaster. Not us; we worked in to the northern side of Ras el Misalla, a low, coral-fringed convex bend in the coast (it could hardly be called a headland), and there dropped the hook to wait for the wind to come to its senses and return to the northerly quadrant. We waited all the forenoon, and when it was clear to me that the wind was not only going to be contrary that day but weak with it, we weighed and beat short, slow—nothing over five knots—tacks down to Ras el Sudr, about twenty miles southeast of Suez, where the indentation in the Sinai shore was deeper than at El Misalla, and there we dropped the anchor again.

There was little harm in all this weighing and anchoring. With a novice crewman on board we could hardly do too much of it. In the Red Sea area there would often be high winds and tiny anchoring space, then there would be one chance to anchor properly, and one chance only. Svante learned how to anchor the boat properly, with a bridle to each ama bow, so that *Outward Leg* like all trimarans, would not yaw in the wind while she lay on the hook.

The climate in the northern Red Sea, in very early March, was not too hot, except for a couple of hours in mid-afternoon, but even then the air was so dry that our lips were already cracking. For me the dry air was ideal; ever since my navy days I have always suffered from breathing problems in moist air.

Some people seemed to think that a life spent at sea must have been necessarily healthy. In my case at least it hadn't been so for a lot of the time. I spent many of my young years on the crowded mess-decks of British warships; and later I had been far too cold and wet, and much too hungry too many, many times, to make for a pain-free later life, even had I not been amputated. These days it was different. There had been great advances all round in knowledge of healthy practices with food and living-conditions and survival at sea, for which we could all be very thankful, and doff our hats to fine men like Dr. David Lewis and Dr. Alain Bombard, who had put themselves to much trouble, hardship, and hazard to make it so.

The sea off Ras el Sudr was discolored, so that we had to feel our way carefully in to anchor, watching the echo sounder the whole time. We got very good holding ground with the sandspit on the Ras bearing 177 degrees and the one, single, solitary, lonely, sad-looking palm tree thereabouts bearing 086 degrees (29°35′ north, 32°39′ east).

Toward evening, as the crew were in the galley preparing supper, I noticed a sailing craft heading north, running free before the southerly breeze. At first I thought it might be a dhow. I had been surprised that we had not encountered any Arab sailing craft in the Gulf of Suez; and disappointed that I could not watch my crewmen's faces when they saw how fast they were, and how well they went to windward. The last time I'd been in these waters, in 1971 (farther south, it's true) the dhows and zhambuks had been like flies around a jam pot at every possible haven, every shallow niche in the shore, every gap in the coastal reef.

As the sail drew ever closer I saw that it was a Western-style yacht, and she was making straight for our anchorage. This was another surprise; last time I'd been in the Red Sea waters I never saw one yacht the whole way from Israel to Kenya; in fact *Barbara* had been the first Western-style sailing craft to call in Djibouti in *twelve years*! At other small ports on the Red Sea shores she must have been the first ever.

The strange yacht turned out, when she was close enough for us to see her ensign, to be French. By this time the lads had served

up supper and we were eating it in the cockpit—boiled Suez beef
and rice—watching the French yacht. By now she was a mere fifty
feet away from us. Her skipper, a slight man of about thirty, at a
wild guess, was at the helm, while his crew, an "arty"-looking
woman, probably in her late twenties, stood on the foredeck ready
to let go of the anchor. As we silently gawped and munched away,
she freed the chain and the Frenchman's anchor rattled down onto
the sandy bottom, *right alongside our own anchor.*

"Bloody marvelous," I said to the boys. "I mean *abso-bloody-
lutely, splendifuckerously, bleebuggererysoddingly wonderful*! He's got . . .
fu— miles and miles and bloody miles . . ." I swept my arm away
across, toward the coast of the Sinai. "I mean you could anchor
the whole of the bloody British, American, and the sodding Soviet
navies in just half the room that bloody French twit has got . . ."
I choked on a piece of hard Egyptian beef.

"You think the French are anchored far enough away?" asked
Svante. "It looks to me like she's a bit close." His English was very
fluent, and he had a distinct English Midlands accent, gained from
his English teacher in Sweden.

Thomas, not knowing whether to laugh or cry, looked over at
me, as I had sat there, speechless, fuming as the French yacht,
dropping back on her anchor chain, slowly bore ever closer down
on our bows. I must have been giving Svante a very dark Stan
Laurel stare. Everyone was silent.

The French yacht settled down, with her anchor chain all paid
out, her cockpit only twenty feet or so from our own, in all that
vastness of anchoring space off a wilderness shore. Her skipper's
voice, in a well-modulated Parisian accent, carried itself over to me
in the now still evening air: *"Bon jour, m'sieur,"* it said. *"Vous venez
ici souvent?"* "Good evening, do you come here often?"

I decided to Play the Game. "Yes," I told him, in my rusty
French. "You see that tree over there? Yes, that one. It's the only
one for miles and miles on this coast of Sinai. I own it—it's my
property. I come to check it out every week or so, in between tides.
But we're going to have to shift soon, about a mile farther north.
The tidal rips here are extremely fierce. You'd better shift too"—
my voice must have dropped an octave—"only you'd better go
first, *because your anchor, m'sieur, has been dropped over mine.*" I must
have pulled a face as fierce as my mythological tide rips, because
in less than five minutes the French yacht had cleared off. Sure
enough, just as I'd said she would, she made for precisely the *exact*

same spot where I had lied to him we were going, but now the Frenchman was well clear of *Outward Leg*, which was what mattered.

Darkness fell; apart from their little anchor light in the night, we saw no more of the French couple; they were gone when we rose at dawn to find the beginnings of a good blow, very fair for us, springing up out of the north-northwest.

That day was the best day's sail *Outward Leg* had had since she had been in the Atlantic Ocean. We spread out both roller headsails on the running poles, wing-and-wing, and let her fly; and fly she did, all the way to a point five miles off Ras Sharatib. That was about seventy miles in seven hours, before the wind dropped in the late afternoon. Then we frigged about with the headsails, trying to squeeze out more southing, until at dusk the wind died, and we hove to, to await a fresh wind next morning, hopefully again from the same direction.

We were off the shipping lanes marked on the charts, between the northbound lane and the Sinai coast, which was about five miles to the east of us. There we could wait. When you've seven or eight thousand miles ahead of you there's no point in breaking your balls to cover distance under power, or wearing yourself out, wasting the energy that comes from hard-earned and carefully stowed food. Easy does it until the wind joins in to do the work.

Being hove-to (stopped in the water but still drifting south with the slight tidal current) wasn't as good as being at anchor off the coast, in some calm haven; the sea was too lively for that—but we could not be sure where the Egyptian Army was stationed on the coast of Sinai. To heave-to out at sea was better than the risk of being shot at, or held to rich ransom, as we knew had happened to other yachts on the Egyptian coast.

In the Gulf of Suez the shipping lanes, always busy day and night, were clearly defined, and most ships stuck to them, but there was always the odd ship out, dodging the traffic, that was a continual menace. Also there was local traffic, small ships, zhambuks and dhows, that plied across the Gulf of Suez, athwart the shipping lanes, and farther south, the Red Sea. They had to be watched out for. So we kept watch all night and in the daytime, too, whenever we hove to, to be that much safer.

In the southern half of the Gulf of Suez another hazard were the oil rigs. There were fields—whole cities—of blazing light, dozens and dozens of different rigs, spread right across the Gulf. That night it was eerie as we negotiated our passage, before a stiff

norther, both headsails winged out, in between the oil rigs, each
one with gigantic flares spluttering huge golden phoenix-wings in
the darkness of the night sky. We could hardly see Venus rising
in the east, nor the moon's passage, nor sniff the breeze for the
glare of man's greed and the stink of black gold.

Sometimes we could see unlit structures, helicopter pads and
unused rigs, with no lights on them at all, but their outlines were
quite clear against the harsh golden light of the working rigs. Still,
we had to keep a sharp eye out, so as not to collide with some
danger or other.

All night we rolled on before a twenty-five-knot breeze, until
daylight at dawn showed us the mountains on each side of the
Strait of Gubal, where the shipping was thick. We even raced a
Norwegian tanker for some miles, and almost kept up with her,
which shows our pace, for she was loaded and in a hurry.

"Where do you think she's heading?" asked Svante.

I'm never at my kindest in the morning: "To some place full of
bloody Skywegian 'environmentalists' waiting to pump gasoline
into their frigging motor cars and motorbikes, so they can get to
some rally to save a local species of toad, I expect." I grunted.

"Wearing plastic anoraks, too," added Thomas.

Svante, wearing a week's growth of beard now, surprisingly
red, had been standing at the galley companionway hatch. He had
raised himself up, using his arms now like a sailor, instead of trying
to use his legs like landsmen do. Svante stared at the Norwegian
tanker for a full minute, and let himself down again into the galley.
There, he was silent for another minute, then he looked at me with
his blue eyes wide open: "Do you really think so?" he murmured.

On the Egypt side of the Strait of Gubal (as opposed to the Sinai
side) there was a mess of small islands and reefs: the Gubal Islands.
In the midst of that maze was the island of Tawila, and there it
was rumored the Egyptian Army did not go, the island having no
water, and the Egyptian soldiers, most likely, having no stomach
for the heavy seas and intricate passages through the islands. It
was also reputed to have the safest and most beautiful haven in
the whole of the Red Sea, Endeavor Bay, named after the Royal
Navy ship which had first surveyed it for the world back in the
mid-nineteenth century.

Endeavor Bay turned out to be on the south side of Tawila
Island, which was mostly dead low and flat, behind a fishhook-
shaped sandspit, open to the winds on all sides, and overlooked,

4 Kastellorizon, Greece

5 Kastellorizon. The self-proclaimed frontier of the East

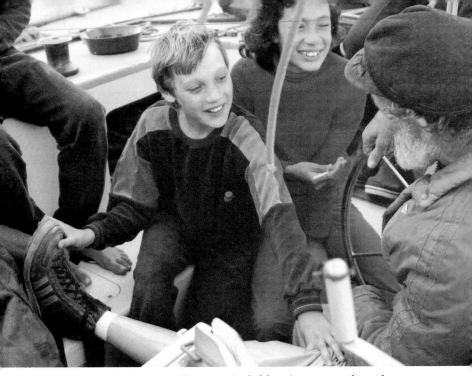

6 Larnaca, Cyprus. A children's party on board

7 Larnaca. Relaunch of *Outward Leg* attended by U.N. Forces
Commander, Major Robin Duchesne, and a piper from the
Royal Ulster Rifles

by three massive oil rigs close by. In the anchorage were six yachts at anchor: two voyaging vessels one on passage from Australia and one from New Zealand, and *four charter boats* on their way back north from the Sudanese reefs. There these charter boats had spent the European winter, catering to Western urbanites who, after watching Commander Cousteau (a paid, serving officer of the French Navy) poking around underwater on their living room TVs, wanted to poke around disturbing and killing undeserving Red Sea fish in *their* living rooms.

The small fleet of yachts had taken up all the good anchoring ground. I couldn't blame anybody for that, except perhaps us, for not getting to Endeavor Bay first. There was anchoring space left only over soft sand, and a hard northerly blowing, up to forty-five knots, in the afternoon.

Twice *Outward Leg* dragged her anchor that day in Endeavor Bay, until I got her bows up close to an old iron jetty close to the throat of the bay inlet, and tied her up to that with two long lines. Then we supped in peace, away from the noise of rock "music" blaring out from one Italian charter-vessel, for the skipper of which I profoundly prayed, and as I told the lads, "There must surely be reserved a place in Dante's Inferno."

In Endeavor Bay I first noticed another big difference from the last time I had been in Red Sea waters fifteen years before: There were some seabirds about now. I could not recall ever having seen any, outside the big seaports, back then. So I slept peacefully, despite the wind howling overhead, having found at least one consolation for the presence in the Gulf of Suez of so much evidence of mankind's heedless exploitation and destruction of earth's precious heritage in that part of it.

There was a port—Hurghada—about twenty miles southwest of Tawila, but we didn't intend to call there. One of our New Zealand friends from the cruising boats told of meeting up with an American sloop which had been held in Hurghada for weeks after refusing to pay three hundred dollars for a twenty-five-gallon barrel of diesel oil, the originally agreed price for which had been twenty-five dollars. I decided to make direct for the first anchorage south of the Sudan-Egypt frontier.

But first we hove to off Umm Qamar islet, about eighteen miles southwest of Tawila. Umm Qamar was so neatly designed, so perfectly round, so perfectly a flat rock, about a half mile across, that it looked as if it were, perhaps, part of a film lot, made of plaster smeared on a wire frame by someone with little idea of what a Red Sea islet should look like. All it needed, to complete the illusion, was a Hollywood plastic pirate ship in the background. There, in waters almost solid with fish, we caught breakfast and lunch. We might have caught dinner too, only we had no refrigerator to keep the catch in, and there was simply no sense in killing for the mere sake of it.

Thomas, always an enthusiastic student of navigation, always the perfectionist, had been studying our chart of the Gubal reefs. "Why isn't that beacon on the north end of the Umm Qamar reef shown on the chart?" he asked me.

"Look at the date of the chart, Thomas," I replied, "the date when the islet was first surveyed, and see the date when the last corrections were inserted on it."

Thomas bent to the chart again. "Yes, 1868 and 1972 . . . I see what you mean," he said. "Why is that chart so old?" asked Svante, who was with us in the after cabin.

I told him: "If we were to buy all new charts for the voyage from Suez to Singapore it would cost well over a thousand dollars. In the old days they cost about one tenth of that. Then we could afford them, but now only a few people can. That means that we either have to find a source of old, used, out-of-date charts, like I did in London, or we have to copy charts, which is illegal. Anyway, copied charts are sometimes badly distorted, or the lettering and symbols are deformed or mangled, so you can't read them properly, and that can lead to disasters on remote shores . . . or anywhere. . . ."

South of Umm Qamar islet we found ourselves headed again. Now the wind was southeast and limbering up to blow a good old Red Sea *hamsin*. I recognized the signs all right—a golden-red glare right over the south horizon and a sea far too wild far too soon, as though, like a boxer limbering up for a forthcoming title fight, it was practicing for the combat ahead. The barometer over our navigation table was plunging, too.

"We're in for a duster," I told the lads. The boat was pitching and heaving now. "I'm going to head for Sharm el Naka. It's just to the north of Ras Aba Suma here." I pointed at a tiny indentation on the coast of Egypt, at 26°52' north. "There's supposed to be a village to the north of it, but if my reckoning's right the sea off the village will be too rough for anyone to leave in a small boat. The possible anchorage"—I pointed at the root of the tiny bay—"is far enough from the village that the Gyppos may not even see us, especially when the storm hits the bay and raises a sandstorm with it. Anyway, it's worth a try."

In an hour's time the wind was howling its head off from the south-east and the air was thick with blown sand which penetrated everywhere. *Outward Leg* was now beating her way into Sham el Naka, with one reef in the main and the yankee drum-skinned. On a close haul she was making nine knots, even loaded down as she was. Now she was hammering and drumming, flying and flailing and the devil take the hindmost as she raced for the golden beach along a deep-khaki desert shore, dodging the reefs which showed turquoise in the blue, blue sea.

By high noon we were tucked away at anchor in calm water right in the corner of a narrow bay pointing southeast. Normally the wind in those parts blew from the north, and normally the wind and current beat right into the bay, pushing any detritus of ships' passages onto the beach. It showed, too: The beach around the bay was entirely covered with a band of brightly colored or dirty-white plastic jetsam, spattered with black oil, for a width of *a hundred yards*, right around the bay, for at least *a mile and a half*, and most likely more.

Inside the bay it had been a job for us to find a bottom shallow enough to anchor in. It was only in the very bight of the bay that there was a narrow ledge, perhaps no more extensive than a tennis court, where the anchor line, at two hundred feet, was not too short for the hook to reach bottom. But once it dug in, the anchor held fine. Because of the rising wind—it was now a regular forty-five knots—we ran out the Bruce anchor as well as the CQR.

As we ate our fish from breakfast-time I looked over toward the shore, in the direction of the village, which was hidden from us by sand dunes. There, on top of the highest dunes, were two tiny figures. I broke out the binoculars and gazed at them. They were two Egyptian soldiers perched atop two camels, one inspecting us through a pair of binoculars.

I handed the binoculars to Thomas. "Now what do we do?" he asked, after we had inspected the sight. The Egyptians were now waving their rifles and shouting to us, their voices thin in the wind. We ignored them.

"Nothing. We're out of rifle range here, and it looks like they don't have any boats. Even if they did have there's no way they're going to get out into that sea."

Thomas and Svante looked toward the north of us, beyond the lee of the headland of Ras Abu Suma. The sea beyond the bay, under a thick cloud of sand, was boiling in white ferment.

The Egyptian soldiers had approached the beach, and there, amid the plastic junk, we watched them as, magnified in the clear, hot desert air, they dismounted from their camels and sat down, one to hide below his djellaba hood, one to stare at us through his binoculars. We all three in *Outward Leg* sat in the cockpit, behind the dodger, staring back at them.

"Perhaps they only want a cigarette?" suggested Svante.

I looked at him for a brief second, then back at the soldiers. They were armed—we weren't. "Listen, Svante," I told him, "nobody . . . nobody, south of Rome or the Mexican border, and not many north of them, merely *wants a cigarette*. Okay? Got that?"

"You mean they might want something else?" asked Svante, his innocent blue eyes wondering.

"Always. A cigarette is only the thin end of the wedge, and that goes for the offering as well as the taking," I replied.

"What is it they want?" persisted Svante.

"Everything. They believe, the vast majority of them, that what you, with your white skin and blue eyes have, is theirs, and what they have is theirs, too. They want everything, Svante, and they'll kill you, if need be, to take it. And if you don't believe that is true—and I won't blame you for not believing it, because it may not be—but if you act as though it were not true, among these people around the Red Sea, then you will very probably be either very poor, very hungry, very wounded, or very dead before long."

"But we in Sweden have had no colonies," Svante informed us. "We have no colonial problems or anything like that with Egypt or the others."

I nodded over toward the soldiers on the shore. They sat, crossed-legged, immobile, the hoods of their coats pulled over their faces, holding their rifles in front of them. "Tell that to them," I said. "Do you really think, Svante, that they give a monkey's tit about that? It's what you *own now* they're after, not some kind of compensation for some legendary wrongs in the past."

I lowered myself down the after cabin companionway and left the two Egyptians, and our German and Swede, to contemplate each other over the windswept mile, too far for Egyptian bullets to fly, between them.

All that day we sat at anchor in Sharm el Naka with a regular sandstorm beating around our ears, and all that day, until dusk, the soldiers, silent on the sand dune, kept us company. Then night fell, and we saw them no more; when the wind died at midnight we weighed as quietly and as fast as we could and got the hell out of the bay, before the sea calmed down enough for the Egyptians perhaps to reach out to us in small craft.

That next day the wind backed right around the compass so that it blew from northwest, and it carried us around 450 miles, in two days and a night, to an area of the Red Sea where we would, I calculated, be comparatively safe, south of the Sudan-Egypt border. The exact location of that line, though, was disputed between our British and American charts. The British charts showed the border sixty miles farther north than did the American. I decided to be a pessimist, and followed, in this matter, the American chart.

So we set our course to steer not less than forty miles from the coast, so as to avoid any possible hazards, and let her go. The second night out of Sharm el Naka we got a full gale and more, and reefed down the twin headsails until they were little bigger, together, than a kid's kite. Then the wind anemometer read at times 40 knots, while *Outward Leg* was bowling along herself at a good 11 knots and more as she surfed over the steep, long seas. If we added our boatspeed to the wind-guage reading, we got a total true-wind speed of something like 50 knots on average, so it was, we concluded, blowing quite hard that night. In the morning the wind diminished to around a steady 25 knots, and we unreefed the headsails to their full extent, forty feet from clew to clew on the running poles, and Lord did she go! On one longish surf of about ten seconds the log boatspeed indicator gave 20.14 knots! This was in a boat, don't forget, loaded down with stores for three men for a voyage of three months . . . which must have weighed an extra two tons at least.

On the third night out we got a repeat performance; a full gale and more, all the night long, straight up *Outward Leg*'s arse so that she took off and surfed and twisted, and climbed and fell and shot forward hour after hour after juddering, shuddering hour, under a black velvet sky; a million gleaming stars reflecting the phosphorescence of the angry, bewildered, froth-whipped seas. No flat lake for such as we, that heaving, boisterous, Red Sea.

On 13 March we sighted the Abingdon Reef lighthouse early in the morning, passed it close to starboard (there were turtles sunbathing below the light), and made our way inshore, through intricate reefs, past the forlorn islets of Shambaya and Mayatib and a big, barren, hot, and waterless (we knew) island known as Mukawarr to Inkeifal, a gap in the rocky shore no wider than a linnet's throat, and there, in Sudanese waters, anchored, just over seven hundred miles to the south of Suez.

8

The Sudanese Reefs

On the way into Inkeifal haven, we on board *Outward Leg* discussed the political prospects ahead in the different countries around the shores of the Red Sea.

Sudan, we knew both from the voyaging grapevine and the BBC overseas service, although wracked by bitter civil war in her southern, inland provinces, was, for the moment at least, on her long coastline, peaceful, although presidential elections were only a month or so away. Then, we suspected, there would probably be some fireworks, and not the festive kind, either. We knew, from the grapevine, that the port charges in Port Sudan were not heavy by Mediterranean standards—five dollars a day for a boat the size of *Outward Leg*—but with a month to go before the change of monsoon we were in no hurry, and staying out of Port Sudan would not only save us that five dollars a day, but feed us with fish, too. It was well known that the Sudanese Army was too busy fighting the civil war in the Upper Nile and Equatorial provinces to be concerned, as the Egyptian Army had been, with spending Western aid on guarding rocks and sand from the depredations of voyagers in small sailing craft. Watching for and guarding against natural hazards we could slowly cruise down the Sudanese shore, behind the offlying reefs, biding our time. Then we could make a shorter stopover in Port Sudan before heading farther south in

April. By that time, the present prevailing south wind in those latitudes might diminish or even change to a northerly, and so help us greatly through the notorious Straits of Bab el Mandeb.

Saudi Arabia, on the opposite, eastern side of the Red Sea, was closed to all yachts except in the big expensive oil-ports of Jedda and Yenbo, where, it was said, eighty dollars a day was levied for moorings alone! Elsewhere, all along the long Arabian shoreline, any yacht was likely to be arrested and the skipper and crew thrown into jail until the payment of a galactic fine. So for *Outward Leg* Saudi Arabia was out.

Farther south on the western side of the Red Sea, Ethiopia was strictly out-of-bounds to any Western vessels except big ships carting food and other largesse for a population brought to starvation by the stupid policies of a callously inefficient government. Eritrea, the coastal province, was still in ferment, fighting its own war of independence, as it had been when I visited there sixteen years before, in *Barbara*. The word on the grapevine was that the Ethiopian Navy was likely to shoot first and ask questions later. That we could do without.

That left only North Yemen to consider. There had been rumors heard in the boatyards of the eastern Mediterranean that North Yemen was open to foreign yachts now, but there had been very few, or conflicting, details, as to their reception.

Outside the Red Sea, in the Gulf of Aden, the only two possible havens, Djibouti and Aden, were ciphers. We knew from the BBC that Aden had been in the throes of a rebellion by "party factions," but that seemed to have died down. There was no news, no way of telling.

We decided to cruise all the way down the coast of the Sudan to Suakin, about halfway down the length of the Red Sea, and then head direct for either Djibouti or Aden, depending on what we might gather by way of news of those places. From either port it would be a long voyage of over two thousand miles to the Seychelles Islands, Sri Lanka (if the Tamil rebellion allowed it), or India.

I remembered the last voyage I had made that way, sixteen years before, and told the lads that the situation had been completely reversed. In those days, because *Barbara* had been in Israel, it was Egypt and Sudan I couldn't call in at, while I had been able, the accepted risks of pirates and marauders of the Eritrean "Liberation Force" apart, to call in at Massawa and dirty, dusty, beggar-ridden Assab ("the arsehole of the world"), in Ethiopia.

For the time being, though, we decided to take it easy on the Sudanese coast, day-hopping south from one anchorage to the next. We could expect a fair north wind, it was the least torrid time of the year and we had plenty of fresh water and barter items on board for trade with Sudanese natives.

When I had first used the word "natives" with Svante, he had objected politely. He said that it had "colonial overtones."

"Everybody speaking English says 'locals' now," he had protested.

Of course I knew that was the fashion among "modern" "expats." I didn't agree with it at all. "Bullshit," I told Svante. "In the old days the word 'native' was used just as much at home as it was overseas. If a British ship was in a port that was someone's home port that someone was referred to as a native, and got special leave privileges. There's nothing derogatory about 'native' at all. It means 'born here' and in that context it's a noun, not an adjective. And anyway, in modern English 'local' is used by someone when he refers to a pub he uses regularly."

"I wouldn't call you a native," persisted our Swedish crewman.

"Of course you wouldn't"—I glanced around at the desert shore—"we're not in Wales, but if we were I wouldn't mind one bit being called a native . . . in fact I'd be bloody proud of it!"

As we entered the narrow inlet of Inkeifal we saw dozens of herons lift up off the waters of the lagoon and hover overhead. When they landed later and stood on the shore we saw that some of them were well over six feet tall. Inkeifal lagoon was about a quarter-mile wide and a mile long, a wonderfully safe, natural haven. I have seen many man-made ports less safe. The bottom was about thirty feet deep on average, hard sand. There were plenty of fish among the fringing reef inside the lagoon, which kept us well fed, and small crabs on the rocks by the entrance which weren't bad either.

Spear fishing was supposed to be illegal in Sudanese waters without a license (which meant some official was probably feathering his nest with the collected proceeds *and* fines). But considering the huge shoals of fish and the absolute lack of people, apart from ourselves, in almost all the havens we called at, the risk of being seen was minimal, and our need to conserve our canned food for the Indian Ocean outweighed all over considerations of conscience.

The crew found that the time needed for spearing enough fish for the day was about an hour in the morning and an hour just before sunset. The energy and willingness were limitless.

Most of the mornings were spent in maintenance work on the boat and the engine, while the hotter afternoons whiled themselves away.

The only people we saw, once, at Inkeifal were camel herders, whose coming was heralded by a vast, lone high sand-cloud far away along the desert plain. We stared at this for an hour, wondering what it might be, before we saw the dark line below the cloud resolve itself into two hundred or so animals, moving sedately along the ground like one huge living being, while their herders, sheltering from the fierce sun under the hoods of their djellabas, hunched in their saddles and wobbled steadily from side to side. As we watched them from our boat through the binoculars and by plain eye, the herd drew along the shore of the lagoon, only a hundred yards away. Two or three young bloods among the herders cut out from their companions, beat their camels with their feet, and raced away, their red and blue robes flying behind them in the wind they raised by their speed. Then, when they were a half mile ahead of the herd, they turned their camels in unison and trotted triumphantly, it seemed, back to the shore by the boat. There they waved their camel sticks in greeting, while Thomas took a picture, and Svante and I, in return, waved a towel and a walking stick. It was a glorious gesture, a stirring sight against the background of majestic mountains across the plain, and it left all the crew of *Outward Leg* silent in wonder. It reminded me of my encounter in *Sea Dart* with the Paraguayan gauchos on the River Paraguay in South America back in 1974. Like this salutation in the Sudan, so far away and yet so similar, the gauchos' gallop over the pampas had been unexpected; a gesture full of the warmth and the delight of recognition of kindred spirits.

In Inkeifal we tested a water-making device. It was an ex-United States Air Force unit, a plastic "balloon" with a black material inside it, originally, we supposed, issued to aircraft crews in case of ditching over the ocean. The unit came in a tightly packed plastic brick and was dated 1947. I had bought it in a government-surplus store in San Diego while *Outward Leg* was being fitted out in 1983. To our intense astonishment, it worked! Floating on the lagoon waters, under a hot sun, it turned out about three cupfuls of brackish, but definitely nonsaline liquid. Carefully we packed the unit up again, and stowed it away. The unit was old—it obviously might itself not last long—but Thomas and I had closely studied it, and knew now how to construct a reasonably efficient water distiller. That knowledge made all the difference, then, to our view of the wide stretches of the Indian Ocean that lay ahead of us. . . .

Our next passage was south through the channel between the offlying reef and the fringing reef on the coast itself. At first we towed the dinghy, but by the time the sun was up ten degrees above the horizon, the wind was blowing a near gale, *Outward Leg* was surfing at nine knots, and the dinghy was yawing like a crazed bullock, so we hove to and brought it on board to sit quietly on the wing deck. We needed it on board in any case; there was a rent in the rubber bottom. This we repaired while the boat plunged on and on between the reefs, to reach the entrance to another haven by dusk. Despite being for the most part in the lee of the offlying reefs, there was even so a steep, wickedly short, sea in the Inner Passage.

As *Outward Leg* plunged and rinsed, pickled and surfed, bound south, off Dara, a one-hut (literally) village, we sighted a camel rider perched atop his intently striding beast, clapping his stick against its haunches, racing along the sea-fringing desert, leaving behind it its own little trail of dust which the wind picked up and swept over the head of the rider.

The first gap in the coast was Marsa Salak, a wide bay full of shoals and islands. By mid-afternoon, when we reached it, the sun was way over the mountains to the southwest and shining right in my eyes. We had no detailed chart of the area, but we did know there was a Sudanese Army post somewhere near the bay. We had no permits, as yet, to land in Sudan, so I bore off, and headed another few miles down the coast, racing away to beat the fast-sinking sun, to sight the beacon off the entrance to Marsa Fijab, fifty miles to the south of Inkeifal. Against the setting sun, and with Thomas forging ahead in the dinghy to sound the passage for *Outward Leg*, we slowly entered the narrow-mouthed haven and threaded our way easily (in the sailor's sense of the word, meaning *carefully*) through shallows until we were about a mile and a half inside a wide stretch of water cluttered with dozens of small low islands, many of them teeming with birds, and dropped the hook in six feet of water over mud. The rise and fall of tide in

Sudan at that latitude was only around two feet, even at springs, so we turned in and slept soundly. I kept "one ear open," though, in case of any attempts to board the boat by uninvited night visitors.

The following morning, as daylight showed the five huts which make the "town" of Fijab, we received our first visitor in Sudan. He was Terif Mohammed, a young man who told us, in a mixture of basic Arabic and English, that he was "about twenty-one." He was tall, lean, very black, with regular features and his hair, black and wiry, stood out from his head all round at least a foot, in the fuzzy-wuzzy style traditional in the Sudan. He was dressed in a length of cloth wrapped around his waist. Over that he wore a belt and dagger. Terif brought with him six small eggs, which he exchanged for two packets of American cigarettes. He held his cigarette between finger and thumb, in the cup of his right hand, as do all people who know deprivation. He told us that four other yachts had called at Fijab: two that year and two the year before. He took the people from the yachts on camel rides along the shore, he said, and they paid him the equivalent of six dollars American for the use of his two camels the whole day. Mainly his family of six brothers, three sisters and his parents lived from the fish they caught. Their only cash income in the past two years, he said, had been the money for the camel rides.

"How many yachts took the camel rides?" I asked him in my mixture of some English and some hand weaving.

"Two," he gave me to understand, "one this year and one last year." I made a quick mental calculation; the total cash-income of Terif Mohammed's family of twelve, over the past two *years*, had been *twelve dollars*, or fifty cents per head per year!

Then Terif, his face fallen into deep gloom, added, "But times were good then. One of our camels died last month, of old age." Which is why, that forenoon, Thomas and Svante and I (feeling rather stupid and thanking Allah there were no other observers apart from my crew and the whole of Terif's family) took it in turns to ride Terif's one remaining camel up and down, up and down the glaring hot, blinding white stretch of sand, about fifty yards long, between the miserable hovels of Fijab, and the fierce, hot rocks on the shore.

It was also the reason why we weighed anchor early next day and shoved off for the next haven down the Sudanese coast. If we hadn't we would have probably ridden that skinny, bad-tempered beast again, along that sizzling shore.

No sooner had we emerged from the narrow, shallow entrance to Marsa Fijab, than our satnav showed signs of a failing ability to pick up signals from satellites passing overhead. As the boat shot off under twin headsails with the wind strengthening to a near gale, and reefs all around us, I found that the antenna had failed us yet again. This was a new antenna unit, only four months on board, the *third* replacement since *Outward Leg* had left San Diego. Each one had cost me 280 ill-afforded dollars, as the makers of the satellite "navigator" did not guarantee that part of their equipment that was most exposed, most vulnerable to sea and air-borne sand. That was annoying enough, but what made me angry was the knowledge that had I expected this fault I would never have dreamed of navigating the Inner Passage of the Sudanese Reefs. Even though both Thomas and I could take quick, accurate sun-sights to find our lines of position at any time during the day or night, those lines in the daytime would be almost all north-south. There was only one fleeting period, over the noontime, when it would be possible to get anything like an east-west line to show our latitude. Besides this, in the noontime, as the sun passed overhead, the beating heat on the coastal reefs raised a white mist which drifted inland and soon completely obscured the inland mountain peaks, which, off that otherwise almost featureless shore, were our only landmarks for finding our position along the coast.

We had met people in Cyprus who had made the voyage from Australia, even, with little or no knowledge of celestial navigation, who had beaten or motored up among these selfsame reefs, against the wind, depending only on their satnav units. These people I had considered lucky fools. As long as electronic equipment in small craft depended on a reliable supply of electricity, it was prone to failure. Anyone who reckoned otherwise, and was not an electronics equipment salesman, or believed otherwise and was not an electronics-expert technician, was headed for trouble. Anyone who headed into the Red Sea, and especially between the offlying reefs and the coast, without a good knowledge of celestial navigation was either an idiot or a potential suicide case. What made me angriest, when the satnov failed, was that I was to blame. Not for navigating inside the reefs, but for trusting that bloody satnav unit any more than I would trust in a boat a psychotic but sociable soul met perhaps in a pub.

Fortunately we knew how to rig a "temporary" antenna, using an old coat hanger but it was nowhere near as frequent in picking up signals from passing satellites, nor as accurate in the end result, a "fix."

What was aggravating, too, was to know that out here, off the beaten track, away from the equipment dealers, there would be no way we could replace the antenna unit before we reached our next major "yachting" port: in our case, Singapore, all of seven thousand miles away and more.

Between Inkeifal and Suakin, on the southern end of the Inner Passage, a total run of about one hundred miles, we sighted eighteen wrecks which looked as if they had struck recently. Of those, six were bigger ships, coasters and such, four were large zhambuks, and the remaining eight were the remains of yachts, of which three had been powerboats and five sailing craft. These were wrecks which we were close enough to see, and which had remained on the edges of the reefs. It stood to reason that there must have been many more on reefs beyond our sight, or sunken. It was sad to see the lone, rusting keel and shattered ribs of a sailing craft all alone, a skeleton on the edge of a dead shore, but it was a continual reminder to us to keep our eyes open and stay *pessimistic* when it came to judging distances off reefs, or depths of water.

Apart from the ailing satnav, the hazard of being among reefs in frequently bad visibility, with its attendant risk of shipwreck on a waterless shore, our other main concern was piracy. It was common knowledge among small-craft sailors at all familiar with the Red Sea and Gulf of Aden that smuggling in those waters was rife. Usually it was carried out in swift motorized zhambuks, and the main trades in 1986 were electronics equipment and household "white goods" (radios, tape players, refrigerators, etc.) from Saudi Arabia to countries on the western shores of the Red Sea.

The other way, from west to east across the Red Sea, the main commodity carried seemed to be drugs, but there was still, it was said, a trickle of the slave trade remaining, and zhambuks carrying African children and women over to Arabia had been sighted.

Another main cargo going across the Red Sea to Saudi Arabia was sheep and goats for ritual slaughter on religious feastdays. I had encountered Arab smugglers before, and had found that as long as I had looked the other way and had kept quiet, they had left me alone, but there was always the prospect of meeting up with more aggressive smugglers in one of the remote, lonely anchorages, far away from any hope of official intervention.

Usually the *sharm* (anchorage) inlets were so narrow that if a piratically inclined zhambuk were to enter while we were inside, there would be small hope of escaping her without putting up some kind of fight. For this reason we all three practiced daily with our powerful hunting bows and arrows. If we were attacked, we were able to, and most certainly would, take at least three pirates with us.

The very configuration of many of the *marsas* made us feel very exposed and vulnerable to marauders. There was usually a narrow inlet in the fringing reef, and that was the anchorage, or it penetrated into the desert, but then there was only flat land all around, with no buildings, no trees, no rising features, so that the tall mast of a sailing vessel was as visible all around from as far away as it would have been had she been at sea. I personally was always glad when dusk was upon us, to hide us from the sight of any passing vessel, or even potential trouble seeker in the desert. But the Sudanese shore dwellers that we met were so poor, and so intensely involved in merely obtaining the means to live through yet another sizzling hot day in their stony desert, that they seemed as if they would have had no energy left over for making trouble, at least not against two sturdy lads and a wily skipper.

Theft from our boat was not so much a concern although we never left the boat without someone being on board the whole time we were in the Red Sea. The possibility of damage to the boat from grounding on a reef, on the other hand, was a major concern. We knew that although there were repair facilities in Port Sudan and even slipways, the rules and regulations would have made a six-months job of dealing with the paperwork alone. Then the amount of baksheesh that I would have to pay out in bribes of one kind or another to different officials and middlemen did not even bear thinking about.

Our next "port" of call was Marsa Arus, about two miles south of Fijab; and there, sitting on the low headland by the entrance, which was about as wide as a bishop's smile, in all their glory, was a row of five *holiday chalets*! There was nothing at all, all around them, but the desert, which stretched from here to eternity on three sides, and the sea, the steely-blue "Red" Sea, on the other, and a rusting oil can which marked the entrance to the *marsa*.

Which reminded me to tell the lads, as they handed the sails and we motored up handsomely to anchor, that the Red Sea was *not* named so because of any legendary redness caused by "floating organisms" or "livid sunsets," but simply because the ancient Arabic geographers, and the ancient Greeks before them in some cases, named the seas they mapped after different colors. So they had, and we have to this day, the "Black Sea." The Mediterranean was, to them, the "White Sea," and so on.

Marsa Arus, despite the "touristy" ambience lent by the newly built chalets, was deserted, except for an old Arab who paddled out in his rags and offered us two fish, which we gladly accepted and gave him two cans of beef in return. This was the only occasion when we swapped canned food for fresh; and we did it then because the old man looked so utterly poor and starved of solid meat. Later in the day we found that Marsa Arus, which widens to a great lagoon inside the entrance, was teeming with fish, and we could have them for the catching any time we cared to sling a line and hook over the side, baited or not.

In the three days we were at anchor in Marsa Arus, we saw and noted in the log four waterspouts out at sea and *fifteen* dust devils (the desert equivalent) over the coastal plain. One of the dust devils headed along the desert plain seemingly straight for the boat, and we battened down all hatches to prevent being "flooded" with sand dust, but as soon as it touched the water in the anchorage, it collapsed, leaving half the "harbor" sand-colored, and us three to discuss the other greatest anticlimaxes of our lives.

Very often, all along the Inner Passage of Sudan, when the wind backed a few degrees to the west, and picked up loose sand from the desert plain, the whole sky darkened and we would be subjected to "sand rain" for hours. Then fine sand would get into every nook and cranny on the boat, so that our hair, our eyelashes, our skin, our sails, our bedding, our shirts, our pants, our underpants, our sugar, our tea, our homemade bread, were all, before long, the same light khaki color.

It was now approaching mid-March and time for our stay in Port Sudan, where we hoped to collect mail. We took off from Marsa Arus out into a much wider part of the Inner Passage and sure enough, by the time the sun was fifteen degrees above the horizon the wind was blowing Force Five, north-northwest. We could depend on its direction and speed now every day, as regular as clockwork.

The barometric pressure also changed every day almost mechanically. At dawn it would be about 30 inches, by noon down to 29.5, where it would stay for all the daylight hours. At sunset it would start to creep up again, until by midnight it would be back

to around 30 inches once again. When we first witnessed the forenoon plunge on the barometer, Thomas was alarmed. It looked as
if a cyclone was on the way in. I told him not to fret; although the
wind in that part of the Red Sea got up to gale or near-gale force
every day, practically, between December and April, real storm-
force winds were rare.

The entrance to Port Sudan was marked for us by the number
of big ships anchored in the offing, in the lee of the reefs, waiting
to enter the port. There were one or two wrecked steamers rusting
in the sun. The entrance to the harbor was wide and well marked,
and we soon found ourselves cozily tucked into the South Basin,
with two anchors out: one to hold us against the wind, and one
to stop our stern from swinging into *Captain Hamid*, a rusting,
gutted old coaster, which looked as if it had been abandoned years
before. We heard later that *Captain Hamid* had been arrested for
arms smuggling only a year or two previously.

There were a half-dozen other yachts at anchor in Port Sudan.
Of these, three were passage making north from the Indian Ocean.
Two were Australian and one American. The other three yachts
were large Italian motor-sailers engaged in the charter trade. They
were crammed with diving gear and compressors which seemed
to be run noisily day and night when the Italians and their paying
guests were not holding noisy parties on deck. Port Sudan had an
airport; the Italians picked up their charterers there, then took them
to the offlying reefs, there to annoy the fish. Every time these big
boats came back into port we saw that their decks were littered
with coral ripped from the reefs. Every time a party of "guests"
left the Italian boats to return home, they were loaded down, men,
women and kids, with string bags full of bits of pink, white and
gray coral that had taken their fancy.

From the "blind eye" attitude of the officials that observed all
this in Port Sudan, we wondered how much baksheesh the Italians
must be paying out, for their passengers to take all that coral out
of the port and through the airport, and decided it must have been
a pretty sum.

There were many big ships in Port Sudan, mostly Western
European and American, offloading relief supplies for the starving
hinterland. All day long and most of the nights, too, the roar of
trucks loaded down with grain could be heard from the docks.

Thomas, while collecting fresh water from the tap on the coaling
dock, had struck up an acquaintance with a young Englishman,

and he, weary of his exile, had ridden back with Thomas in our dinghy.

The young Englishman, a trained engineer from a red-brick university in northeast England, told us he had been involved in organizing the transport of food for a big, internationally renowned British relief agency. Our Englishman also told us that the truck crews paid for their meals in the roadside cafés with bags of donated grain, and that he estimated that on average only about 70 percent of the food landed in Port Sudan reached the south of the country. The rest, he told us, found its way onto the open market, mainly through the corruption of officials, and the theft of it was rampant. He doubted if 30 percent of the donated food reached the starving people for whom it was intended. He was thoroughly disillusioned. All he wanted to do was go home. Now he was waiting for money to arrive from his parents.

He was a slight, fair man in his early twenties, who spoke with a northeastern English accent. From his appearance—dirty shirt, torn pants, and tangled hair—I was at first inclined to doubt his tale of having worked for a relief agency, but he showed me, in the course of our conversation, several papers that proved that he indeed had been doing that for over two years, until very recently.

"Where are you staying?" I asked him. He also looked drawn and hungry, as young white people so often do after some time in the tropics.

"In a shipping container on the docks," he replied. "I've cleaned it out, and I've got no money, so nobody bothers me. . . ."

9

Of Crows and Hawks

There were three parts to the city of Port Sudan: the South and East, which were the port and oil-refinery areas, and the West, which was the main area for shopping; the mile-wide central *suq* (market) was there, and what "entertainment" existed; the main post office was close to the suq. We confined ourselves to the West Town; it was about a mile from the South Basin and I could get to it in a taxi, usually at least thirty years old, expensive at one dollar, rusty and rattling. The four taxi-drivers I met were all middle-aged; two of them were very pro-American, but that might have been their version of public relations—they had seen *Outward Leg*'s ensign and knew we had some dollars. They all admired the British, though, but their fondness was more nostalgic for what one of them told me had been the "easy" laws when Sudan had been under British tutelage; a subconscious hankering, if you like, for good old habeas corpus, rather than anything like a loving fascination with "Swinging Britain" or "Beatlemania," or gratitude for free-food donations over the years. On that matter one of the taxi drivers told me that everyone in Britain and America must have too much food, so they should, each and everybody in both countries, by law, be *made* to send food to Sudan. "You have friend, he send me food every week, yes?"

That same taxi-driver, when I asked him what he thought of

the terrorist attacks on Western European airports a few weeks
earlier, deplored them. He could not understand why the Western
Europeans did not attack Libya. "Why not?" he demanded, "The
Holy Koran says, *'An eye for an eye, and a tooth for a tooth. . . .'"* He
went on, *"We* think that Qaddafi is crazy. If he bomb somebody
and they don't bomb him in turn, then they crazy, too, and not
only crazy, but they go against the will of Allah!"

The market in Port Sudan was huge. It was a warren of filthy
lanes lined with stalls almost as dirty, selling every kind of wares
imaginable, from cheap Japanese radios (smuggled in from Saudi
Arabia) to camel saddles, real American underwear to ancient swords,
some of them genuine Damascus steel.

The meat market was worth a visit, even if the stink and the
filth and the sight of thick blankets of gleaming black flies over
each and every piece of meat made it a short visit. The most shock-
ing thing in the meat market, though, was to see comatose or
sleeping men and boys on the greasy, filthy shelves of sold-out
meat stalls, almost naked except they were covered all over with
those disgusting, gleaming insects, from head to toe, and to see,
now and again, a pair of human eyes flicker open under those
masses of flies. One of the boys, no more than, perhaps, seven
years old, had no toes on his one and only foot.

"He's probably a leper," I told Svante, who silently clutched
his shopping bag alongside me.

Outside the old Central Hotel, now a peeling-paint, monstrous
fleabag on the main square, hordes of young men hustled a living
exchanging foreign money. Their rates would vary against the dollar by as much as 30 percent in as many feet along the broken
pavement. These young men could always be recognized before
they said anything by the cheap imitation "London fashion" clothes
they wore, many even wearing waistcoats under their jackets in
the full heat of midday in Sudan! But they seemed a gentle, friendly
lot, even despite the wild appearance of some.

When Svante, always eager to recognize the essential *goodness*
of *any* third-worlder, however wily, had pointed this out to me
later on board, I had told him it would be very bad for their business
if they were any other way. "The cops would come down on them
like a ton of bricks; imagine spending a few weeks in a Sudanese
jail. You've seen the meat market—imagine the jails! I'll bet the
guys in charge are real Goody Two-Shoes; just up your alley, Svante!"

"Real family men," had put in Thomas, "tennis and billiards

and all that. . . ." For a German, Thomas had learned British English, and not only our language, swiftly and well. "They give the prisoners a day off every week, to go into town," he went on.

Svante had stared at Thomas for a few seconds then had started to say, as Thomas and I had joined in, in chorus, *"Do you really think so?"*

On our shopping trips along the sand-dust-blown streets of Port Sudan, we had no occasion to enter the main post office—its reputation as a nest of petty extortionists and thieves reached far beyond Suez. It was known all along the cruising grapevine that any letter mailed there would have its stamps removed by bent clerks, then be thrown away. Any letter sent from abroad to "Poste Restante, West Town, Port Sudan," would either go missing altogether or eventually be found in some dusty cupboard in the East Town, or the South Town, or perhaps in Khartoum, on the banks of the River Nile, four hundred miles away across the desert. Any parcel mailed in Port Sudan, or sent there from anywhere else, would, as we small-craft sailors knew from the bitter experiences of many of our predecessors, go the same way as much of the vast consignments of food aid shipped from abroad, whether the contents of the parcels were edible or no. For those reasons, and for the only time in any of *Outward Leg*'s main ports of call until then (except in Egypt) all the way from San Diego, we gave the main post office in Port Sudan a miss.

There were a few bright spots in Port Sudan. One of these was the Hotel Palace, a small, but clean place on the road to and from the port, where there was air-conditioning in the foyer, which had been converted into a milk bar where excellent ice cream (!) but almost inedible food were served. Most of the customers there seemed to be merchant seamen, Italian and Greek for the most part, from the ships in port. There was no wine to be had ashore; no booze, except beer as weak as tea; and so they crowded into the Hotel Palace, mostly the younger ones, to eat ices and, I supposed, to dream of the romance, adventure, and excitement of the seafaring life.

Sometimes an apparently well-off Sudanese would enter with his wives, often as many as four. One of the waiters, who spoke good English, told us that these were mostly pilgrims from the interior, on their way to Mecca. Our crew and I would while away a cool hour out of the dust and the beating heat and away from the continual whines of beggars outside, trying to estimate which of each man's wives was the senior. Most times it was easy, from the amount of gold she was wearing (in a couple of cases enough to start a small jeweler's shop on Fifth Avenue); rarely, it was not.

Another consolation for being in Port Sudan was the tailors' stalls. There, for a song, we could buy real cotton shirts, bush jacket-style, made with four pockets, and these were the best bargain I ever found on all the voyage, until then, in *Outward Leg*, excepting perhaps the exchange of one cigarette for a live hen in Rumania.

In the town market we could buy, for our stove, paraffin at a reasonable price, and methylated spirit, at twenty times its cost anywhere else. We were told there was a "great shortage" of meths, and yet we saw it stocked rows upon rows of bottles of the stuff, in just about every market stall dealing in hardware. What would have happened if a fire had broken out, with tons and tons of meths stored all over the crowded suq, would have made the burnings of London, Chicago, and San Francisco look like minor celebrations.

In Port Sudan town and in the port, vast flocks of huge crows (as big as gannets), loudly cawing, set up a deafening cacophony, toward sunrise and sunset; a harsh clamor, a dissonant pandemonium as they wheeled round and round overhead, over the hulk of *Captain Hamid* by our mooring, or crowded the branches of precious, shady ancient trees planted, it seemed, before the Mahdi had defeated the British-Egyptian force at Khartoum a hundred years before. I wondered how many prisoners from that debacle had rested their weary bones in these shadows in the years between the death of Gordon and the mass slaughter by the British Army under Kitchener of the Sudanese warriors at Omdurman.

There were even yet, here and there, relics of the days of British tutelage in Sudan (the old "Anglo-Egyptian Sudan"). In the middle of the West Town was a fine old park, complete with what had once been an elegant tea shop and rococo bandstand, but left to wrack and ruin, to be the haunt of the mindless, the legless, the armless; even, in some awful cases, the faceless, of Port Sudan. There they existed, sleeping on piles of leaves gathered by those who could do so, and, hardly stirring from the rats' nests they inhabited, made their living by silent begging, the most moving, the most touching, of any kind of plea. Not so the younger boys: From the port to the town, all around the town, from the town to the port, never were we without an accompanying treble chorus of "Monee? . . . Monee? . . . Monee?" They were not poverty-stricken by African standards; a couple of them even trailed us on bicycles.

"What do you think of that?" asked Svante, as yet another squad of small boys, hands outstretched, descended upon us. We were on our way to the Scout Café on the waterfront, to eat rice and beans (with our *right* hands) off tin plates.

"As it was, is, and always shall be," I replied, "forever and ever, amen". My mind was too much on the long voyage ahead of us; too much on overcoming the possible, to dwell too long on ways and means of trying to overcome the impossible. If Aden was not safe now, we were in for some very thorny problems, like how to sail four thousand miles with the chance of little wind, or the reverse—cyclones—ahead.

On 25 March we weighed anchor and headed out of Port Sudan. Surprisingly the departure formalities had been carried out swiftly. The way the officials had zoomed through the paperwork, in only *four and three-quarter hours,* had been as if they were eager to be rid of us.

By early noon *Outward Leg* was off the Totawtit Reef; with a good fresh northerly wind which gave her six knots and more down the Inner Passage, which, south of Port Sudan, was busier than it had been farther north. Most of the traffic was fishing craft, but now and then we would sight a motorized dhow heading for one of the gaps in the offlying reef, on her way over to Saudi Arabia, most likely.

By late dusk we had wended our way into Suakin haven and were tucked in well behind the reef, and as the swift tropical darkness descended, we dropped our hook in twenty-two feet, over mud, by what I thought were craggy rocks, and snugged down for dinner and the night.

We were always, in port, awake and about before dawn. The late morning and early forenoon were the only times, in the tropics, cool enough to get any work done without sweating away good fresh water and energy. By eleven o'clock the heat was too fierce for any sustained effort of mind or body. At sea, or in the open anchorages, it was different. In March the wind over the Red Sea rose early and cooled everything down nicely, so that the climate was like a hot, dry summer's day on the coast of New England.

The first dawn in Suakin showed us an astonishing sight.

I was first up in the cockpit. I stared about me for a full five

minutes, gawping. Then I said quietly to Thomas, who was below
in the galley making tea: "Every bloody politician in the world
should be sent here to have a look at this. . . ."

Thomas stuck his head up above the galley companionway. He
screwed up one eye and stared at the sight.

Against a background of stark khaki desert receding into a hazy
mist over distant blue mountains, the "craggy rocks" of the night
before were now revealed as the ruins of a whole city, glowing
pink and gold in the dawn light, over the emerald and turquoise,
green and blue waters of the haven. The ruins stretched almost as
far as we could see along the south side of a huge bay crowded
with rotting and wrecked Arab dhows. Apart from five other passage-making small craft at anchor, it was if everything in the world,
except us, had suddenly been ransacked, vandalized, smashed,
destroyed, blasted, and pulverized. Over the ruined town there
hovered a half-dozen hawks; apart from that there was no sign of
life. It reminded me of the sight of the bombed center of Bristol in
1943. It was as though a nuclear Armageddon had left everything
and everybody in the world demolished, except for a few survivors
hopefully clinging, chastised, onto the edge of nothing.

As it turned out, the cause of all this ruin of a once-busy port
had been not war, but simply the silting up and coral encroachment
in the harbor.

As for the dhows and the zhambuks which lay forlorn all along
the northern edge of the bay, these had all been arrested by the
Sudanese government for smuggling; thirty and more finely built,
beautifully formed, once well-rigged, handsome sailing craft, up
to one hundred feet long, lay dying under the hot sun, with not
a soul to tend them. Yet outside of Suakin we had not seen many
zhambuks, and they had all been emasculated and now ran under
power only.

Over the causeway which led from the once-city, on its perfectly
round island, was the "modern" village of Suakin, a filthy, flyblown dusty shitheap on the edge of a desert so vast as to make
the Red Sea itself, all the reaches of it, small in comparison.

There, in the suq, tribesmen from the most remote regions of
the Sudanese desert, from northern Ethiopia, from Chad and the
Cameroons, the Central African Republic and even the Congo,
arrived in Suakin and camped, after Allah only knows what travail,
together with their camels, their wives, their offspring, goats, sheep,

and piles of baggage, to await passage in dhows on their *hajj*—
their pilgrimage to Mecca.

In the suq fine old swords were on sale by local tribesmen for
a matter of a few dollars. I was surprised to find that the Maria
Theresa thaler (an old Austrian Empire gold coin—the origin of
the word *dollar*) was still in use, but not as much as when I had
last passed through the Red Sea.

Another surprise was to find that some of the ruins of the old
city of Suakin were still inhabited, even despite their dangerously
crumbling state. Often we would hear parts of a building collapse
with a rumble in the dark night, and wonder if anyone had been
trapped under the fall. We could not land to search; the ruins were
prowled by packs of dangerous wild dogs reputed to attack and
even devour humans. Even the hawks that nested in the ruins,
were bold enough to swoop on men, I was told by one of the
ragged denizens of what had once been the Turkish governor's
residence, and was now a jumbled, tumbled heap of stones.

The young man, who spoke very basic, but good, English, told
me he was an Eritrean refugee. He and his companions, six all
told, all between seventeen and twenty-four, almost navy-blue in
their blackness, had *walked* the three hundred miles from their
home region near Massawa, to escape hunger and impressment
into the Ethiopian Army. Barefoot (no civilian shoes under Colonel
Mengistu) they had tramped for fifty days, over the stony, sizzling,
waterless coastal desert, to find refuge in the ruins of Suakin.
Eventually, they said, they hoped to "reach America." They showed
me their "home." It was two old wooden doors balanced on a heap
of rocks. Under the doors they kept a tiny supply of rice and tea,
which they offered to share with us. I, lying, politely declined,
saying we had already eaten. Nevertheless, our hosts pressed some
dates, wrapped in an old newspaper printed in Arabic, into my
hands. The young man and all his companions were covered with
festering cuts and gashes from falls among the crumbling rocks
and boulders. We gave them some antibiotics and stomach medicine from our small stock, and a few cans of Venezuelan fish,
carefully hoarded since the spring of 1984, and wished them well.
They, in turn, bowed their heads slightly, every one, their hands
pressed over their hearts under their djellabas, and called down
on us the blessings of Allah, as our crew jumped nimbly, and I
slid, clattering, down a long-fallen wooden beam, into our dinghy.

So, although we were not sure we were doing it at the time, and apart from a brief anchoring off Cape Gardafui, we left the shores of Africa.

Motoring back to *Outward Leg* we were all silent for a while, until Svante piped up, "They were good people. It's a shame they have to live like that."

As I grabbed the shroud wires and heaved myself up onto *Outward Leg*'s deck over the guardrails, I remembered the living conditions in Massawa sixteen years before. They'd been far worse. Besides, a youth spent in the crew's quarters of British warships would cure anyone of sentimentality over living conditions where fresh air and light were freely available. "What those lads have now is probably an improvement over what they had at home, Svante," I told him, gasping. Getting on board from a bouncing rubber dinghy is quite an exercise for anyone on one leg. Before Svante, awaiting his turn to leave the dinghy, could ask me if I really thought so, I continued jokingly, "But those blessings might come in handy. We might need them." My mind was still on the long, long traipse ahead of us if Aden was in ferment.

It was Thomas's turn. Quick as a flash, as he clambered on board *Outward Leg* he turned and grinned at Svante. "And Tristan really thinks so!" he teased.

Little did he know how right he was!

One of the voyaging yachts in Suakin was *Sybaris*, American, on her way west-about (the "normal" way) from the Far East to Europe in "easy" stages. We swapped some charts with their skipper, Carlyle. For him some of our Mediterranean charts, which we would never need, and for us some of his Far East issues. As I told Carlyle at the time, some charts must have been swapped so often between so many different yachts, bound on so many different voyages, that a few of them must have sailed the world far farther than any person had done.

Then it was anchor aweigh and out into the mess of shallows and reefs among the islands southeast of Suakin, so as to make for the open sea sixty miles or so away from the ruined city. Navigating the Suakin reefs kept Thomas and me busy most of the passages, either eyeballing the shoals or taking snap-sights of the sun. Our satnav was well and truly awry in many of its "fixes," so, although it had about 60 percent accuracy, we could not trust it.

The first night out of Suakin we spent anchored safely in the lee of the tiny island of Sha'ab Muru only a hundred feet away from the island's starboard-side light structure, which, every fifteen seconds or so, flashed an eerie emerald flash over us as we ate supper (line-caught fish and beans) in the cockpit. I told the lads about the "green flash" which is sometimes seen in the Southern Ocean or the remoter reaches of the South Atlantic. Then, far from any air pollution, when the sun goes down it shines, for a fleeting moment, across the curve of the world, *through the ocean*, and its light causes everything to turn bright emerald green. "It's like a trip to Mars," I told the crew. "If you look at your skin, it glows bright green."

"Just the thing for Saint Paddy's Day," observed Thomas. Which showed how colloquial his English had become, and I again mentally congratulated him.

On the thirty-first of March we reached our last Sudanese anchorage at the island of Taller-Taller Saghir. I was taken back in my mind sixteen years before—when I had anchored here with Conrad Jelinek in *Barbara* to shelter from a roaring *hamsin* gale from the south. Then, it had been our only Sudanese call, because *Barbara* had sailed direct from Sinai, which was then in Israeli hands. If we'd headed into a Sudanese port then, they would have either shot us or locked us up and thrown away the key.

Now, in *Outward Leg*, with the wind blowing from the north, we went to anchor on the south side of Taller-Taller Saghir, under the lee of bluff, stark, red cliffs (18°45.7' north, 37°41.45' east). The bottom was deep—our anchor just about reached it, even on the end of four hundred feet of line and a hundred of chain, but there was little fret; as long as the wind held its direction. If the anchor dragged there was nothing but the deep sea to our lee, and we always kept anchor watches in any place where there was any risk of the anchor dragging.

The following day I had a bad case of diarrhea so we decided to delay sailing for Aden for—perhaps—twenty-four hours. The crew were not affected, and I concluded my affliction must have been caused by eating raw dates. Then we found that Thomas, with his typical generosity, had handed to the Ethiopian refugees in the ruins of Suakin our one and only bottle of stomach medicine in return for the proffered dates!

Thus, I thought, as I sat on the bucket for most of the forenoon, the corrupt, inefficient, starvation- and disease-facilitating mach-

inations of the minions of Colonel Mengistu, head of state of the
Ethiopian People's Socialist Republic, reached even into the bow-
els, and the head, of *Outward Leg*.

As I sat, stomach aching painfully, with my head thrust up
through the foredeck hatch, shaded from the heat of the sun by
two cushions thoughtfully provided by Svante, I stared at the blank-
faced cliffs of Taller-Taller Saghir, and bitterly recalled how often
people, who probably sat and watched programs about refugees
on their living room TVs, had gushed about "How wonderful it
must be to be able to get away from it all . . . just take off into the
blue and say good-bye to all the problems of the modern world. . . ."

While I "rested" on board, the crew both went ashore on the
island, to find the cairn on the far, north side where in 1971, I had
left a note in a bottle telling of *Barbara*'s passing. After a long traipse
over the dazzling, hot rocks for a mile, they found the cairn all
right, atop its hill, but no bottle, no note. Which, on their return
on board, made me feel better; I was glad, then, that I had written
The Incredible Voyage, so that more people could know of our Red
Sea passage in 1971 than could ever have read about it in a stranded
bottle. I had often had my doubts about the wisdom of entering
the book-writing game. It was an arduous, lonely job; probably the
loneliest activity known to man; certainly more lonely than single-
handed ocean sailing. It wracked and drained the body as thoroughly as the mind, and even more so when attempted while on
the move. But the thought that the voyage of *Barbara* had not left
behind it a mere wake in the waters of the seas and oceans through
which we had passed helped my stomach recover much faster than
any medicine. The real voyages are not in the voyages themselves,
but in the telling of them. Many will disagree with that; but it's
inside me, true, firm and well, well learned.

All the while we had been passage-making down the Inner
Passage of Sudan, Svante had been learning the intricacies of good
sailing and boat-maintenance. He was not a fast learner, but once
he had a grip on something, it stuck. The life in a small sailing
craft on long-distance voyaging must be a kind of life of its own,
rather like a gypsy's, I think. It is not a job, not a pastime, it is
definitely a *life*, and so every facet of it, every particular way of
thought and of tackling problems, so different from the landsman's
ways, must be learned. Nothing can be taken for granted, and
every possibility, good or bad, must be considered and allowed for
with cool, unsentimental, hard-nosed detachment, yet keeping to

the aims of the endeavor. Everything must be considered as either right or not right, and there can be no half truths, no half measures. Anyone doubting the veracity of my words should try, without holding to those truths, organizing a long voyage in a sailing craft of any kind, and successfully carry it out.

Svante had, besides "learning the ropes," also and more importantly, learned some of these truths, and he learned them well, which is not easy for a landsman, born and bred, to do. It needed a lot of patience on his part, and perhaps more on mine, but between us we found it, and were friends through all the sometimes painful (for both of us) process. His lack of humor, at the start, did not make our tasks any easier, but humor was another thing Svante learned in *Outward Leg*, and by the time we anchored at Taller-Taller Saghir he was, from all appearances, enjoying our banter as much as we.

All the way down the Sudanese Inner Passage, Thomas, besides fish hunting wherever that was possible, to augment and conserve our stocks of canned and dried foods, had other projects continually in the making. Ever busily inquisitive about anything new to him, anything he hadn't done before, he was experimenting with cooking and food processing. He was, by the time we reached Taller-Taller Saghir, baking good, tasty bread in our pressure cooker, making laver from the tiny green lettuces and other measly-looking vegetables available in the suqs. These lavers he stored away for future vitamin supplies on the long ocean voyage ahead.

As for me, our Red Sea passage had been more in the way of a relaxation than anything else, apart from conning the boat, teaching the lads this and that, and checking that all was well with the hundreds of different items on board any ocean-sailing craft. Ever since Suez we had no contact with the world, outside of the silent, lonely desert anchorages, busy, closed-off Port Sudan, and ruined Suakin. My distrust of the Sudanese postal service (warranted, from all accounts) meant that I had already been completely isolated from my publishers and editors for more than two months. The British edition of my book *The Improbable Voyage* was now being readied for printing. With a good six or seven thousand miles still ahead of us, before we reached Thailand, there was no way I could set up a communications base for more than a few days at a time. With many parts of the Middle East along our route of voyage in a state of war, civil war, rebellion, or anarchy, I could not even tell them where I would next be, nor when.

To all intents and purposes, as *Outward Leg* weighed anchor, bound—perhaps—eight hundred miles for Aden, we were as isolated as any craft in the farthest reaches of the Southern Ocean or the Arctic, and in far more danger from human ill-intent or violence than they could possibly be. As we prepared to set sail into the blue, over the BBC overseas service came the news: The presidential elections two days before had brought a state of siege to Port Sudan; there had been severe rioting in the port area, and several people were known to have been killed and scores wounded.

"We got out in time," observed Thomas.

"Four days to spare," I added.

Svante wasn't convinced that the news was at all accurate: "Do you really think it's true?"

"Svante," I told him, "stop sounding like a book reviewer, for Chrissakes!"

"?" His Swedish blue eyes looked at me from his sunburned face for a minute.

"Some of them are like that," I explained. "They'll say I dreamed up all these political problems, so as to bring about tidy climactic chapter endings. Or they'll say I looked for trouble, or what the hell was I doing going east this way anyway?"

"But there's no other way, unless we had headed around the Cape of Good Hope," muttered Thomas. "And if they say you're in the wrong, trying to voyage peacefully east, then they are saying that all these tin-pot self-proclaimed revolutionaries are in the right. . . . Whose side are they on?"

"But that's what they'll say," I persisted.

"Do you really think so?" said Svante.

It was April Fool's Day, 1986.

10

"Yachting," and "Hanging On"

There were some regrets in *Outward Leg* on departing the island of Taller-Taller Saghir. For two weeks we had cruised swiftly, amiably, and gently almost every day from one stark, but lovely, peaceful, isolated anchorage to the next. Under way the scene had been one of continually shifting desert, orange, blue or gold, according to the time of day, backed often, except when there was a mist hiding them, by majestic mountain ranges in the far background, and underpinned by the ever-changing, glowing turquoises, blues and greens of the sea in the passages between the coral reefs.

There was a lot of relief, too. With the satnav not operating at maximum accuracy, the Inner Passage had meant many nerve-wracking moments for the skipper and mate, while we worked out the results of frenziedly hurried sun-sights. Svante, too, had paid his price for our enjoyment of the Inner Passage. He had spent many a long, hot, weary period balanced halfway up the mast, perched at the top of the ratlines we had rigged on the shroud wires, searching for reefs that the charts (originally drawn up by heroes in the last century) told us might, or might not, be there.

As we weighed the hook off Taller-Taller Saghir we knew we had the deep open sea ahead of us. We were not yet in the clear from hazards human, but we were comparatively free, for the next couple of hundred miles, at least from natural dangers, the weather excepted, of course.

Outward Leg, too, seemed to know that she was now clear of the ever-threatening reefs and rocky shoals. As soon as her working rig—main, staysail, and yankee—were hoisted, she was off, yielding stiffly at first to the fresh norther, then, darting forward, humming with purpose, she lay her cheeks down in the inky-blue waters and sang her own song of the open sea, accompanied, strangely enough in the Red Sea, by two gulls, who jealously thought she might perhaps, with her rigging wires zinging, be trying to outscreech them.

As the desert island on the very edge of the reef dropped into the hot haze astern, there was on board that feeling of fellowship most peculiar to a sailing-craft running for clear waters, with good gear, a willing, trained crew, and plenty of food on board.

I had known that ambience before: It was felt not only from and among the people on board, but also between the boat and the people. I knew that because I had often felt it when I had been alone in a boat. It was almost as though the craft herself were a living, thinking, breathing person with a will of her own, and her will was devoted to the success of the voyage. It was, perhaps, similar to the air of a loving marriage.

There could be no other relationship between a thing and a person (for what is a sailing vessel if she is not a thing?) quite the same as that between a good boat and her crew. I had heard some small-plane pilots, and motorcycle daredevils rant on about their piece of machinery, but, compared to the silent love of the sea-bound sailor for the thing beneath his feet (or foot) their rantings and braggings sounded to me more like mere reflections of their own intense admiration for their own skills at handling their own pet speedy vehicle; not at all like a good sailor's love for his boat.

A sailor actually falls in love with the thing that he helps to guide over the seas. It is almost as if there were a subconscious wish for the thing to forgive any of his failing.

I often had watched sailors who loved their ship place their hands on any part of her. I had seen the way their feet moved over her moving decks. I had observed their reluctance, their lingering slowness, to leave her when they clambered into their dinghies to go ashore, and the many looks they had cast in her direction as she lay at anchor. Some people said that it was a mere fetish, but what counted, surely, was where love came from, and were not fetishes love—of a different nature perhaps—yet love, too?

There was a fresh northerly blowing outside of the lee of the island, but not too strong for our genniker, which was soon hoisted and heaving, and breaking up, with its brave colors of green, white and red, the hot, steely-blue, monotony of the Red Sea sky.

As soon as *Outward Leg* settled down under her genniker only, and before the heat became too intense on the deck, I slid out onto the starboard ama. (I didn't wear my leg at sea when we were running free before the wind—going to windward was different and hellish.) There, balanced on the forward edge of the wing deck, I blissfully listened to the hiss of our three hulls as they sliced neatly and cleanly through the blue, blue water. But in a matter of minutes the tropical sun climbed onto his throne and glared at me for my temerity, so that I was soon forced to retire, sliding on my stern over the deck, back into the shade of our cockpit awning.

There used to be, years ago, even in the crowded waters of the United States or northern Europe, a sense, when a small craft let go of her lines or weighed her anchor, of *departure*. I don't mean a knowledge that we were merely leaving a place, but that we were "cutting the trammels of the land" and "heading out into the blue"; that our craft was to be, until she reached her next haven, a little self-contained world all of her own.

That had been in the days before the advent of modern navigation aids, when radar had been something only seen atop the masts of big ships, and radio had been a thing in the pub, a box with knobs on it, that told us the football results. Electronics had then been something that only tweedy, pale little men knew about—men who sounded and looked like secretive assassins with unintelligible conversation, their low voices, long hair and thick glasses.

On this voyage, so far, I had not had that true feeling of departure, of cutting ourselves off, since *Outward Leg* had sailed out of the Azores eighteen months before. Not in the English Channel, not in the North Sea, nor the Black Sea nor the Aegean, nor, God help us, not even in the eastern Mediterranean, nor yet the Gulf of Suez.

It was only then, seventeen degrees north of the Equator, in the Red Sea, with nothing between us and the ocean but a mess or two of barren, waterless islands, the vicious straits of Bab el

Mandeb, and a thousand miles of hard headwinds between us and
Gardafui, the Cape Stiff of the Horn of Africa, and no possibility
of turning back, that I experienced once again the old delicious
sense of utter freedom.

The ability to choose lines of action is one of the factors that
distinguish people from animals, and yet at the same time it is
choice that imprisons us. Take away our ability to choose and we
sense a loss of responsibility which we can choose, or not, to call
freedom. But in a small craft a great deal of responsibility remains
with us always to ensure her well-being and safety from hazard.
With a vessel we know intimately and love, this is a small effort,
for she and our loves for each other will work for and with us.

It is thus only in a well-worked sailing craft, making a good
departure, a voyage, an arrival at a predestined haven, with a
trained, efficient, willing crew, that the real sense of being as close
to utter freedom as we shall ever approach in this life is gained.
In a vessel with which we are not familiar inside and out, this
simply cannot be. So it is only long-distance, longtime cruising
sailors who can ever possibly know what freedom, in the uttermost
meaning of the word, really feels like. But they can only know it,
only approach it, in the more remote areas of the world's waters.
Anywhere else, the attempt, which we all indulge in at one time
or another, to catch the elusive sensation of utmost independence,
can only be like grasping straws in the wind.

The effort to describe the feeling of self-sovereignty in a small
sailing craft with all the world's oceans before her, must be, surely,
like trying to describe colors to a person who has been blind since
birth. That knowledge of the absolute freedom to *choose*, I thought
to myself, as *Outward Leg* plunged and rolled, lifted, hovered and
surfed, forging south, the wind dead astern and the Jebel At Tair
Islands ahead of her, was the difference between "yachting" and
voyaging.

Dawn showed us to be twenty miles off Taclai, where the frontier between Sudan and Ethiopia joins the sea, and where the
Eritrean refugees back in the ruins of Suakin had, they said, swum
out three miles to round the line and so avoid the trigger-happy
border patrols.

I had been off Taclai before: in *Barbara* I had stood in to the
coast seeking shelter from a full storm, but had found there in the
desert shore only a broken wall.

We were giving Ethiopian waters a wide berth. We knew that

a hundred miles or so southeast of us the barren, waterless Ethiopian island of Harmel was supposed to be uninhabited, as it had been when I last called there briefly in 1971, and that a couple of northbound cruising yachts had recently anchored there peacefully in the south bay, near the relics of the World War II Italian Army fortifications, to rest between hard bouts of beating. But I decided against heading for Harmel, in case some detachment of Ethiopian soldiery had mustered the courage, the resources, and the craft to cross over to the island from the mainland. If they had, we would certainly risk detainment, if not being shot up, wounded, or killed. I didn't want to die yet; I had too much to do. Besides, I was reluctant in the extreme to let Colonel Mengistu's minions succeed where the Nazis and a hard life had failed.

By the third of April, in latitude 16° north, we knew by the wind shift to southeast that we were approaching the North Tropical Convergence Zone. This is the area where the monsoon winds meet the winds from other systems, in our case the north wind blowing south from the Mediterranean. The meeting of warmer tropical winds with cooler breezes from the more temperate latitudes causes a cloud layer.

In the Red Sea it hardly ever rains at sea, but the high coastal mountains catch the clouds, and this causes a seasonal rain, in different areas, to move north as the Convergence Zone moves north with the sun's declination. This provides, or not, depending on the amount of moisture in the air, the harvests in the countries bordering the Red Sea.

It had been the lack of rains over the Ethiopian mountains, we ruminated, as we gazed at the dark clouds hovering low over Africa, to starboard, which had caused the terrible drought and starvation in Ethiopia and the south of Sudan.

Thomas said: "And people are always telling us how nice it must be to get away from it all at sea!"

Svante observed: "Back home in Sweden they think they are seeing reality on their TV screens. . . ."

I said: "And so they are, but it's the reality that other people put before them. Unless they switch off they have to accept it. If they want to have any idea what's going on, they must watch TV presentations. But what they really see is a version of the truth which is distilled to distortion, so that Bugs Bunny gets mixed up, in many of their minds, with famine and they think that pouring money into relief will solve the problems. We know it won't because no amount of money will shift that bloody Convergence Zone one inch!"

Then the wind rose, now heading us. We hauled in the sheets of the yankee and main. As I grunted and heaved in hot effort, I prayed that this year the rain would fall for the Ethiopians and that (despite the blundering, blustery bodging of Colonel Mengistu and his bloody tribe of troublesome trigger-fingerers, who evidently had about as much idea of the true precepts of real social organization as I had of the names of the progeny of the late Emperor Haile Selassie's pet lions) everyone in that unhappy land, now thirty miles immediately under the lee of *Outward Leg*, would have enough to eat.

We beat close-hauled all that day and the following night, until the forenoon of April 4, as it should be, immediately after breakfast, showed us the low, hazy, gray profile of the South Yemeni island of Jebel At Tair, shyly and slowly rising out of the southern horizon. We knew from the cruising grapevine that the islands were barren and empty except for a few fishermen who, in the "winter" season, based their zhambuks there. By repute, the islands were safe.

I decided we should head for the main island of the group and rest there, before tackling the harder winds and steepening seas farther south. We were still waiting for the Tropical Convergence Zone, stuck solid over southern Somalia, to move north and change the prevailing wind direction of the monsoon from east to west.

In all that follows, this should be borne in mind: We were in no great hurry. We were early on the doorstep of the monsoon change; only if it should be late would we have to press on for logistic reasons.

"How much, when and where," I told Svante, when he asked me what the word "logistics" meant.

By noon we had the Jebel At Tair light structure, the one solitary man-made thing on the whole mountainous island, as far as we could see, bearing 090 degrees. The wind, off the island, had swung around back to northerly, and had freshened, sending monstrous breakers pounding onto the rocks of the northern shore. I decided, in view of that, to head around the western point of Jebel At Tair and nose around for a cozy spot to rest to the south of it.

When we rounded the point, we saw there were a few small, obviously, from their graceful shapes, Arab craft at anchor in the bay immediately south of the lighthouse. I decided not to join them at anchor, but instead to heave to about a mile off to the south, where the sea in the lee of the island was still relatively calm.

Those waters abounded with sharks, but where they had plentiful food they were cowardly beasts; although the lads did not care to swim, the sharks did not bother us, except they scared away all the fish we could have caught for supper, so that we had to make do with canned herrings from Scotland via Cyprus.

The reasons I hove to were not only to keep clear of the Yemenis, in case they should bear an American-ensigned vessel ill will, but also because the wind might shift to the south during the dark hours, and we would then, of course, find ourselves on a lee shore with perhaps a gale about our ears.

At dusk, as the Yemeni boats moved out to the offing to fish, their crews, a raffish-looking lot in their flowing robes and turbans, knives at their belts, hollered and waved to us in a friendly fashion. Onto one zhambuk which came close under our stern, we threw a packet of cigarettes, which raised a great cheer for us, and her helmsman, a stout, piratical-looking man of about fifty, with a white beard and a huge paunch, saluted our flag. Even so I demanded deck watches all night, and the crew willingly agreed that it might be wise.

All night long *Outward Leg* with her little white oil-lamp hoisted up the forestay, her staysail hauled over to her lee and her wheel tied over to weather, moved merely a few yards back and forth, despite the lively breeze. She was as submissive to our command to her to stay put, as a fond, obedient retriever, and remained quiet faithfully. We, in our turns, kept watch, listened to the crackly voice of a BBC radio announcer until the atmospheric interference obliterated it, ate canned Scots herrings, read, drank tea, slept, and loved her.

Getting under way again was no problem; Thomas untied the wheel, let go the weather sheet of the staysail, hoisted the yankee, and there we were, close-hauled and hard at it, with, soon, a strong northerly-running current and a hard southerly breeze, both against us, of course. The sea was in a short, frenzied chop for most of the day: abrupt, steep lumps of water, as hard as brick walls, hurtling at us, one after the other, millions and millions of them, all trying to stop *Outward Leg*, all bouncing and jerking her, so she rebounded and recoiled from every single sea, and with every single sea as it passed she jumped, vaulted, sprung, hurdled, leaped, and cleared, then crashed down, all in a matter of three seconds, up and down, up and down, all the hot, weary day long, and most of the night. No matter how efficient a hull was, no matter how well rigged any vessel was, no matter what hotshot whiz kids her builders and designer were, a sea as short and steep as that sea was would make any boat damned uncomfortable. On one leg it was, much of the time, purgatory.

And so it would be, and I knew it would be, all the way, at least, to Cape Gardafui. There was little saving grace about it. For me it was an exercise in pure, bloody-minded determination. If we were to get *Outward Leg* to the Far East I simply would have to go through that torment. The thousand miles of heavy beating ahead of us was but another hurdle among hundreds.

The stretch between the southern Red Sea and Cape Gardafui was one of the main obstacles that had, so far, prevented the successful circumnavigation of the world, east-about, north of the Equator, by any small craft in history, sail or not. It was one of the great hurdles that makes that route the Everest of voyaging. Anyone who doubted that had only to look into what was involved. A couple of hours' thought and research would show right away what a Pandora's box it all was. To the critics of that—the scoffers—all I would have needed to say to them was, *do it!*

Early morning brought the northernmost of the Zubair Islands, Jebel Zuquair, in sight, low, rounded, hazy, "rather sinister-looking" as I told the lads at the time. I didn't know why I said that; there was no particular reason, except perhaps that the barometer had dipped to an all-time low for the whole voyage, and we had been through a very nasty night, with water slashing over the cockpit. There had been electric storms east and west, over both shores of the Red Sea, frightening in their sudden violence. The yankee halyard masthead block had snapped with an explosion in the small hour after midnight. Thomas, little, slight, lionhearted, had clambered aloft, somehow, in that windy, wet darkness, the boat pounding like a bucking bronco, the mast weaving like a lunatic orchestra-conductor's baton, to replace it; there was a strong current which had been pushing us back all the time, and maybe it was the way I felt that day.

There was nothing vastly different about Jebel Zuquair, as we approached it; bouncing and hurdling, now in a southerly gale, under black and gray clouds hurtling across the sky. That is, nothing too different from Jebel At Tair, our last island, until we were only a mile or so away from the north shore, and saw that it was like a stormbound moonscape, if there ever could be such a thing.

From the north, as we, now under shortened sail, probed around, searching for the double-dogleg entrance (formed like a W on its side) to the little lagoon behind the reef, the island appeared to be one vast, black, craggy volcanic peak looming up over two thousand feet into the stormy heavens. Its crater was lost in the flying clouds. I remember quite clearly saying to Thomas as, bleary-eyed from the night's endeavors, he and Svante stared at the stupendous sight, "All this bloody place needs is Heathcliffe."

After I'd explained that to them, we renamed the Jebel Zuquair mountain Wuthering Heights.

We beat our way close inshore between small rocky islets white with sea foam on their south sides, and made for the almost invisible double-dogleg passage. The wind now howled a full storm; the anemometer showed a wind speed of fifty knots, until we were right under the lee of Wuthering Heights. There the wind dropped to nothing, with sudden, vicious gusts of thirty knots or more which swept down off the black slopes of the awful volcano, driving clouds of black dust before it that clogged up our eyes and made us squint and left a bitter taste on our lips, so that we looked and sounded like South Welsh coal miners calling a strike.

As we carefully and slowly hauled our way into and through the double-dogleg entry and as close to the rocky shoreline as we dare, I said that it was shaped exactly like an old-fashioned rattrap. So we named the tiny lagoon Rattrap, and swiftly, holding themselves braced against the violence of the gusts, and me clinging to the wheel and maneuvering it like mad, our crew set both the CQR anchor and the Bruce anchor out, about 60 feet apart, on all the lengths of their rodes (anchor lines), which were each 40 fathoms long, or 240 feet. Only the CQR had a 60-foot length of chain on its anchor end; the Bruce had no chain.

There was a limit to the amount of weight that a trimaran could carry and still haul to windward well, and the anchor chain was, for the amount of time it would be useful, very heavy.

Outfitting and storing any ocean vessel was always an exercise in compromise; in a multihull it was a whole game of concession, trade-off, conciliation, and reconciliation. What it boiled down to is that we couldn't have our cake and eat it, too. Either we had lots of anchor chain on board and went to windward about as efficiently as Westminster Abbey, or we had a little chain and could slog it out as good as any monohull, and far better than a lot of them. So *Outward Leg* had little chain.

Having said that, I should add that the experienced sailors among you should by now have guessed what was in the offing; and they are right. We were in for one of the most worrying times I have ever spent in a sailing craft at sea or at anchor, or anywhere, except perhaps up in the Arctic during the long night with *Cresswell* twenty-seven years before.

The lagoon, no more than four hundred yards wide, was squeezed between the offlying reef and the base of the volcano. The shoreside was a scene of tumbled black rocks, dust, and desolation. Above the shoreline the mountain loomed over us so near that we stretched our necks to peer up and see if we could espy its crater, which our chart indicated was somewhere up in that forlorn, dreary waste of bleak barrenness.

From our boat straining at her anchors, holding now against a full storm, all we could see on the foreshore was some cast-up old tree trunks, from Allah only knew where in that treeless part of the world.

At the far western end of the lagoon, amid the boulders above its shore, was a single, solitary tombstone sticking up, so that as the sun went down its shadow almost reached to our boat.

I told Thomas that all the scene needed was a vampire bat, but all we saw of any life were a few boobies and pelicans. Even they were sheltering between the rocks.

I turned to look astern. There, only a matter of perhaps twenty yards away, the offlying reef lay. At high tide there was a small sandy island above water. The rest of the reef was a mere shadow under the turquoise sea, except for around the islet. There, the reflected swells from the storm raging around the island beat with a threatening roar every few seconds. Then, every time an unexpected, unannounced, unwanted, and unloved storm gust ripped maliciously down from the volcano, strong, forceful, with evil intent, making *Outward Leg* scream in her rigging, the water at the top of the swells was blown off in a delicate, innocent-looking line of sparkling spray. It was, I thought to myself, like watching Christmas-tree lights through the bars of a locked door of a dark dragon's cave, with a fire-breathing monster rumbling about in the inner passages. But I kept that thought to myself. There was no sense in depressing the crew.

No sooner had we made sure the anchors were set and holding (Thomas and Svante had both dived down to check them, while I had kept watch for sharks), than the wind shifted very slightly; no more than two or three degrees, to the southeast, and all hell was let loose upon *Outward Leg*. We felt, then, the full force of a storm.

Before midnight the wind reached fifty knots, gusting up to sixty, and it stayed like that, and sometimes blew even harder, for two whole days and nights.

All we could do was set watches and hope to Allah that the anchor lines would not part, or the anchors shift in the sandy bottom of Rattrap Lagoon.

Now we realized how well we had named that place, with its entry passage of two right angles, no more than thirty feet wide, bordered by reefs, its offlying reef, a passive but dangerous threat, a ship killer if we should drag, and its looming black mountain, around which the wind howled.

We couldn't get out of the lagoon; in that storm, with no sea room, there would be no controlling the boat. She would be blown sideways onto the reef. Even if we did not attempt to shift and the anchors did not hold she would be blown swiftly astern onto the offlying reef, and there, in a matter of minutes, be pounded to bits. If that happened I, unable to jump around, would probably either be seriously injured or swept away by the undertow of the huge swells and drowned. There was no outside help, that I could imagine, for hundreds of miles. The lads might, if they could make it to the mountain base in the rubber dinghy, stand a chance of surviving, if they had fresh water with them, and fishing gear.

All through the night I sat in the after cabin and stared up, as if hypnotized, at the wind-gauge needle in the cockpit showing fifty . . . fifty-five . . . fifty-seven . . . sixty knots.

I made up my mind. In the light of the oil lamp, I dug out all three passports from their stowages, and the cashbox, and set them on the navigation table, ready for a quick grab if the worst happened: the anchors gave way and we hit the reef. A few minutes later I ordered the lads to stow and lash ten fresh-water cans, their fishing gear and six bags of canned food on deck, where they would be more easily seized should *Outward Leg* drag and hit the reef only yards away under her stern.

In the darkness, up in the howling storm, the crew quietly and purposefully did my bidding, bracing themselves on deck, and latching their life-harness hooks onto our rigging, in case an extra strong gust should blow them over the side and they be lost in the roaring, screeching night. In that cyclonic wind, in that darkness, there was no hope of ever being able to find anyone who did fall over the side.

Now, at high tide, the sea was beating straight over the offlying reef, even against the wind, and spray was flying up and away well over the height of our mast, while the boat reared and jerked to her anchor lines, so that we had to reset the chafing rags, where the warps came on board over the fairleads, every few minutes.

Apart from that, there was nothing more we could do. I myself could do nothing anyway but drill a hole in the upper limb of my plastic leg, in case it should fill with water when we were dashed on the reef. If I took my leg off I would not be able to remain upright in the water. At least I would give myself a fighting chance, perhaps, of reaching our dinghy, which through all this was gently bobbing in the lee under our main stern. But I doubted I could manage that. If *Outward Leg* was smashed onto the outlying reef, I would most probably be killed.

I didn't mind the prospect of death so much, after all the pain I had gone through, especially in the past three years, but the thought that the work I wanted to do would be left undone, to try to ease the pain in others, was too much for me to bear.

All through the night, as the storm roared above, and bits and pieces of gear broke away topside and were hurled into the darkness astern, and as the two anchors of *Outward Leg* somehow clung on to their grains of sand, as our boat trembled all through in her effort to live, and our weary crew, brave lads, tried to gain some sleep, I bowed my head, and for the first time since I had been in inexpressible pain in Amsterdam, in February of 1982, four years and one month before, I prayed.

I couldn't cry; there had been no tears in me since the Arctic; and it would have been futile anyway, better another good anchor; so I prayed.

11

Gate, Tears, and Epithet

As the wan light of false dawn filtered into the after cabin through a murk of billowing, black dust blowing over the boat in the screeching wind, I lifted my head from my hands and found myself staring, unwittingly at first, at my little library on its shelf over the navigation table.

My row of books was far smaller than the collection I had gathered and cherished when I had lived ashore in the U.S.A., and I remembered all my heart-searching back in San Diego when I had sorted out the books I should take with me on this voyage. Books weighed. Weight in a multihull vessel was anathema. I'd had over three hundred; I'd given away all but thirty-five of my precious books so as not to carry that excess weight, and so slow the boat down. Now I stared and stared at my thirty-five books. They had been thrown about a lot; the soot from the defective cabin-heater back in the freezing winter in Germany had covered them with gray grime, I'd had little chance to read any of them since. . . .

I heard the crew stirring forward, even through the noise of the wind roaring overhead. It is amazing, when you love a boat, how the slightest untoward noise or movement could be felt, almost telepathically, no matter what hell was let loose topside. My bleary gaze returned to my books, and I realized that someone, something, somewhere, was telling me something, demanding

139

something of me, and that something was heartbreaking. I had to reduce the weight on board, so as to reduce the load the anchors had to hold against that screaming wind. To reduce the weight on board I had, among other things, to *dump my library overboard*.

Resisting the thought, my mind raced through the list of every conceivable weight in *Outward Leg*. Anyone who knows anything at all about voyaging craft, and especially one stored up and victualed for three months minimum, knows roughly how many weights that made.

I couldn't ditch any food; neither Aden nor Djibouti, in those strife-torn times, might be open to us. I could hardly consider dumping any fresh water, except as a last resort. All excess clothes, winter gear and footwear, blankets and sheets, would have to go. We didn't—wouldn't—need things like that until we reached colder regions.

Thomas came into the cabin with a cup of coffee for me and one for Svante, who was huddled against the shrieking, stridulate wind keeping watch on the anchor lines. He too was bleary-eyed, after only an hour's attempt at sleep. It was almost as though, if we raised our voices, we would add to the ship's strain and agony. I spoke quietly. "Thomas, get rid of all excess clothing," I said. "Everything—all we don't need to sail to India. Dump it overboard. We could have given it away to those poor buggers in the Sudan, but now it's too late . . . we have to get rid of all extra weight." I didn't mention the books. My mind was recoiling from that horror.

In a few minutes, with Svante giving him a hand, Thomas had dumped all the winter jackets and trousers, thick underwear, woolly blankets; as it was passed topside I mentally calculated the weight going overboard. The clothes weighed in all about four hundred and fifty pounds. It wasn't enough. The anchor lines were stretched like violin strings.

I remembered all the charts stowed under my bed mattress. Mostly they were of the Mediterranean; all of it, from Suez to Gibraltar. We had not needed most of them, having made the passage across Europe via the Danube and Black Sea. But I had hoped to be able to exchange them with westbound yachts for charts of Oriental waters. Each chart was worth, nowadays, a few pounds, both in monetary value and weight. There were about fifty of them. Thomas stared at the treasure trove of charts lying there under my silent gaze. The boat shuddered under a particularly violent gust of wind. Heart stopped, I listened for any movement—any juddering—of the anchors. None. Thomas stared at me. I nodded. The charts were heaved topside and so overboard. That was another three hundred pounds gone. One third of a ton so far.

Then I demanded a thorough search of the forward cabin for anything—*anything*—(anything to save my books!) that was un-used, unlikely to be used before landfall at a place where it could be replaced. That rendered up old hand-lamps, a rusty stove with ruined burner, a heavy old toolbox which need not be used as we had an alternative stowage for our tools, several old yachting mag-azines, a rotted canvas dinghy-awning—anyone who has ever cleared out a boat at the end of a sailing season knows the kind of things we found and ditched. They rendered up another three hundred or so pounds of excess weight. But that did not satisfy the god of the sea, when I pleaded with him that it should be enough.

The god of the sea shook his head. Half of our precious fresh water, ten cans of it, was next to go, emptied in a spray over the side. Still unmerciful, unforgiving, he turned my head continually back to my library shelf. Desperately I remembered all my old files. I always kept old letters and records. Every now and again I would gather them together and send them somewhere they would be safe: to a friend, so he might keep them for me more safely in a drier air. Then, in Jebel Zuquair, I had on board files from the time I had left London. You can't keep everything in a writer's life in your head, besides all the things in a voyaging skipper's life. The mental strain would be enough to send you crazy. The excuses not to dump the files raced through my mind; but over they went, two and a half years of work, of memories fond and bitter.

In despair, I hobbled into the engine room and dragged out of their hiding place in the bilge a ruined, ancient pair of deck shoes, their soles ripped from the uppers. I'd known for ages they were lurking there. Seven pounds weight. Over they went. But the old god of the sea still shook his head.

Finally came the moment I had been dreading, when the only possible further weight to be ditched was my books. I gazed at them again, in their worn, torn covers, some with the titles hardly legible: *The Voyage of the Snark; Decline and Fall of the Roman Empire; Origin of Species; Admiralty Pilot for the East Coast of Greenland* (the one I'd used in *Cresswell*); Gerbault; Kipling; T. E. Lawrence (I could never stomach D. H.); Slocum; Bill Tilman (oh, the *pain* of handling his books for the last time!); Henry Miller; Mark Twain (the *agony*

of farewell!); and my three books of poems by Emily Dickinson . . .
Thomas Chatterton . . . as I, swallowing hard, handed my books,
the only *things* (apart from sailing craft) that had ever meant anything to me in my life, up the companionway to Thomas, who
wordlessly handed them on to Svante, out of sight on the stormy
deck. I thought to myself, "If hell has no worse than this, then I
need never again be afraid of death."

I cheated though.

Another sudden shock sent the boat hurtling back on her anchor
lines, and knocked Thomas off-balance up at the top of the companionway. While he recovered himself I swooped on my battered,
scruffy, bedraggled, thumbed and worn little volume *The Oxford
Book of English Verse*. I'd had it since I was boy dekkie on the old
sailing barge *Second Apprentice*, and it had subsequently kept me
sane during my lower-deck navy days. Feeling like a petty thief in
a dockside warehouse I grabbed it willy-nilly, and swiftly stashed
it away under my berth out of sight, praying that neither Thomas
nor the old sea god had noticed my deception, and half knowing
that if they had, they surely could do no other than forgive me for it.

So the awful sacrifice was made to the gods; half of my life in
Outward Leg—the part that mainly made living it worthwhile—
was consigned to the northerly running current in the gale-ripped
Red Sea. *Outward Leg* was left with no excess weight, except *The
Oxford Book of English Verse* and the lead in my own bereft heart.

A few moments later, the barometer needle started to move
again; two days after the storm had risen, and a half hour after
my precious treasure had been dumped overboard, the barometer
rose, so suddenly, so quickly that we could see the needle *rising,
twenty-six millibars in twenty minutes!* The wind, which had swept
and rampaged around Wuthering Heights down onto Rattrap Lagoon dropped completely, then sprung up from the west, and it
pissed down. The rain was so heavy and thick that it was impossible
for me to see the bow from the cockpit for a good half hour. We
quickly refilled all our water tanks. In less than the time it takes
to tell it, the rainstorm completely disappeared, the sky cleared,
the sun shone, and the wind dropped entirely. It was all so sudden,
this calming, that we felt almost embarrassed by it.

By early forenoon we silently and damply lit out of that awful
place and were on our way around the west coast of the Jebel
Zuquair Island, heading south in a flat sea, with not a breath of
air. Under way with the Yanmar engine chugging away at eco-

nomical revolutions (the only revolutions that ever are), *Outward Leg* was a quarter of a knot quicker now. We all appreciated that increase in speed, but I would still rather have had my old books on board. There are some things in this life which are far more important than speed. I think the lads knew I felt that way; they kept their rejoicing quiet. I think they looked on me with new respect. I think they liked me; they knew I would always be far harder and more demanding on myself than I would be on them. Which is how a good skipper must be; anything else would be a contradiction in terms. They had both volunteered to dump their own skimpy belongings back in the rattrap, but I had not allowed them to do it. I had got them into the trap; I must make any sacrifice needed to get them out. There was nothing more morale-destroying to a crewman than snatching other people's irons out of the fire, and especially his skipper's irons.

On the southern point of Jebel Zuquair Island, between it and the maze of islets and reefs, there was a passage not much wider than *Outward Leg.* Carefully we sounded our way through, under high, frowning black cliffs on both sides of us, and made our way into a vast lagoon, as calm as a millpond and teeming with basking sharks. Apart from the heat of the sun, almost directly above us in mid-April on those latitudes, the day was perfect. I steered the boat under power, through the blueing, indigo water of the deep passage, surrounded by small islands and the variegated colors of the water over the reefs around us: azure, virescent, sapphire, olive-green, emerald, cyan-blue, pea-green, aquamarine, turquoise, lapis lazuli, viridescent, glaucous, grue, and every possible combination between and among those glowing hues, all around us.

We decided to hold a sailor's holiday to make up for the misery of the night before. After ripping up the floorboards to air the bilges, our crew carried every scrap of our remaining clothing on deck, laid on the lifelines our mattresses and sails, hoisted a trail of damp shirts and pants up the signal halyards, and stopped blankets and blue jeans to the shrouds and stays, so that *Outward Leg* looked like an old-clothes shop chugging along. Then they brought the two stereo speakers out on deck and played Beethoven and Brahms over them for the forenoon, until lunchtime. We had trolled a line astern all the way from Rattrap Lagoon, just about, and had caught two walloping doradoes. We had a slap-up meal, fish and rice, and, taking turns on the wheel, dozed away the afternoon as the boat drew ever closer to the big, now-safe southern bay. There we anchored, only a mile east of the only sign of the existence of living humanity we had seen outside of the boat since we passed Jebel At Tair, two hundred miles to the north: a torn, tattered blue plastic bag blown against the crumbling wall of a ruined fisherman's hut.

In the south bay of the Zubair Islands it rained again heavily during the night, though with little wind. Again we refilled our empty water cans, and I recalled the last time I had been in this area, in *Barbara*, when we had no sign of a single drop of rain the whole passage from Israel to Mombasa. My crew now saw how good an idea it was to have the whole of *Outward Leg*'s main-hull deck fitted as a rain-catchment area. With a drain hole in each "corner" it gave us a catchment of about twelve square yards. Filling the cans, from the pipes down below, each of the four fitted with a tap, was an easy, dry job. We had never had to take on shore water anywhere there had been any rain. I could not recall taking on water from a shore tap anywhere between the Azores and Cyprus. The water we had dumped in Rattrap Lagoon had been from Port Sudan. Now we had rainwater to replace it. We thought that perhaps it might be a salubrious exchange.

I told the lads that this rainfall was probably the first to fall on the Zubair Islands for years. I don't know if that was true, but it was probably the first to fall there in twelve months. There was no soil on the islands, no greenery, except some lichen clinging to the rocks close to the shore, which, strangely enough so near to the Equator, in one of the hottest areas on earth, reminded me of the polar regions. There was no other wildlife that we could see, no animals, no birds. The land and the sky were utterly dead. It was as if all life on earth had suddenly disappeared. Only the sea had life in it, and in it life *teemed*.

Next day we weighed at false dawn and shoved off for the Bab el Mandeb (the Gate of Tears). As the sun rose, the wind sprang up out of the *west*, which is about as frequent an occurrence, in those parts, at that time of year, as me doing the Highland fling. It was perfectly obvious to me that my sacrifice to the gods had not been in the least in vain. A west wind at the southern end of the Red Sea is like manna, the Comstock Lode, and the Star of India sapphire all rolled in one. I had laid my treasure in the lap of the sea god, and he was rewarding me. My delight almost outweighed my surprise.

There must be an old Arab sailor's saying somewhere: "If there's ever the slightest chance of getting through the Bab el Mandeb, out of the Red Sea and into the Gulf of Aden, without having a headwind and being ruthlessly pasted, take it!"

We took it.

We hoisted all working sail and the big roller headsail and shaped a course slightly east of southeast and headed in the direction of the Yemeni port of Mocha. We had no intention of calling there, unless the wind turned fickle and headed us. Our intention was to seek the lee of the high mountains of South Yemen, so that if the wind did veer southeast we would be able to close-haul in fairly sheltered waters (if there were such a thing in those conditions in that area) and hopefully slam our way through the strait in one tack. If that happened it would be all or nothing and no half measures. The northern approach to the Bab el Mandeb was fraught with the hazards of heavy shipping and a string of islands, the Hanish, which, ill lit if at all, were slap-bang under the lee of any close-hauled sailing craft heading south.

Tense and taut, our instincts sharpened by the hard lesson of Rattrap Lagoon, we zoomed toward the Bab el Mandeb, much lighter now, of weight as well as fanciful wishes, making ten knots on a broad reach.

The old god of the sea was even yet playing with us, though. No sooner were we five miles off Mocha, around lunchtime, than the wind died and we were left wallowing around in a measly chop. Through the binoculars we could plainly see the town of Mocha, and the shipping lying off it, with a background of high, hazy mountains.

Our motoring forty miles down the coast of North Yemen, in a flattening sea, all the hot afternoon, all the evening, was an anticlimax. Weary, at nine o'clock we hove to. The light on the cape of Bab el Mandeb was now well within sight. To the west of that cape, across the smaller, eastern strait of Bab el Mandeb, we could see the dark mass of the island of Perim, which sat in the middle and guarded both straits. That island, we knew, was South Yemeni territory (and so a Soviet fief). We also knew there was no love lost between North and South Yemen. We decided to bide our time, until we got a wind. The tides were strong in those waters, but we were well out of the way of the heavy shipping passing through the western, larger strait.

We did not light our riding lamp. There was no sense in advertising *Outward Leg*'s presence in Yemeni waters, North or South.

The Yemeni frontier guards—in fact the whole population—were renowned for the nervousness of their trigger fingers, and we had no permit, as is required (illegally according to international maritime law), to call and rest for a few hours in their waters before heading on out into the stiff resistance of the Gulf of Aden.

We had reason to congratulate ourselves; we were exactly where we should be, at the southern end of the Red Sea, and when we should be, which was at the time the monsoon was due to change direction. We were now three thousand miles from Istanbul, from where we had set out eight months earlier with the boat in a sad state. Now, after voyaging south, south, ever south for months, we were ready to round the Bab el Mandeb and start off again east, with our boat in good order and full supplies and water on board.

The first suggestions of daylight showed an innocent scene. To the southeast, over water as flat as a baker's tray lay the low, surprisingly undramatic headland of Ras Bab el Mandeb. South of us the island of Perim rose out of the still-seeming sea.

To the south again, beyond Perim, a line of unmoving cumulus cloud on the horizon showed us there was no wind. Fresh bearings on the Ras Bab el Mandeb and on Perim indicated that we were being pushed back north at the rate of around two knots. I decided to find anchorage, so that with our hook clinging to real estate we would stay put and give nothing more to the Red Sea. We knew from the grapevine that Perim was out of bounds and heavily guarded; we headed, then, for the cape itself, and anchored under its lee, out of the north-running current (12° 41.78' north, 43° 26.67' east).

As our crew took a quick nap to refresh themselves, by the dawn light, peering through our binoculars, I inspected the surroundings; the scene was idyllic. I could see a fort about a half mile away, above the rocky foreshore, where placid waters gently lapped against the boulders. Clean and unsullied by smoke or fog, the strongpoint looked exactly like the toy forts of my childhood; perfectly square, with crenelated walls. About its walls drooped a few date palms. On the far side, facing inland, was a drawbridge, and over the main gate was erected a flagpole. There was no flag on it. There was no sign of any occupants in the fort, and it looked to me deserted. Away to the east of us, about two miles along the shore, a small village betrayed itself by showing fishing craft drawn up on the beach, and smoke from the houses. It all looked peaceful enough. I scrabbled down the galley companionway and set to preparing breakfast. Oatmeal patties.

I'd no sooner finished turning the last of the patties in the frying pan (nothing like the odor of freshly cooked oatmeal patties to wake up a soundly sleeping crew) than the faint sound of a bugle call, hardly ascertained over the sizzling of the patties, sent me shooting back to stick my head above the top of the hatchway, grab the binoculars, and stare in the direction of the fort.

What I saw was incredible; straight out of a scene from a movie on the French Foreign Legion or the Bengal Lancers; up the flagpole a flag was being hoisted, probably the North Yemeni flag, but I didn't wait to check its colors. A quick glimpse of a score of running figures, all in flowing robes and turbans, all toting rifles or submachine guns, all making fast down the hill toward the foreshore boulders, sent me diving for the engine starter key. Images of being blown up only fifteen miles to the north of here, thirty-five years before, when the Yemenis almost killed me, flooded my mind. I was too anxious to get the hell out of there to be afraid.

I shouted to the crew, "Right lads, let's have you! We've got a reception committee! Get your continental arses up here as fast as Christ will let you!" or something like that.

Within seconds Thomas, now the Bavarian Bullet, and Svante, the Stockholm Cannonball, were both on the foredeck pulling like crazy on the anchor rodes. We had dropped the hook in deepish water—about one hundred feet—and as soon as the crew felt the anchor come out of the sand I stuck the Yanmar into Ahead and let her go, at full revs, so that we were dragging the anchor underwater as it was being hoisted. I just hoped to hell there were no fishing nets about.

No sooner were we under way and even before the anchor was up on deck, even as Thomas swung himself over the bow rail to hoist its heavy weight on board, out of the corner of my eye I caught a glimpse of something moving farther east, along the shore. I grabbed the binoculars and turned to stare aft, guiding the wheel with my rump, watching the wake so as to hold a straight course. Sure enough, and no doubt about it, even as I heard the thump of our anchor hitting the foredeck, I saw a big open boat, full of figures, leaving the shore, and heading straight for us, fast, as I could tell by its wake.

Now was the time for Yanni to prove his little kamikaze self. I shoved the control lever as far ahead as I could. Thomas, now back aft, dived below at my nod and rammed the fuel-control cable wire at its full distance on the fuel pump. I glanced at the engine-revolutions counter. The needle was almost off the gauge.

I yelled at Svante to get back aft; he'd been standing on the foredeck like a speedboat-club race-committee commodore. As the first yells from the chase boat reached us I grabbed hold of Svante's shoulder and dragged his head down, alongside of mine, below cockpit-top level. As I did so I glimpsed the speed log—seven and a half knots!

Svante made no sound. "Keep your bloody head down, mate, they may start firing any minute!" I gasped, as I raised my head just high enough to watch the compass and hold our course, *west*. So, with our engine roaring away, our anchor laying loose on the foredeck, where Svante had abandoned it when I had yelled at him to get aft, Thomas down below in the engine compartment straining at the fuel-control cable, exhaust smoke pouring from our main hull, Svante wordlessly trembling alongside me, and me crouched in the cockpit, steering and peering, we left the peaceful, quiet anchorage off Ras Bab el Mandeb. If that sounds like nothing much, try it on one leg!

The distance across the little strait of Bab el Mandeb was about two miles, give or take a few yards. I reckoned silently that if we could stay ahead of them for eight minutes, we would be in South Yemeni territorial waters, and the North Yemenis would not be able to catch us.

At the end of the second minute, they were about three quarters of a mile astern of us and gaining. By the end of the fourth minute they were half a mile astern; the sixth minute a quarter of a mile; near enough for me now to hear, even over the roar of Yanni, their shouts, and for me to see them shaking their fists and rifles at us. They were close enough for me to see, as I somehow balanced on my good leg, crouched down in the cockpit, my eyes just at deck level, that their helmsman was a man about my age, stout, dressed in white robes and an Arab headcloth, with red and gold head-bands around it.

By the end of the eighth minute the North Yemeni boat was no more than two hundred yards from *Outward Leg*'s stern and I could clearly see the anger on the faces of the tribesmen who crowded her . . . but by the middle of the ninth minute of the chase the North Yemeni boat had stopped dead in the water, and as I stooped to holler through the hatch for Thomas to lower the engine speed I saw that we were close to the shore of Perim Island. Then we stopped the engine, and, as the boat's way carried her forward as she slowed down in the flat sea, we felt a breeze rising from the southeast, and knew that we had won the race, and that, short of being fired on from Perim Island, we were safe.

As the lads hoisted sail I inspected Perim Island through the binoculars. Much of the rising land from the foreshore, and the hills above it, was occupied by concrete fortifications. Then, atop one bunker, a flash of color caught my eye and I did a double-take. Figures dressed in khaki and in white robes were waving at us. I hollered to the lads to desist in shifting the sails about while I listened, and sure enough, there it was, faint from this far away, but unmistakable; the South Yemenis were cheering us! I swept my gaze through the binoculars over other pillboxes along the shore—and saw that almost all of them had figures standing on their roofs, or crowded in front of them, overlooking the shore and us, and cheering us, like racecourse punters yelling on a Derby favorite.

Once the sails were up and drawing, *Outward Leg* moved forward gracefully, and headed for the open sea to the south, with our Aries wind-vane gear steering. Our crew stood on the main deck and cheered the still-waving and shouting soldiers on the island of Perim in their turn. I, New York walking-stick in hand (thereby hangs a tale!) clambered onto the main deck to join the lads. I grabbed hold of the staysail stay, but didn't face the west and Perim Island. I faced *east*, into the rising sun, toward the North Yemenis still wallowing on the frontier line in their boat, and shook my stick at them. I turned and saw Thomas and Svante grinning at me.

I remembered, just in time, as I thought, my promise to the old sea god in Jebel Zuquair, when I'd made my deal with him to save *Outward Leg* for a better fate than being pounded to death on the reef. I'd promised to moderate my language, in speech as well as writing. Well, he'd had my library, what else could I offer him?

I shook my stick again at the North Yemenis and hollered, *"Go take a running jump at a galloping gander!"*

I turned again and saw Thomas silently, curiously, staring at me, boring into my expression with his blue eyes. We looked at each other, me half grinning, but with my face gradually falling. I realized that despite his mastery of most colloquial English phrases, there were yet some he hadn't heard before, that he had yet to learn. "Surely," I silently begged of the sea god, "this is not the time, in the glow of our little victory, for me to be teaching my mate a new English phrase? Flat ones, at that? *Surely one last time?*"

I thought I heard the old sea god harrumph in an agreeable way. I turned again toward the North Yemeni boat with its now-downcast crew of marauders. I raised my stick as high as I could as I held on to the staysail stay. Then in as loud a voice as I could muster without my loose false teeth falling out, I slowly pronounced a good, time-honored Anglo-Saxon phrase, renowned the world over, wherever English-speaking people have sailed or trodden, from the searing sands of the Kalahari Desert to the freezing Arctic wastes, from Valparaiso to Vladivostok. As I shouted I moved my teeth, lips, tongue, and jaws to roll the consonants and vowels around lasciviously, deliciously, as it came out, so I could taste every nuance of the words, as I hurled them at the elderly stout Arab helmsman.*

As I yelled, a lightning flash had struck out of a hammerhead far to the south, followed by a dull, distant roar of thunder. I clambered back down into our cockpit to plot our beat out into the Gulf of Aden; I knew the old sea god had turned his head for a split second, so he wouldn't hear me. I thought he might have winced a bit, too.

And that's how *Outward Leg*, her triumphant crew, and her *reformed* skipper, sailed out of the Red Sea.

*Author's note: For young friends and those few of you who object to my true reporting of good old honest English words (but not their Latin-derived equivalents) and for some book reviewers, who, despite all the evidence to the contrary, suggest that seamen and sailors do not use such words, I have in the main text omitted the epithet I yelled at the armed North Yemenis who had been pursuing *Outward Leg*, and whom she had outrun. It is below. You can, if you wish, miss this note, and so reserve your seat for some Celestial Cup Races. I, not being interested in races—except in emergencies—shall not be there.
"Fuck you, Jack!"

12

There Aren't No Ten Commandments . . .

As soon as we rounded Ras Bab el Mandeb the wind showed its full force. The current, of course, was against us, with all the Gulf of Aden trying to rush up north through the straits to replace the daily loss of billions of tons of water evaporated by the heat of the sun throughout the whole of the Red Sea. All that day, the twelfth of April, and all that night, were spent beating in a Force Five southeaster, navigating on soundings and dodging shipping intent on its way to and from the Indian Ocean, eight hundred miles to the east.

In the western Gulf of Aden the satnav seemed to be almost useless. In thirty-six hours our temporary coat-hanger antenna picked up only one signal. This was against its usual six or seven signals a day north of the Straits of Bab el Mandeb. We didn't know at the time, of course, but we were to find that this would be so until we were well clear of the island of Socotra, off the coast of Somalia, almost a thousand miles to windward.

As *Outward Leg* smashed her way through the seas, hour in, hour out, that first night in the Gulf of Aden, I turned on our radio to the BBC. Even an easy-sounding exercise like that was a little purgatory for me, in the bouncing, heaving after end of the boat. The only way I could manage to do it without being jerked around violently was to throw myself backward, horizontal on my berth,

aft, and fiddle around with the radio switches from a prone position. I couldn't have the cabin lights on because that would de-
stroy my night vision, and our only red light had given up the
ghost weeks before. Boats and electronics are bad companions. But
there was no news of Aden; all seemed to be peaceful.

If there had been news of troubles in Aden, our plan was to
turn around and head west to Djibouti. I had been there last in
1971, when it had been a French colony. Because of the closing of
the Suez Canal my boat, *Barbara,* had been the first Western yacht
to call there in twelve years. Then we had been feted by the Foreign
Legion. Now the word on the cruising grapevine was that ship's
papers were confiscated from any yacht by notoriously resentful,
bullying officials (of the Afar or Issa tribes) and the papers were
held for ransom against payment of exhorbitant and vastly inflated
"harbor fees."

Djibouti, still home of a French Navy base, was by reputation
very expensive because it was geared to catering for French naval
ratings, with their regular monthly pay-packets well filled by farm-
ers back home who themselves were drawing subsidies the size of
queen's dowries from the EEC. So for us, if there was any alternative port of call, Djibouti was out and that left no alternative at
all.

Banging up and down against serried ranks upon ranks of steep
seas, against a never-changing backdrop of barren mountains to
the north, spray to the east, and whitecaps south and west of us,
about eight to twelve miles off the coast of South Yemen, we in
Outward Leg discussed what we had read and heard of the political
situation in Aden.

I remembered when Aden had been a British colony, a major
port of call on the shipping route from Britain to India and the Far
East. There had always been a small Royal Navy presence there in
those days, to keep an eye on the shipping lanes and to discourage
piracy in small craft in the Gulf of Aden.

The British had left Aden to the "workers" and "peasants,"
with their Soviet advisers and Chinese arms, in 1967, after the Suez
debacle. In time South Arabia became the People's Democratic
Republic of Yemen. Like every country in the world that had "People" or "Democratic" in its title, government had nothing what-
soever to do with people, except for an elite minority, who forced
upon their fellowmen a political system which the vast majority
either barely tolerated, detested, or half starved or died under. The

country's short history had been a brief chronicle of bloody-minded strife, intrigue, and bastardy against everyone in contact with it (except the Soviets, of course). Inside the country, internal feuding between tribal factions had been continuous.

We knew that the Soviets had established military and naval bases in Aden, and that they had electronic listening (and satnav-signal-jamming?) stations on Perim and Socotra islands, so that they now supervised and controlled, thoroughly, the gullet of the main and shortest sea route from Europe to the East. With South Africa a potential client state of the Soviet Union in a few years, followed by Chile and Panama as possibilities, we calculated that probably by the end of the century no ship would be able to sail from Europe to the Far East or Australasia without Muscovite let.

From Aden, only ten weeks before, there had been radio reports of vicious infighting among different party and tribal factions. H. M. S. *Britannia*, the royal yacht, on her way to New Zealand, had been diverted to Aden to evacuate foreigners from the strife-torn city to Djibouti. Eleven passage-making yachts that we knew of had been resting in Aden before tackling the Red Sea. We knew that one British yacht had been set ablaze by gunfire as she tried to escape the holocaust of fires and explosions all around her in the port. We also knew that other yachtsmen had abandoned their craft and escaped to Djibouti aboard a Soviet freighter.

What we did not know was how things were now, and how our reception would be. I decided to be like the cat and pad about outside in the garden awhile, quietly, before making for the door. "When in danger or in doubt, take your time and work it out. . . ." I told the lads. But they knew I had one of these little rhymes to suit every occasion, and they merely grinned. When I told them that we were supposed to have an Adeni permit to enter their coastal waters, unless we headed straight for the port, their grins faded. I explained that it would hardly be seamanlike to press on past Aden for the minimum two-and-a-half-thousand-mile voyage to India, and that we would need to replenish fresh stores and canned food; that we should top up with fresh water and have a good check around all the boat's gear, and give the old monsoon a few days more chance to stop blowing from the east and haul around to the west; that it wouldn't be sensible to head straight in to Aden, with its recent history of violence and random shooting at craft in the harbor. They agreed, and their faces again lit up.

What I didn't—couldn't—tell them, though, was my secret other reason to head in to Aden: my leg-stump was one red-raw mass of sores, caused initially by heat rash. I did not dare to risk any diminishment of my crew's morale. What I did tell them was that after two hundred miles or so of heavy beating to windward in a hot climate I was ready for a rest, and anyway we should clean up the boat a bit before we headed in to what had once been a Royal Navy base, regardless of what it was now. The ghosts, I knew, would still be watching.

I headed *Outward Leg* in to Banda Imran, which, I recalled from the old days, was a great shallow bay, bordered by high mountains which sent vicious katabatic squalls sweeping down from the heights at night. Most of the bay was wide open to the southeasterly wind, and there the whole Gulf of Aden simply piled in and beat on the beach to set up tremendous surf and spray. The waves beat so heavily on the sand that a roar could be heard, I remembered, five miles offshore. The spray, and the mist that it set up, was so thick that nothing could be seen of the coast itself for the whole length of the twenty-mile bay. But on the eastern end of Banda Imran, closest to Aden, and a mere thirty miles from the port, there was a steep, bold headland, Ras Imran, and below it a small horseshoe-shaped island, Jebel Aziz (12° 44.43′ north, 44° 42.91′ east), where I knew the shelter was good. So we made for Jebel Aziz, and anchored there by the soft light of a full moon, in flat water over twenty-five feet of good sand. There had been a few lights out in Banda Imran bay, and we had seen the dark shapes of small craft around us as we hauled into the anchorage, so we set anchor watches but did not light any lamps, not wishing to advertise ourselves.

Daylight showed us two wrecked and deserted Adeni gunboats, of Soviet design, on the sandy beach inside the bight of Jebel Aziz. From what I could tell peering through our binoculars, they showed no sign of combat, and it looked very much as if they had dragged their anchors and simply drifted ashore, and been abandoned there once everything portable and of any intrinsic value had been removed. Both the wrecks had rocket launchers on the sides of their wheelhouse, so they must have been of fairly recent design.

We spent all that day at anchor, squaring up the boat, oiling the deck wood, cleaning the sides and the bottom growth. I believe very much in entering a port of call, if it's at all possible, with as little work to do on board as can be managed, and especially a hot tropical port. We did more work on board in that one day, at anchor in a stiff breeze, with air rushing through the boat, all hatches open, than we could possibly have done in a week inside Aden harbor. For sure we knew the bottom should be scrubbed outside the harbor. The pollution in most tropical shipping ports that were not open anchorages had to be seen to be believed. Every one I had ever been in had been one vast sewer and oil-fuel dump. It was probably the same in temperate climates too, only there the odor of it didn't hang around us, nor stay with us in our boat for days after we had departed.

At false dawn, delighted with a fresh *northerly* breeze, we weighed and set off along the mountainous coast east for Aden, hardly believing that we might have a broad reach, in a flat sea, the whole thirty miles. But no sooner had we rounded Jebel Aziz than the old east-monsoon wind slapped us in the teeth and got us back to grinding in the winches to close-haul again, and tack, and tack, the whole distance, so that we covered the passage in sixty miles instead of thirty. The wind picked up early that day, as the heat on the mountains sent the air over them shooting over the Arabian Desert and dragged inshore the monsoon wind. By tea break at ten o'clock we were off Ras Abu Quiama, staring, in between tacks, at old British forts on the heights. Once we had rounded the headland the monsoon became a friend on our starboard beam, and on a broad reach we shot through the offlying shipping, mostly Soviet, and hauled around the narrow breakwater entrance, to anchor off the old British-built Customs wharf, just over three thousand miles from the Golden Horn at Istanbul.

The scene in the port of Aden was much the same as I remembered it from the early fifties in my Royal Navy days. It was crowded with craft, large and small, at anchor and moving about, and the town around the shore seemed busy enough. But there were some differences, which were immediately obvious: burned and shell-pocked ruins of many government buildings on the hill of Steamer Point, including the old British military hospital where I had once lain racked in pain; and the number of Soviet ships, merchant as well as war, which lay off the town.

Many harbor launches, packed with Adeni workers all dressed in the same style (and size) blue overalls roared past *Outward Leg* as she sat waiting for instructions, her U.S. ensign wafting in the oil- and shit-scented breeze. As the boats passed us by, every single overalled dock worker waved to us enthusiastically, and there were many shouts of "America okay!" and "Lucky Strike!"

Two Soviet cruisers, and a supply vessel, *Volga*, lay at anchor only thirty yards or so away from us. During the time we lay in Aden I was, of course, very interested to watch the Russian sailors go about their day's duties. After some time studying them it came to me that except for the different uniforms and flags, and the gear on board the Soviet ships, I might have been looking at Royal Navy cruisers and supply ships of thirty years before. The routine was *exactly* the same: morning divisions and evening fire- and damage-control parties mustered on deck for work allocation to the youngsters by older, time-serving petty officers who reported to the junior officers standing nearby, looking, apart from returning the POs' salutes, useless; and always a couple of "skates" (wise guys) at the back of the mustered platoons, with their caps at a jauntier angle, quietly and very efficiently mocking the whole show.

The one glaring difference that I saw from RN ships of my day was that in the Soviet ships no one ever seemed to work alone, or even to *be alone,* unless they were walking or running somewhere along the deck. They were always in groups, parties, large or small, but never less than three sailors together, all the time I watched them.

Even when officers went ashore in the ships' boats, they never went alone. The exception was one civilian who was continually being ferried back and forth over the harbor to the nearest, flagship cruiser. He I marked down as the local KGB agent. He was the only Russian, apart from the boats' crews, to return our waves when no one was watching, or, with his jacket flung over his shoulder, to look at all casual.

The Soviet ships were very smart, but there was less polished brass about than we'd had in the old Grey Funnel Line. This Russian Navy presence was obviously a show-the-flag visit by them to an ailing client-state. The sailors' uniforms were clean and pressed, even their working suits, which, like every other navy's, were dark blue shorts and light blue shirts.

I stared at these descendants of the Soviet sailors I had seen in the Arctic in the early forties and remembered (so far away, so long ago!) how they had painted with their bare hands in the freezing cold of the Arctic (no brushes in Stalin's Russia) the sides of the old battlewagon H.M.S. *Resolution*, which Churchill had handed over to them, along with a couple of tons of gray "Pusser's crabfat" paint. Apart from the old *Resolution* a couple of coastal submarines and a seagoing tug or two, had been the Red Navy

Arctic Fleet in those days. If anyone had ever suggested to us Royal Navy men then, that one day we would see Russian cruisers and supply ships in *Aden, in operational control*, we would have said he was crazy.

The same old bullshit that had been our bane in the Royal Navy was even yet rife in the Soviet ships; the same shouts and barks, the same officious junior officers now and again coming down on some much older chief or petty officer who, when it came to knowing what he was doing, was probably miles ahead of the snotty; the same stupid saluting, the same flag-worship, the same old bugle calls morning and evenings.

"What do you think of them?" asked Thomas, as I stared through the binoculars at an array, on board the closest Soviet cruiser, of hands mustered for what looked like pay day.

I had been grinning at the antics of one little chap at the back of the parade who had been pulling the collar of a taller lad in front of him. Every time the taller lad had turned around, obviously annoyed, the little'un had sprung to attention. I felt fondly for the short chap, recognizing him instantly.

"As it is, was, and ever shall be," I murmured.

From what we could see on board the ships, and in the passing ships' boats, as they ferried Soviet sailors to and from the shore, there was little of the awe between sailors and their officers that there had been in the British Navy in my day, little of the distance; but on the other hand they did not seem to be as familiar, even chummy, as the American Navy seamen had been toward their officers.

In the ships' boats (which sported *wooden* ensigns, to save wear and tear—a good idea) we never saw Soviet sailors, nor their officers, going ashore or returning on board alone or in groups of two or three, as we would have in my navy. They were always in organized groups, platoons, of a dozen men or more, and the libertymen were always, it appeared, under the control of a petty officer, even ashore.

At first, when we in *Outward Leg* greeted, as sailors do the world over, the helmsman and crew of the Soviet ships' boats, we were either frowned upon or ignored. But little by little we wore them down with our insistence on the courtesy of showing a passing boat's helmsman that we were aware he was passing, and that there was no underwater obstruction to foul his propeller. Which was why a sailor greeted a passing boat, and not merely out of natural friendliness, although that, too, was important. But Ivan is really a land animal, and it showed in many other small ways, like their ships' boats tearing across our bows, which is something usually done only by car drivers who steer motorboats as though they were out on a highway, or "Mediterranean cowboys" escaping a marina fee, to everyone's peril, including their own.

On April 15, after twenty-four hours of watching Soviet ceremony, I decided, despite the sores on my stump, to get away from the sights and sounds of the Red Navy and head for the shore. Like rock "music," militaristic bullshit and imperialistic baloney might be all right at twenty; at sixty-one it was just plain intolerable. I donned my sun hat, and we all three crowded into our dinghy and set off, for the first time since Suakin and Africa, for the bullet-scarred and shell-pocked Aden Customs and Immigration wharf.

Before we went ashore I reminded Thomas that he should not take his camera with him. They were forbidden.

The scene inside the main hall of the wharf was strange indeed. The hall was divided by that favorite ploy of obstacle-ists the world over—a long line of tables. On one side of the tables, all around the periphery of the high-ceilinged, cool, Betjemenesque great hall, where open doors and broken wooden louvers overhead let in shafts of hot sunlight and cooler, oil/shit-scented breezes, loitered a couple of hundred European men of all ages and conditions. One swift glance at their rolled-up shirt sleeves, their "short back and sides" haircuts, and their wide-bottomed pants and big boots, and their dozen parcels each, half of them, and pale skins, most of them, was enough to tell me that these were the modern inheritors of the old British maritime empire: Eastern European crewmen from the Soviet-bloc merchant ships in the port. There was no talking, that I could hear, among them, and they reminded me for all the world of penned animals. I didn't think I had seen any group of people looking so "out of place" since we'd seen the Russian "tourists" on the shores of lovely Lake Balaton, in Hungary. But there were no spring flowers, no buds, in Aden. They just sat or stood around, silently, expressionlessly, with their eyes downcast, showing not one glimmer of interest in the scene about them, nor any interest in the people on the other side of the table-barrier.

These were the Adeni Customs, Immigration, and Harbor police. There were about thirty of them, sitting and standing behind the tables, some drinking tiny cups of coffee, some smoking cigarettes as they inspected me, with my sun helmet, and my crew, dressed all smart in their shoregoing rig of clean shirt and pants. The officials were all in uniform of one kind or another, mostly, except for a few red stars here and there, looking like hand-me-downs from the British days. But the Yemeni, bless him, as always, was incapable of wearing any Western-style uniform as it was meant to be worn, in *uniform style*. One had his cap askew this way, the other that. One had on his feet Arab-style slippers, another tennis shoes, one had brass buttons, the next silver. Most had buttons undone or missing.

There was a tension all about as the officials, all unsmiling, inspected us, from the tops of our heads, our wind-creased faces, our lean bodies, my stick, to our salt-stained *Timberland* shoes, now all cracked and worn. Now it was we who felt like intruders from another world, as indeed we should, for we were.

There's an old sailor's saying: When you're beating offshore, get to the wind before it gets to you.

Before we got to the nearest official—a thin, hungry and dangerous-looking man, with a hooked nose, his face darkening even more than it already was—I stopped, pressed my right hand over where my heart was supposed to be, bowed lightly at the officials in three directions at once, as they all gawped at me, and said, as clearly and distinctly as I could manage: *"Mahaba, Salaam Aleikum!"* ("Greetings, the peace of Allah be upon you!").

There was a moment of consternation, of shocked surprise, which seemed to hover in the high hall right over our heads for a second or two, then each and every one of the thirty officials, all like puppets jerking as their controlling strings were pulled, all together, instantaneously, all bowed slightly toward me and murmured, each one, *"Salaam Aleikum . . .,"* and looked up at me from under their raised eyebrows with respect. As I produced our passports for Eagle Features, he thanked me shyly and called me *"Effendi"* and we knew we had won him, at least, right over.

We were through the formalities with Eagle Features before you could say *"Allah akbahr!"*. In less than a minute our passports were stamped and we had been warned of pickpockets and "crooked" money-changers in the town. Then, as the Russians, Lithuanians, Estonians, Poles, East Germans, and others all around the room gawped in silent amazement, and all the other Yemeni officials gazed kindly upon our passing, Eagle Features marched with us, he on one side of the line of tables, and we on the other, and escorted us to the main door of the Customs wharf. There, in daunting heat, he took my elbow and helped me down the crumbling steps in the street where, producing a whistle from his chest pocket, he flagged down for us an ancient taxi and told the puzzled, disconcerted driver, to take *"my father and his two fortunate sons"* to the main market square and not to overcharge us if he valued his license. As he turned to leave us Eagle Features murmured something about "You cannot tell the sweetness of the dates from the height of the palm tree nor the age of a palm tree from the sweetness of its dates." Then he left us and we never saw him again.

There were a few towns grouped around the area of Aden. The one closest to the port was Steamer Point, and there, because of my pain in moving around ashore, I stayed in the slightly less (I knew) dank heat around the waterfront. The lads I sent to have a grub around in Crater City, a huge, sprawling, purely Arab place on the eastern, breezy side of the Aden peninsula, as I had done when I had been their age. They were gone a couple of hours and returned all aglow with tales of the strange things they had seen, just as young sailors had in the days of Ulysses, and as they will, no doubt, in years to come, return to some spaceship docked on some faraway planet on the far edge of the universe.

But I, too, saw and heard strange things. There were shell holes in many, many buildings in the town. Many others were burned out, while more than a few places that had once been streetside shops showed by every sign that they had been looted. In the main square of Steamer Point, at the park gate, an old British cast-iron pillar box (mailbox), was still, I was content to see, painted the old "imperialistic" bright red. The original royal monogram, *"GR VI"* (standing for King George VI) was still on the pillar-box, but not now picked out in black, as it had been in British times, when much of the mail had been posted to London and not Moscow.

In the park, at a little open-air café, where I awaited the lads' return from Crater City, I was accosted by several men, old and young (purdah—the isolation of the sexes—is still the order of the day in Aden). This is a normal Arab thing, and means only attempts at passing the time of day, friendliness and the chance to talk with a stranger and perhaps learn something new. Some of them spoke reasonable, basic English, which relieved me of the strain of dredging up what Arabic I remembered. They started, each one, by greeting me, then asking if I were Russian. Of course, at first, and to be honest with them, I replied that I was British, and then they were curious as to what I was doing in Aden, and when I told

8 Leaving Tel Aviv, Israel. Svante in the foreground. Israeli ship
Peace in the background.

9 *Outward Leg*. Forward cabin and galley

10 Shipping in the Suez Canal

11 ...and more shipping: *Outward Leg* on passage

them, "Oh, just passing through," they expressed surprise, but were pleasant enough, and we parted company with due farewells. Then, feeling a little bored with the usual conversation between traveler and native in languages neither understood properly, which brings the level of exchanged ideas down to about that of three-year-olds (I thought—and still do—that a lot of land travelers, "trekkers" and such, to "exotic" lands, mostly merely wished to revert to conversational infancy), I decided to experiment. The next couple of men who came along and spoke to me were in their thirties, decently dressed, in djellabas and wearing ties. They looked like small-business men, but could just as well have been police-men. Upon their asking from whence I hailed I replied—in half truth—"America," and they took off from that open-air café, exposed to the view of all of central Steamer Point, like greased lightning, hardly staying long enough to mumble a good-bye. The word must have flown around the park and its environs; I was left severely alone after that to await in peace the return of my crew although several passers-by stared at me curiously.

After a meal in the main square, in a "restaurant" for which the advent of Marxism among the Yemenis had done nothing— neither for the food nor the standard of hygiene (greasy chicken leg, dark-spotted lettuce, half-black potatoes, chappati, and warm, brackish water from a tin cup that looked, with its chipped rim, as though it had been purloined from a British Army barracks during the Second World War)—we browsed around the town, slowly making our way back to the Customs wharf.

There was a shop on the main square which sold the best ice cream I have ever tasted anywhere. Being only two yards square it was too crowded, with four people in it, for me to get inside, so I ate the ice cream standing on the pavement, in the evening heat, with Thomas and Svante either side of me to prevent my being pushed off-balance by passers-by, who hurried along with glazed eyes, as though they were in a trance. I was somehow reminded of Rumania.

While I watched the passing people, Thomas and Svante talked with several young Adenis, all male, mostly about pop music and living conditions in Western Europe and Great Britain. Without exception every Adeni they spoke with wanted to emigrate to West-ern Europe. I told them they'd be better off in America. The average American, I observed, didn't know a Yemeni from a Turk, and their well-known Adeni entrepreneurial ability and simple needs would stand them well. The young Yemenis, I thought, did not believe me, but I put that down to the shirtsightedness of youth and turned again to watch the crowd.

Watching humanity was always a favorite pastime of mine before I set off on a long ocean voyage. Most sailors who wrote rambled on about going off into the mountains or the woods to commune with nature; but I didn't think they could have been at ocean sailing for very long; not me—there's always "nature" enough out on the ocean. Give me, when I had the choice, the sights and sounds of the towns and cities every time. I could never get my fill of them before I shoved off again into the blue. Besides, they filled my memory batteries with food for thought and vast entertainment for many a long night at the wheel.

In the streets of Aden, between the revolution-wrecked buildings, several squads of Soviet sailors passed us by, all hurrying back, arms loaded with parcels of Western and Japanese goodies, so our young informants told us, to their ships before nightfall. They were not allowed to stay ashore after sunset. The Russians were ignored by the Adenis. The Adenis were ignored by the Russians. It was as though they lived on two different planes, in different time-warps. There was none of the old occasional spark of interchange, none of the frequent recognition, none of the periodic disdain, none of the iterative sense of clashing cultures and backgrounds, none of the pure *fun* that I remembered so well from my shoregoing Royal Navy days. Between the Soviet sailors and the Yemenis, there was, I felt, *nothing*. A *glum, surly nothing.* They were ships passing in the night, all right, but there was a wide, empty ocean between them.

We called into a shop to buy a little gadget—I won't say what it was for fear that the people involved will be drastically persecuted. Neither will I say what race the shopkeeper was, nor what age he was. When Thomas inspected the gadget offered, the shopkeeper's assistant asked him, in good English (no fear of identification there; all the shopkeepers we met in Aden spoke good English), what nationality he was. Thomas replied, "German."

"East German?" the counter hand asked.

"No, West."

"Not Russian?"

Thomas laughed and shook his head. Everyone in the crowded shop, a dozen people or more, who until then had been watching us suspiciously, broke into smiles and chatter.

"Good," the counter hand told Thomas. "German, English, American very good. Russian bastard!"

Everyone in the shop agreed with this, and those who could speak English interpreted for those who could not, and even tiny tots were told the tale.

"Why do you say," I asked the counter hand quietly, "that the Russians are bastards?"

"Because they not buy anything."

"But I've just seen lots of them loaded down with parcels on the street . . ." I told him. (Fair's fair.)

"Yes." The counter hand was emphatic now. "They are only allowed to go to special shops owned by the Party . . . but they cannot handle the goods there to inspect them. Instead they come here, practically take everything apart, then leave and buy at the Party shop."

Someone else rushed into the shop. "When are you leaving Aden?" he asked me breathlessly.

"Oh, in a few days' time, I think," I replied casually, as I always did when asked that question anywhere. No sense in tempting the old sea god by advertising our departures.

"I think you better go very soon," he exclaimed. "You must leave Aden now!"

I stared at him for a few seconds, wondering who he was to be ordering us away: "Oh, why?"

"The American Air Force has just bombed Qaddafi's headquarters in Libya! Already the students are out on the streets in force . . . there will be another rising! They are going to attack anything Western!"

"Suffering Muhommad!" I thought to myself; "that'll make a good chapter ending!"

Part Three

The Dawn Comes Up Like Thunder

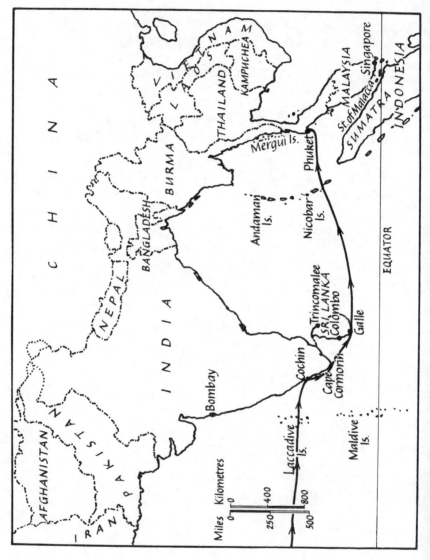

The Arabian Sea and Bay of Bengal

13

Free!

"Better get back on board, lads," I said calmly after the first shock of the news had passed over us. "This is one for the book; we can't—I wouldn't anyway—go back to Port Sudan. We can't head for Djibouti—it'll cost a fortune. We can't stay here in Aden; the balloon's going up as soon as those mountain tribes hear the news about Qaddafi—all hell'll be let loose. And the bloody monsoon is late changing—there's no sign of the easterly dying yet." I thought for a moment: "We can't go back—and we can just about go forward . . . against the monsoon—unless it changes."

"So we sail for somewhere safer?" half suggested Svante.

Thomas stared at Svante for a second, then half grinned at me. From somewhere far away came the noise of what sounded like rifle fire.

I smiled at Svante. I was getting used to him now. His stating the obvious was now part of our routine. "You bet your Swedish arse we sail. We sail to anywhere out of Aden, and as soon as we can. But the problem is that the nearest port east where we can be sure of not being thrown out of—or worse—is either Mombasa, in Kenya, or Cochin, in India, and they're both well over two thousand miles away. All we can do is beat like hell for Cape Gardafui and see how the monsoon is there, if it has changed, then shape our course the best way. It'll take us a good week to get to the Cape anyhow." I told myself that my stump, burning, covered in sores and bleeding at times, would have to wait for treatment. I'd smear it with penicillin ointment . . . and I thanked God that it was me, and not one of our crew, who had the complaint; otherwise I would have had to stay long enough to make sure he got the right medical treatment, regardless of any risk to the boat.

I sent Thomas and Svante ahead back to *Outward Leg*. I was too slow on my foot ashore.

"Make sure she's all right, lads," I told them. "And hoist the British, German, and Swedish flags on the starboard signal halyard. Then if there's any trouble they just might think twice bfore attacking the boat, if they know there are several nationalities on board." It was a faint hope, but both Sweden and Germany were involved in "aiding" (i.e., paying the danegeld) to South Yemen.

The crew protested that I should not, in my state, hobble back on board alone. The roads and pavements were in sad repair, they said, but what they really meant was that there was a chance I might be attacked by marauding "students." (God save us in days when "student" was a word which might arouse fear in ocean sailors!)

"When in danger or in doubt," I told them, "defend the vessel. Now you two get back on board as fast as Christ will let you. I'll manage." I put on bravado: "No Yemeni yob is going to attack an old crock like me, and if one does I'll ram my stick up his jacksy and have his balls for breakfast! Now you two trot on ahead. Light every lamp on board. Don't let anyone get the idea in his shitty Shi'ite head that we are hiding or afraid. If anyone tries to get aboard without explanation, clobber the bastard and heave him over the side."

"He might drown . . ." Svante started to elaborate, ". . . in the harbor. . . ."

A bleeding stump is not a friend of long, involved explanations: "Good. Then you can shove the bastard under with the sodding boathook! . . . And Svante you come back to the Customs wharf with the dinghy and wait for me there. And while you're at it you can hum a hymn or two!" With that I started painfully shuffling my way the half mile back to the Customs wharf, while the lads hurried ahead through the suspiciously dark and silent streets.

This is going to take some believing, I realize, so, exactly one year after the event, I'll write it slowly; all the way back to the

Customs wharf, as I limped my way along the ill-lit main street of one of the—usually lively—most strategically placed ports in the world, all the way along the moonlit waterfront, all the way through the dark, vast hall of the Customs wharf, and so to the jetty, I neither saw nor heard, close by, *one* solitary *living soul* until I was within sight of the Russian warships, and saw the night watch on her quarterdeck. Then I heard Svante call to me softly at the landing steps. "I think everyone is at home having dinner."

"Yeah, under their beds," I added. There had been tears in my eyes, almost, when I had finally reached the jetty.

Back aboard, we set watches for the night. I was tempted to move out of Aden harbor right away. But we still needed to top up our fuel and water tanks, and the port authorities were holding our ship's papers. I knew that we would probably be challenged and stopped by a harbor-police launch anyway, and then we would really be in trouble for departing without official permission. We were, after all, behind another little Iron Curtain.

Before the crew turned in and I took the first night-watch, I said that as everything was quiet (too quiet?) we would take our chances, and stay put. Tomorrow, in the broad light of day we would fuel and water as fast as we could, under the eyes of the Russian cruisers, and then get out. Fast.

The night passed without incident. I noticed there was not even traffic from the Soviet ships to and from the shore. I remembered that I had considered, when we had entered Aden, asking the Russians for medical help, but I'd changed my mind. I was damned if I'd ask the builders of the Berlin Wall for *anything*. Their minions in Bratislava had cured me of any ideas like that almost a year before when they tried to sink my vessel in the Danube. I'd never forgive those sons of bitches, I told myself, and asked the old sea god to forgive me for thinking that of them. "If we ever needed Neptune or Poseidon or whatever you call him on our side, by Allah it's now!" I'd concluded.

"We haul up the American flag?" was Thomas's first question next day.

Bleary-eyed I stared at him from where I sat on my bunk. I'd stayed on night watch until five o'clock, to relieve my young crew of sleepless hours. It took a minute for me to gather my wits. It had once taken me only seconds; now it took a full minute. Thomas repeated his question. "We haul up the flag aft?"

"It's not a flag. I've told you fifty times, Thomas, it's an ensign.

Haul it up? Of course we haul the bugger up. What do you think we are, bloody *Bulgarians*?"

I told myself: "I'm not what is called a stickler for flag etiquette, but I do like my ensign hauled up properly before breakfast. I mean if we don't do that, where will it end?"

Thomas disappeared and a moment later the scrabbling sound of our Old Glory—the same one *Outward Leg* had worn on the Danube as she busted through the granddaddy of Iron Curtains —being hoisted on the starboard backstay, sweetened more my morning tea.

The Yemeni faces as we pulled alongside the bouncy, rusty, filthy-oily fueling pontoon in the morning were, to say the least, surly. If insults had been bullets, if tones of voices could have been daggers, if looks could have killed, we would have been stone-dead before *Outward Leg* was even tied up alongside. As it was, it cost us two cartons of American cigarettes, instead of the customary one (as the grapevine had it) for the fuel attendant to unlock his ancient hand-cranked diesel pump. The lads carted away the fresh-water jerry cans under strict instructions to let no one else at all even come near them. Thomas and I padded into the Customs wharf where our ship's papers were practically thrown at us, crept back to where the boat was tied up, started the engine, and took off swiftly out of there to a hundred curses, a hundred scowls and a chorus of Arabic imprecations from everyone around. As we headed out into the anchorage, past a burned-out British yacht, a relic from the "Party-factional squabble" of a few weeks' before, a harbor launch roared past *Outward Leg*; every Yemeni on board it either shook their fists or gave the old one-finger sign to our American ensign.

"That's America's fault," observed our Swede, true to pro-gramming.

"Bullshit," I told him. "That's Qaddafi's fault for blowing up women and kids in Rome airport, the bloody twicer!"

As we had on the Danube, we played our bagpipes tape of "Lochaber Gathering" and "Lament for the Old Sword" as we passed the Russian ships, at full volume, and the Stars and Stripes waved aft in the breeze. "If the crocodile's going to get you, you might as well sound your best and wear your good clothes," I silently told *Outward Leg*.

In the midst of my anxiety about getting *Outward Leg* and us out of Aden in one piece, and tackling the problem of where we were to head now in a highly complex situation rife with problems, I was finding Svante's automatic, knee-jerk rejection of everything that was Western or Western-derived, and his consignment of it, without thinking about it for one moment, to some kind of dustbin in his head, *aggravating*.

I had more important things to think about than all this nonsense ashore. Like why in God's name hadn't the monsoon changed from east to west? It was supposed to ease off from the east in April. Here we were halfway and more through the month, and it was still blowing its head off at us all the way from the Gobi Desert. If it continued to blow from east when we passed Cape Gardafui, the Horn of Africa, we would have no alternative but to head south for Kenya, to await the west monsoon in Mombasa. That would delay by months our arrival in the Orient.

And here was this youngster, from a country that had stood by, busily getting rich, for years while the most monstrous, murderous political and military system the world has ever known raged and rampaged all around it; this scion of a people who had done little but lecture the rest of the West ever since on "proper" attitudes to the Third World, trying it out on me.

By now, if we'd been anywhere but off Aden, a day after the American raid on Libya, I'd have dropped Svante ashore. There was no way I could do that in Aden. Swede or not; Norwegian, Portuguese or Yugoslavian, he was white, and that was his measure as far as the Yemenis were concerned. Not even the Russians were daring to tread Yemeni dirt. Svante's life that day, ashore, would not have been worth a krona. I knew it; Thomas knew it; Svante was as innocently blind as a newborn babe. "Thus the welfare state," I told myself, "kills even the survival instinct. The cradle to the grave all right—and nothing in between."

Thomas, good old German Thomas, bless him, intervened as I steered out from behind the breakwater and headed for the offing. "Hoist the sails?" he queried.

I nodded, and he and Svante bent to their tasks, blames forgotten, our only enemy now the vast ranges of salt water which stretched eternally on between us and our destination, wherever that might be, Mombasa, the Seychelles Islands, or India. The important thing—the vital thing—was that we had obtained sixty-one gallons of diesel oil and eighty-two gallons of fresh water, in Aden.

Real adventure consists mainly of mundane chores. While we

were in Aden we had fixed a faulty running light, repaired the broken staysail "horse rail" across the main deck over the cabin, and built a new galley stove from two small Chinese-made burners bought ashore. Our old stove had been defective, pouring clouds of black smoke, all the way from Port Sudan

Out in the Gulf of Aden we didn't stay near the coastline of South Yemen. The monsoon, against us, blew straight along the shore anyway. Nearer the shore, too, it would be less steady, I knew, than it was out in the offing, where it varied between eighteen knots in the middle of the night to a full thirty knots in mid-afternoon.

I was anxious to get out of the Gulf of Aden; away from Yemeni territory; I was biased against the Yemenis as a whole (I had good reason to be), bigoted against the mass of them, distrusted them, despised them; disliked them in the main and hated them in the particular. There were very few I'd ever met that I genuinely liked; and I was alive to say so, and I wanted to stay alive. For those reasons we didn't reef down once in the Gulf of Aden, but kept *Outward Leg* hammering to windward and beat the hell out of her.

The seas in the Gulf of Aden were choppy, lumpy, undulating, jerky, bumpy, uneven, turbulent, and rough. Every single wave of all those billions, for a thousand miles of our zigzag course, was against us, trying to push us back to the Bab el Mandeb. They beat and banged and clattered and howled, while *Outward Leg* yawed and heaved and pitched and lurched and lifted and hammered and banged and broached and righted herself, until ten days later we at last broke free off Cape Gardafui, on the very tip of the Horn of Africa.

On both sides of the Gulf of Aden, in both South Yemen to the north, and in Somalia to the south, we knew, were featureless desert and mountain shores, inhabited only in the west-monsoon season by wild tribes from the interiors. There was, there, no compassion for infidel dogs like us, no ports, no havens, no food, no fuel, and most important, no fresh water. There was also an ever-present risk of piracy by marauding dhows and zhambuks. Some of my more "liberal"-minded critics may scoff at this, but I shall only take notice of their scoffs when they direct them to me from the cabin of a small sailing-boat beating against the monsoon wind, away from what was a client state of Qaddafi's in a state of neurotic anti-Westernism and where their lives were not worth their shadows on their decks. Otherwise their scoffs shall be to me as the drumming of our throbbing yankee jib, a slight annoyance, but still helping me on my way.

We stood close inshore, necessarily, off the coast of Somalia, very close, to avoid the worst of the westerly running current, and to gain any slight advantage from winds which might bend slightly onshore, attracted by the tremendous mountain heat, from the Gulf of Aden.

There was a great deal of shipping for a hundred miles out of Aden, making its way to and from the Bab el Mandeb to every part of the world south and east. But the farther we hauled away from Aden, the less shipping we saw, and so the safer we were—a paradox that many landsmen might not appreciate, perhaps, until fifty thousand tons of steel ran them down in the middle of the night.

For three days out of Aden, we beat against the monsoon, with very little to distinguish one wet, weary, hot day from the next. For the first two nights we were crossing shipping lanes, as we crossed the gulf at a wide angle, from northwest to southeast. There was little sleep as we dodged the tankers and car-carriers charging east and west, to keep humanity in its latest guise charging along ribbons of concrete in iron and plastic boxes.

In the early morning of the twenty-first of April we sighted Ras Adado, a Somalian headland which looked low, undramatic and somehow *suburban*. As there were no suspiciously lurking zhambuks hovering about, we stood inshore. Ras Adado turned out to have only one small white stone hut on it, and even that appeared, on closer examination through the binoculars, to have been abandoned. Still, we knew that with all the reefs around it, stretching out to seaward a few miles, and tremendous seas breaking on them, Ras Adado might just as well have been Croydon or Long Island, for all the visiting we were going to do.

On three occasions, as we forged our passage east, banging this way and tacking that, along the moonscape shore of Somalia, we sighted small craft close to the worn, beaten-looking shore. Each time, as we approached the craft in passing, they headed toward *Outward Leg*; each time we smartly came about, hauled over the sheets, and laid her over, beam onto the puling, piling seas, and, the wind screaming in her rigging, drove her and drove her on a broad, broad reach as far, as hard and as fast as we could, north into the white-capped offing, until we lost sight of what might very likely have been a potential marauder. Then, plunging about, we grinded in the sheets again until they were as rigid as zinging catgut, and headed once more inshore, a few miles more along that hot, seared, barren, waterless, godforsaken coast, where surely no angels had ever trod.

We may have had good reason to run away from every sighting; we may not. But at least we are alive a year later to tell the tale. As I put it to the crew: "When in danger or in doubt, grab the wheel and come about." The Somali coast was not, and never had been, a place to loiter, nor to even try to win friends and influence people. The best thing to do off Somalia was to get past it, as fast as ever we could, as soon as possible and mind our own business, and that was regardless of anything else that might have happened anywhere else on earth. I knew that the attitude of those desert people was very simple: Anyone who had anything they wanted was their enemy and a fit victim. There were not, and never had been, any half measures about that. That they were brave people, and honest—even honorable—in their own way, there was no doubt in my mind, but there was little urban wiliness about them, and so being unable to gain it by other means, they killed for anything that might help them to survive. So we avoided them.

I have never carried arms on board a sailing boat. There is nothing "moral" about this. My contention is that if arms are carried their presence tends to allow you to drift into situations where you might need them. If they are not on board, this tendency is much, much less, and you are very much more wary about getting too close to potential attackers—and distance is by far the best defense on wild coasts where there is no law. A couple of years back, when I had written for a British yachting magazine on the subject of self-defense, I had, tongue in cheek, suggested several very violent and extreme means of discouraging piracy in small craft. These included dynamite, hand grenades, and even keeping a poisoned bottle of drink in the cabin, so that if the skipper and crew were overcome, and the pirates celebrated their deed, they wouldn't live long to rejoice.

These suggestions had all been made in a sardonic way, almost hidden in the context of a long article, in which I had criticized those who *did* carry arms. The magazine editors had lifted out those japes and published them on their own, completely out of context, and made me look like some kind of Hollywood "hero." Nothing could have been further from the truth of my thoughts on the matter of keeping arms on board cruising vessels. The fact was that they seemed to cause much more violence, and even danger, than they guarded against.

I had voyaged in many of the most lawless areas on earth, and I had been present when firearms had been used, but I myself have never handled any gun of any kind, except a flare pistol, since I left the Royal Navy in 1952, and neither do I intend to. Besides, hunting bows and arrows are much quieter, much less prone to confiscation by authorities, and cost less.

The next two days and nights were spent beating hard to windward under all working sail no matter how hard the wind blew, the Aries wind vane steering most of the time, to relieve us of that bane of sailors—the tyranny of the tiller, along the stark, mountainous coast of north Somalia. The moon was filling, the clouds thinning, and there was often enough light to see the breakers on the desert shore, but all this made for little sleep.

At one point, on the second day of this long beat, we were able to steer close inshore, off the only inhabited place we saw, a small village of stone huts in the middle of a forgotten nowhere. All its small craft were pulled up high on the beach, so we stood inshore to take a closer look, and gain advantage of less current. We could clearly see the old district-commissioner's residence, which was marked on our ancient British chart. It was a slightly more sturdy structure than the rest of the buildings in the village, and stood under the one, single tree, a gnarled, twisted dwarf of a thing little higher than the desert scrub. That was the only tree that we saw on the whole of the Somali coast, over the three hundred or so miles that we were able to observe in the daytime.

I told the lads of how, for generations, the younger sons of British families had been sent, willingly, to such God-forsaken holes as that, to administer their districts, to try to bring some idea of sanity, fairness, and balance to places where they had never existed. It had probably, I said, all been to little purpose, if any at all. Yet I hoped, I told them, that the memory of good intent and duty faithfully performed would never die. But they were silent. All this was outside anything they knew of, and Svante pretended, I thought, not to hear.

Fifteen houseflies—yes, we counted them all right—came on board as we passed the village, and were very affectionate toward us. Although we tried hard, God knows, we didn't kill the last one, they were so quick and wily, until a week later, when we had reached 150 miles south of Socotra. The flies and the high humidity, together with the continual pounding and hammering as we fought to windward against the monsoon, were tests of endurance enough to turn any Cowes weekender to break-dancing in a steambath by way of relief.

On the twenty-third of April, 750 miles sailed out of Aden, we hauled around Cape Elephante, which is the smaller, "twin" cape of Cape Gardafui, to the latter's northwest. It really did look like an elephant's head with most of its trunk submerged in the sea. The color was about the same, too—a pinkish gray. Only the eyes were missing, though I had little doubt there were other eyes watching us, more malignantly than any elephant's could.

Often, off the great capes of the world, when you were trying to beat up to them to reach and round them, the wind would blow a storm until you were within a few miles of the actual cape itself. Then there might perhaps be a comparative calm over the meeting of the seas off the continental headland. So it had been, sometimes, off the Cape of Good Hope; sometimes off Leeuwin, often off the Horn, frequently off Farewell, and so it was off Gardafui.

It was teatime when we rounded Cape Elephante and the wind had been mixing it up with us all day, at around thirty knots. Of course in a trimaran, dashing to windward at nine knots, heavily loaded with stores for an ocean crossing, that made for a wind speed of almost forty knots over the deck (if you added the forward wind speed to the real wind). It didn't make for much conversation topside.

But as soon as we got Cape Elephante under our starboard quarter (behind us, to our left, looking backward) the wind eased right down, almost apologetically—or like the eye of a storm passing—and we were left to wallow and lollop around in a stiff, steep sea with little or no wind. That, as we know, is a bit like having your trousers drop down in the middle of a bar fight.

Years before, when I had rounded this cape in a roaring gale, and spent three weary, wet days doing it, I had sworn that one day I would return and anchor right under its bloody nose. Now, as I steered *Outward Leg* in under Cape Gardafui, I could hardly believe my luck. It was not unmixed, however. We tried our best to sail against the weak southeast wind, to make for the lee of Cape Gardafui—what there was of it. But trimarans are very sensitive to heavy weights on board (so is any craft, come to that) and *Outward Leg* moved along, in lessening seas, reluctantly, until I switched on the Yanmar and the lads handed the sails as we motored, somehow shamefacedly, right up the little bay on the north side of Cape Gardafui, and dropped the hook only thirty yards or so away from its shore, so cluttered with windworn, weather-beaten rocks that it looked, by moonlight, like a modern sculptor's show. We anchored knowing that we had beaten, against the full force of the monsoon, the wind and current of the Gulf of Aden, and reached one of the world's five hardest "Cape Stiffs" (along with Good Hope, the Horn, Leeuwin, and Greenland's Cape Fare-well).

For supper we had rice, egg, and curried beef. Thomas said that as we had almost reached Eastern waters we should eat Indian food. I told him this dinner was more like Hampstead or Hamburg. He puzzled over that backhander for quite a while.

"What does 'Gardafui' mean?" asked Svante, in between great spoonfuls of rice and egg, dripping strong curry.

"No idea," I replied. "It's probably Portuguese or Italian. The Portuguese were the first Europeans in modern times to find the cape . . . on their way to discover the land of Prester John, who was supposed to be a great Christian king in the East. That legend was probably a hash-up of half-true rumors about the emperors of Ethiopia, who were Coptic Christians. But the Arab name is Ras Asir, and that's the name that is used on modern charts now that the European chart-makers are so busy revising—even denying—their own history."

Svante grinned, then mouthed the name "Ras Asir. . . . Mmm, that's a nice name," he said, as we stared at the rise of a great, orange, luscious moon from beneath a peaceful Indian Ocean to our east.

"It might be a 'nice' name," I agreed. "And 'nice' is a word used by bookies' clerks and shop assistants, but no bloody ocean sailor worth his salt would ever call it by anything else than 'Gardafui.' You can go to Sydney or Cape Town, New York, Hong Kong, and Bristol. If you say 'Ras Asir' they'll look at you blank; anyone that knows anything at all about voyaging in any craft, big or small. But if you say 'Gardafui' they'll know right away where you mean. It's hard to believe it now," I said, as the ascending moon shone a silver light on the stark beauty of rearing cliffs only yards away, "but that piece of real estate is one of the most dreaded capes in the world for sailors, and always has been, ever since the ancient Greeks made it this far, and Ibn Batuta wrote about it in his journals seven hundred years ago."

"Clever people, the Arabs," muttered Svante, at it again. "They were writing good books when we lived in caves."

"You might as well say all Corsicans are good generals," I flashed, "and wear their hats sideways." That shut *him* up.

"When we gain the offing at dawn," I went on, "we'll be able to look south, and say 'That way is the South Pole'—and east, and say 'There's India'—and beyond that, Thailand . . . and southeast and know that Australia is there, and there's hardly anything at all between us and them but salt water. . . ."

The vision of all that wide ocean ahead of *Outward Leg*, for the first time since we'd sighted England after departing the Azores, was almost too tasty to contemplate.

"And ice," added Thomas, always the German pedant, as he settled down to his anchor watch, and Svante sought his berth. "Ice before the South Pole, hein?"

"And ice," I agreed, but the coldness of ice was another unthinkable thing, too delicious to consider, off the eastern tip of Africa, so I lowered myself down the after companionway to nurse my stump and sleep in an almost-still bed for the first time since we had departed Aden.

For the first time since *Outward Leg* had reached Falmouth, England, nineteen months and almost seven thousand miles before, she was right out of the "narrow waters." Now, with the wide Indian Ocean before her, barring catastrophe, she was *indomitable*.

The sudden calming off Cape Gardafui, and the full moon's passing might mean, I prayed, that the monsoon was indeed changing now; that the Zone of Convergence had now moved north from southern Somaliland, where it had been hovering for a month. I could only hope so. The sun's declination had been north for some days now. If the wind was even yet easterly in the offing, it might mean we would have to tack all the way over the Indian Ocean, and that would double our distance to Thailand, and make it eight thousand instead of four thousand miles.

I fell asleep knowing that there were only a few remaining obstacles to *Outward Leg* reaching the Orient—like getting clear of Cape Gardafui, keeping away from notorious Socotra Island, dodging pirates and cyclones, four thousand miles of ocean; but these were minor things; she was the very first small vessel of any kind, power or sail, ever to voyage this far east around the world north of the Equator. By the log, *Outward Leg* had voyaged a total of

21,600 sea miles since leaving San Diego. That was exactly equal to the farthest straight distance right around the world—at the Equator. She was the first-ever small craft of any kind to reach the Indian Ocean from the Pacific by way of the middle of central Europe, and—a hundred thousand hazards overcome—she was 3,000 miles from the Golden Horn, with another 4,000 to go to reach the Orient, and the start of our realization of our Atlantis dream—but she was free.

I slept short but well off Gardafui.

14

An' a Man Can Raise a Thirst

At the first hint of dawn on April 24 the breeze piped up from southeast. Cape Gardafui was no place to be in any kind of wind at all except perhaps a westerly, and so we weighed up how long it would take for the monsoon night-breeze to wake up, buckle its braces, lace its boots, pull its cap peak down over its eyes, and kick us in the teeth. Then we weighed our disappointment at the wind direction, as well as our anchor, and beat it the hell out of there before we even thought about breakfast.

In harbor or ashore, we rarely concerned ourselves with breakfast, except for a cup of tea or coffee. Under way it was different. Then breakfast, easy, quick and light, took on the air, if not the trappings, of a small ceremony—our recognition, if we liked, of being together, of the start of another series of daylight hours; just as the noon-sight, and Thomas's little hurried flurry of quick calculations to reckon our last latitude, as the burning sun hovered over us for a few seconds, was our salute to another sea day. Sailors reckon from noon to noon. Teatime was another small gathering before the hours of darkness. Apart from that, offshore (and this will probably amaze landsmen), we hardly saw or even, it seemed, noticed each other most of the time, unless there was a sail change, or a drastic change of course, or if (a rare thing) a ship was sighted.

Most of the time we kept ourselves to ourselves, so that we did not impose on each other. This was to be difficult, at first, for Svante to do, but after a few polite but curt responses to more of his questioning the obvious, he got the message, and on the whole the Indian Ocean passage, although drawn out and slow, was to pass without any major frictions. A small craft at sea is not the place for idle gossip, nor for antipathy.

Out of our tenuous hold on Gardafui and Africa we beat close-hauled all day and all night against a wickedly confused and re-sentful sea. The wind was south-southeast, about Force Five, and the current ran north-northwest at around three knots, so every-thing was against us, and it was a wet, hot, weary slog.

If we sheltered behind the cockpit-dodger windows we got no breeze and sweated; if we didn't we got a continual faceful of cold water. If the dodger windows were not up, a stream of spray slashed into the after cabin, and on the port tack straight onto the navigation-chart table; on the starboard tack right onto my berth, unless the after cabin door was shut, when it quickly became a hotbox.

The reason we were tacking so close to the wind, heading south-east was simple. A few score miles off Cape Gardafui, directly east, lies the big island of Socotra. Between Socotra and the coast of Africa lay a mess of reefs and islands, a line of them about fifty miles long, from Abbut Kun to The Brothers, all now known to be unlit.

For centuries navigators had avoided Socotra and its outriders because of treacherous onshore currents around them, and prolific piracy and wrecking, which, it was known, were looked upon as valid professions by the natives. Those dangers still existed, but now there was another; the Soviet imperialists had built one of the world's biggest radar listening posts on Socotra, and any strange small craft approaching the island was liable to be sunk by a surface-to-surface missile, made, most likely, in the Urals.

To the north of Socotra, in the Arabian Sea between the island and the coast of Oman, was the main spawning ground of ferocious cyclones; and the month when they were most frequent was May, as the sun's declination passed over the Great Arabian Desert and baked the land; and May was five days off . . . and to head north of Socotra would have been about as sensible a thing for us to have done as jumping into a pitful of cobras.

Which is why reaching Cape Gardafui had been so vital to us, and to get past it and south and east of Socotra, to avoid the cyclones.

Well to the south of Gardafui, on the coast of Somalia, there was a natural haven for Arab traders in dhows awaiting the change of monsoon. This was at Ras Hafun, and I knew it all right but I also knew from our radio that Arab blood was well up now about the bombing of Libya, and out best course was to get as far as we could from Somalia and the Arab countries. As the Americans say, we had to haul ass, fast and far.

I'd avoided telling the lads about the tricky bit around Socotra and the hazard of cyclones—which in the main make Atlantic hurricanes look like someone switched on a house fan. In them, winds of over 150 knots were not unusual. The boys had enough scary problems ahead, astern, and all around them, as it was. Now, beating out of Gardafui, I let them know, and so they willingly bent their backs to grinding in the sheets just that mite more taut, just that little bit quicker, so as not to give away one damned yard to the Somalian current, which was doing its best to force us to the north of Socotra and into the womb of the cyclones. If that happened, I had calculated, we were liable to be becalmed. Then the name of the game would be to run under the engine, northeast, as fast as we could for Oman. We had just about enough fuel for the five hundred or so miles we would then have to cover. If the engine didn't run for any reason, we'd be sitting ducks for the biggest pasting of our lives, if not for oblivion.

We trusted our engine. It had never once let us down, but there could always be a first time, and so we worked and banged, and slammed, and pounded, and bashed, and crashed, and we worked hard to windward off the Horn of Africa, to stack the cards on our side and avoid the northern reaches of the Arabian Sea. Our slogan then was "Ten or bust!" (meaning the latitude 10° north, of course).

If all went well and the rain monsoon arrived on time, by early May the southwest wind would be well set in, and we might, as we approached India, even expect a welcome gale, or even an acceptable storm or two to help us on our way.

By dusk of the twenty fifth of April we had beat our way to a point 100 miles southeast of Cape Gardafui. It had been a very hard, rough slog at an average of nine knots (don't forget we were heavily loaded with new supplies of fuel and fresh water) through fierce seas, and we had covered close to 320 miles through the water. We were then in a good position to turn east, on our star-board tack, still very close hauled, and so gain our easting past Socotra and its attendant dangers.

No sooner had we turned east, than the wind backed round to south-southeast-by-east and we were headed again and forced northward toward the reefs west of Socotra. It was as if we were in one vast oceanwide trap, and no matter how we worked, and twisted and turned, there seemed to be no escaping it. If we turned south the wind hauled south; if we turned east so did the wind, and this went on for two more days, so that I was more than once tempted (oh, so strongly!) to run on a quarter-reach for the north side of Socotra, and take our chances on a quick dash around the northern side of that island. It was only a mighty effort of will that stopped me.

I don't know, and I never will, if I was right to stick to our stubborn course south of Socotra. But if the weather records, kept over the past hundred years from ship's reports, were right, so was I.

Thomas, down in the bouncing fore-cabin, had been studying the atlas on the third day out from Gardafui, open at a map of the Indian Ocean. Svante was on watch, keeping an eye out on the Aries wind-vane steerer. I was in the galley checking the main battery state on the gauge on the bulkhead. We only ran the engine when we absolutely had to, to save the fuel.

"Perth, Australia," Thomas said. "That's where they will hold the Americas Cup races, *hein*?"

"Well, it's off Freemantle, really. Perth's a bit inland. There isn't enough room in the harbor there even for them to take a turn around the buoy." I started out through the engine compartment door. "But where they ought to hold it," I added, as the boat lurched deep, then tossed herself off a sea with a tremendous crash, and I steadied myself, "is out here, between Gardafui and Socotra. That'd sort 'em out!" No romance off Gardafui; only a wet, sweaty anxiety.

"Who will win?" asked Svante, who'd been listening through the galley companionway.

I didn't even know who would be taking part, except I vaguely recollected there would be a San Diego boat in the race, and I knew that *Outward Leg*, despite her heavy labor, was also listening, as she was registered in San Diego—it was her homeport.

"Win?" I said. ". . . why, San Diego of course!" Then the conversation turned to something else, and I completely forgot my forecast (accurate as it turned out) until almost a year later, after the San Diego team did win back the trophy for the United States in *Stars and Stripes*.

I recount that little tale though, not to boast of my winner's forecast being right—I knew and still know nothing about racing —but to show how the boat herself becomes, and especially on a long voyage such as ours, very, very much a person in her own right, and how responses, remarks, observations, expletives even, are bent with her in mind. In *Outward Leg* it was always as though we had some young, lively, but extremely hard-nosed, wise, rather prudish but very tough and unforgiving Californian (from the most sane latitude of that state) listening in on us. She showed little Australian character, even though her designer, Leo Surtees, was Australian. She was nowhere near loose-minded enough to be anything but somehow descended from the Plymouth Rock brethren by way of the lush Hudson Valley, dusty Oklahoma, the parched Nevada desert, and sunny, rolling, seaside southern California. In her, she had all the faults of Americans—an insistence on doing things *her* way, a reluctance to *listen* until she knew we were *sure*, an always expressed and unmistakable longing to be loved; but she also had that hard, cold single-minded toughness which disdained all normal human emotion when the going was rough, and an unbounded generosity. She was a first-class American *bitch*, and we loved her even though our sense told us it was stupid to love a *thing*; but one tiny word against her and our lives would be pure hell for several days afterward. If she then didn't whistle up one form of torture for us, it would be another, and so we guarded our words in her, and cosseted her at times, lovingly, and sometimes dolled her up where and when she had little need of it. She was our lives.

The Indian Ocean dished up some difficulties that were all her own. At nighttime in the western Indian Ocean, even with a good strong wind, the humidity was heavy, often up to 97 percent. This made everything in the boat soggy and damp, and, together with my sore stump, until we lost the wind and I could remove my false leg, put me through purgatory for much of the passage to India. I had found some old medicated powder in one of my lockers, and this I liberally sprinkled on my stump daily, until it ran out. Slowly, as we made our way east, east, the sores dried up and eventually, just before we fetched Cochin, hardened, but they did not disappear for months.

Reluctantly, but because this account is as honest as I can make it, I must mention the state of my teeth. I had one good tooth left in my head. I'd had broken teeth—stumps, five of them—which gave me agonizing pain from time to time. My lack of dental care had been mainly caused by the poverty on board *Outward Leg* during the first two years of the voyage from San Diego. I simply had not had enough money to support the voyage and attend a dentist. Besides, my time had been so full, either voyaging or writing to support the voyage, there had been no time to spare sitting in waiting rooms, nor could I have waited anywhere long enough for any regular dentist to do a good job. So most of the way across the Indian Ocean I was nursing a burning, sore leg-stump and five agonizingly painful tooth roots. Together with the high humidity at night, the searing heat in the daytime, so close to the Equator, and those afflictions, it was about as far removed from a pleasure cruise for me as I ever want to get.

I know that some people would say that it was stupid of me to continue with a long voyage in such a state, but I had been so accustomed to hardships in my life that it rarely occurred to me that things could be better. Besides, I had to get to the East to start Atlantis, and nothing short of death would stop me. I doubt—I don't remember—if I ever complained to the crew about my afflictions, and I believe that I did not lay the suffering on them any more than I could possibly avoid. I tried my best to be interesting and cheerful. I knew that this ocean crossing was to them a great adventure; to me it was about as close to the abyss of perdition as I shall ever reach in this life. I could have turned away from our eastern course at any time, and headed south for Mombasa or the Seychelles, but I was determined to reach Thailand and the East. I had come too far now for any retreat. It was fight, fight, all the way.

I have no doubt that a few sedentary critics—not many, but they lurk around—might say that this was, on my part, some form of masochism. They have, one or two of them, said that about some episodes of my past endeavors. They are wrong. I hate suffering. I detest it. I have to be dragged even to a dentist's chair. I love my comforts as much as any other normal human being, and some of my comforts perhaps even more. But this was *fight*, and

I'd never turned that down either, and so I fought. I wasn't trying to set examples to anyone—least of all our crew, who I doubt even guessed, or had any inkling of, how much of a fight I was making. No—perhaps I'm mistaken; perhaps Thomas did.

We had never had proper awnings in *Outward Leg*. Their weight was one factor which had told against their provision in San Diego, before the voyage started. Another factor—and the most telling one to me—was the (never explained) drying up of funds to outfit. This had demanded that I spend what money I could provide on more important things, like a life raft and guardrails. I'd had enough, too, just, to provide a cockpit dodger, and now, as we crept at a snail's pace over the sinister-calm Indian Ocean, we thanked God for it. Apart from that, and a small canvas dinghy-cover sewn up hurriedly for us by Liz Purkis before we departed Israel, we had no form of shelter from the sizzling heat of the sun but a couple of tattered old bedsheets which had somehow survived our weight-ditching session back in the Jebel Zuquair Island rattrap. These were now slung over the after cabin, about a foot over the deck, and over the widest part of the main deck, immediately forward of the mast. With, every morning, Thomas's and Svante's light-sleeping bags unzipped and spread across other parts of the main deck, that was our protection against the daily torture of steady, unremitting calefaction of the sun, for twelve hours out of twenty-four.

In this manner, with all sails, except the main, stowed below, and with the cotton cover on the mainsail, to preserve it from the deadly solar rays, *Outward Leg* would have appeared to any celestial observer tiny and lost in that vast waste of water. Looking more like a stall in Port Sudan's market, she plodded slowly and steadily on, crawling, steamy mile after sluggish, hot mile as if she were blinded by the harsh reflection of the sunlight from every sea, minatory, sinister, silent, heaving, each one more extensive than a score of football fields. We could compare her progress with that of a small snail crossing JFK airport.

Morning of the twenty-ninth found us creeping along through heat, across an almost dead-flat sea, with barely a breath of wind, being shoved northeast by what I guessed was an ocean current of about a quarter knot. What hot zephyrs there were crept, too, treacherously out of the southeast.

That day we set the fresh-water ration to three cups per man per day, and two cups for cooking. Of the sixty-one gallons we had left Aden with, eleven days before, we had forty gallons remaining. A quick calculation showed us that we had been using two gallons a day. That was nothing by shore standards for three men, and if the southwest monsoon had been blowing it might have been all right, but on the passage to India, with over thirteen hundred miles of ocean ahead of us, and no, little or contrary wind, our water consumption was far too high. In that heat—100 degrees Fahrenheit in the after cabin by 7:30 A.M. was normal—it wasn't surprising that we'd consumed one third of our fresh-water supply, but we simply had to cut it down severely, and so we did.

At the same time Thomas set to making a water still (our World War surplus unit had crumbled by now), and for the next few days, whenever he had time off the wheel to spare, he kept at it, while Svante and I, on our time off steering, performed all the other maintenance chores which must go on in any sailing craft, at sea or not.

Eventually Thomas managed to drain two or three cups of brackish water from his still. It worked on the evaporation of seawater, and consisted of a clear-plastic bubble mounted on a frame, with another clear-plastic "funnel" running down through the center of the bubble. Inside the inner clear-plastic there was suspended a length of black cloth (part of an old jacket). The plastic outer bubble rested in a bowl of seawater, which was sucked up onto the black cloth and, in the heat of the sun, magnified by the clear-plastic, evaporated. The vapor then rose through the gap at the top of the funnel, and there some of it condensed and fell down the inner sides of the outer bubble, into its bottom, from whence it was drained. It wasn't elegant, it probably was not as efficient as it might have been, but it might have kept us alive, if the old sea god had not been on our side, long enough to reach somewhere—with water—an island perhaps, in the eastern Indian Ocean, one of the Laccadives or Maldives.

We had no electric steering gear; the unit which had been provided in San Diego had been a joke, fit perhaps to steer a light dinghy on a windless, calm day. It had been discarded and left to rot in its own uselessness ever since the first month of the voyage. Now it was resurrected out of its hidey-hole in the engine compartment, but, try as Svante and I would, we could get no useful movement out of the thing, and so we were condemned to sit behind the wheel, fiddling about with it, jigging it this way and that, like idiot-morons (or "Mediterranean cowboys") all the blistering hot days long, day in and day out, one starry, cooler, humid night after the other, all the way to India.

It wasn't the monotony of sitting there in the cockpit, wheel in hand, staring at the compass to hold a dead straight course, nor the discomfort of the scorching heat beating down on the dodger top immediately above our heads that were my main concern—it was that any effort in the hot daytime hours meant the helmsman was sweating; and that meant good fresh water was being wasted to that degree. I had worked out by now that if these conditions persisted all the way across the Indian Ocean—and at that time that was an almost unthinkable horror—at the speed of economical engine revolutions, with the boat making two knots, heavily loaded as she was, one cup of water would have to move us ten miles. Every bead, every drop of perspiration on any body on board was noted, counted and mulled over by me, and silently resented.

When the muggy breeze did slightly stir itself we tried all kinds of combinations of wind vanes on the Aries, from small things that made electrical contacts, rigged up to the old electric steerer, to great huge kites, all of twenty square feet in extent; but nothing except human hands would serve to steer the boat in a dead-straight line east, and in the Indian Ocean, with our fuel and fresh-water supplies diminishing daily, nothing less than a dead-straight line would do. We must hold ourselves against a slight but persistent current forever trying its best to push us north, closer to Socotra, at first, and then into the cyclone area of the north Arabian Sea.

Each noon in the ovenlike after cabin, when we laid the latitude, Thomas would ask, "How much farther to the Laccadives?"

Those islands to the west of India by about six hundred miles were our objective now, as long as the new monsoon sat on its sweltering fence and loitered. When the new monsoon decided to jump down off its torrid perch and started shoving us from the southwest, then we would, I planned, turn southeast and so have the wind on our beam, our fastest point of sail, and so reach Cochin or Sri Lanka, even, in a matter of ten days or so.

With the Yanmar engine purring away behind its bulkhead, and the boat, as upright and steady as a church, gliding at funereal pace across an ocean so vast that each inch over the chart was beginning to look like infinity, I would reply, "Three weeks."

Thomas knew as well as I that there was *only* enough diesel fuel on board to last, with the engine running day and night, two weeks—if that.

"The monsoon should start now, *hein*? The end of April, start of May?"

"Should be rising tomorrow, Thomas . . ."

Then he would climb out of the sweaty cabin to eat an uncooked lunch of canned beans and cold potatoes from the night before, leaving me in the boiling cabin to stare down at the chart of the Indian Ocean and our thin little pencil line of crosses and dots, which looked so short, tiny, weak, and puny against the vast reaches of the ocean which stretched ahead of us on all sides. Every time, my gaze would focus on the southernmost of the Laccadive Islands.

I suppose that many people ashore think that the worst plight for ocean sailors is to be in a storm, or in the inescapable threat of one, and I admit that can be bad. A debate could rage about which is worse when it comes to getting a good stiff dose of the willies: a storm or a thick fog at night near a lee shore or a busy steamer track. But anyone who had been at sea in small craft for any length of time must surely admit that the worst prospect by far for any small-craft sailors is being becalmed in midocean, hundreds of miles from any safe haven, far from a shipping track, in a tropical, hot area where rain is nonexistent. What magnifies, eventually, the double, treble horror of this predicament is its seeming innocence, at first; the quiet, peaceful, impeccable, clean, guiltless way in which it creeps up on us; a real wolf in sheep's clothing if there ever was one. It must be a bit like being mugged by a parson.

At first, and especially after being close-hauled and banged to windward for days on end, there was quiet rejoicing that, as the sea calmed down and the breeze with it, clothes and sheets, papers and cabins could be dried out, and sleep caught up with, and a good meal cooked without the pans bouncing off the galley stove, and accurate, clear sextant-sights reckoned and carefully, tidily worked out on the chart without, at long last, jerkiness or hurry. It was as peaceful and restful, at first, as being in a quiet, safe haven. In the nights and the early mornings, that is. From mid-forenoon until an hour after dusk it was like being on a griddle under the searing heat of a merciless sun almost directly overhead for steaming after simmering hour after hot hour. By ten o'clock no metal on deck might be touched. By eleven it was impossible for the crew to walk on deck barefoot. By twelve the temperature in the cabins would be anything up to 130 degrees Fahrenheit.

There was no rest from the fiery heat in the daytime, and then we would wish we were anywhere—anywhere but in *Outward Leg* slowly chugging away from empty sultry horizon to empty steamy horizon in the middle of the Indian Ocean.

Dusk always descended like a cool benison, to return to our atrophied, burned-out brains some kind of logical sanity under stars so big and bright it seemed we might reach up and touch them. Then we would not have wished to have been anywhere else in the world, as long as our diminishing fresh water could hold out.

In a few hours on that first day of calm the ocean was dead flat, and there was difficulty in seeing where the horizon was and where the sky began. In the morning the humidity turned everything around us to a pale grayish-blue. Now and again, very infrequently, the outline of a dolphin's hump would break the steely, crystalline glassiness of the sea, and sometimes the shadow of a shark would pass under the boat, a dark silhouette, like a sinful memory, glimpsed out of the corner of our eye.

On April 30, as we lay still on the ocean, a breeze came up in the forenoon, from the east. I studied the brazen hot sky for a few minutes and found nothing there. We headed under all plain sail north-northeast, until the breeze died at dusk. Then we hove to again, and found we had made only 22.5 miles that day. At that rate it would take us sixty days to fetch India, if we found a wind, and fifty days, even, to reach the Laccadive Islands. There were rumors of a Soviet Imperial Navy missile base there; we knew, from the voyaging grapevine, that the Indian government was very paranoid about the Laccadives, and that their officials were likely to arrest anyone landing there without permission, but when thirst and hunger drove, there would be no conscience, and official objections could go hang themselves. I decided to make for the Laccadives, under power, but at as economical an engine speed as we could manage, as long as there was no wind. Through the immense reaches of the Indian ocean, through a billion gently heaving, sinister seas and a thousand miles of twinkling phosphorescence we would cut a path, just twenty-six feet and two inches wide, like a meteor wandering through the solar system.

On May 1 we had two causes for quiet celebration: First we were past the longitude of 55° east of Greenwich, which meant that we were well east of any danger of being swept onto the hostile shores of Socotra; and Labor Day (anywhere else but in North

America) was also the first anniversary of *Outward Leg's* cracking through the Iron Curtain in Czechoslovakia at Bratislava. To celebrate, and so that *Outward Leg* would know we cared dearly for her—and had worked hard to make her well—and also cared for our lives, the crew went joyfully over the side and cleaned the bottom of all three hulls, while I kept wary watch for any shadows lurking beneath the surface of the blue ocean. We had saved one bottle of Hungarian "Bull's Blood" wine; that was all the booze on board. Thomas slipped a Dvořák tape (familiar from our Danube passage) in the player. With them we celebrated at supper. *Outward Leg*, as though she breathed and trembled, lifted and rose, imperceptibly almost, in the calm (too calm!) ocean seas, under a billion blazing stars.

There is no concealment of reality for long at sea, not even in a dead calm, as there is on land; no hiding from the truth. The laws of the sea are few, simple, and austere, and take no reckoning of anyone's wealth or wishes. "Wake up," they say, "see the danger—or die!"

By the last hours of May 1, at latitude 11° north, 57° east, I knew that unless we in *Outward Leg* were very, very careful, we could, in a few days, be in an extremely hazardous situation. Food was not the problem. We had a good three months' stock on board, due to our careful hoarding in the Red Sea. Water was the bugbear, and in the heat of the tropics it is not an easy thing to reduce the consumption of fresh water and at the same time maintain efficiency and strength. But it must be done. Even though we had been very careful with the issue of fresh water, we were now down to thirty gallons. *If* the Yanmar engine held up and could manage to move *Outward Leg* at two knots for three weeks; *if* there were no contrary currents, *if* the wind did not blow strong from the east, that gave us a ration, among us, of ten gallons a week; or one and a half gallons a day. But anything contrary to that, any delay in reaching the Laccadives, would mean we would be waterless. It all boiled down to time, direction, and fresh water. I cut the water ration to one pint a day each, and changed course to northeast. When people's lives are at stake there can be no room for false pride or stubborn holding to an ordained course. There, somewhere, I knew, lay the main shipping lane between Singapore and the Red Sea, and where there were ships there was fresh water and, maybe, fuel.

For three days *Outward Leg* motored on, carefully nursing her fuel, to the northeast, through a scorching, torrid, sultry, feature-less, never-changing scene, in the (now dreaded) daylight hours, of glassy, shining sea and a sky of hot-iron blue. No birds, no fish, no life, nothing but a steamy saltwater waste.

We were still within range of BBC overseas broadcasts from London. The weathermen in the Bracknell international weather center, their voices crackling in the ether, told us of the awful heat in India, and the violent rain over Sumatra, and how the Tropical Convergence Zone was motionless, lazying over central Africa and holding back the rain from the then-fashionable parched highlands of Ethiopia. Each night they all agreed that there was no sign of the start, that year, of the southwest monsoon's annual pilgrimage from the lush jungles of the Congo to the stony wastes of the Gobi Desert.

They said it all from their Home Counties studios in much more urbane tones than I; they said it in terms of highs and lows and depressions and sunspots; I said it was as though God was on holiday and had left no one to mind the shop. To myself I stated, without any doubt: If we did not find fresh water within a week we were in danger of a slow, lingering death—and I knew what it was like; I'd had a taste of it when my sloop *Two Brothers* had been sunk by the whale of the Azores eighteen years before.

On May 3, eighteen days and almost one thousand miles out of Aden, at dawn—cool, majestic purple, lilac lavender and plum, apricot, and then gold, on the eastern edge of the world, dawn, always more beautiful the closer to the noose—I sighted it as I rigged yet again our bedsheet "awnings." A mere nuance of change of color on the far horizon to the darker, perse north; no more than a smirch—a smidge—a smudge; but it was there all right.

I forgot, completely, the throbbing pain in my leg-stump and my gnawing, aching gums; now it was succor or suffer; fresh water or the threat of burning thirst; *live or die.*

12 Akko, Israel

13 Red Sea. Zubair Island,
where *Outward Leg* was caught
in a storm

14 Red Sea. Suakin. Stranded Zhambuks

15 Indian ocean calm

15

Beneath the Awnings

We knew we were somewhere near the main shipping lane to and from the Orient; we had sighted and signaled a Japanese freighter the day before, from a distance of about two miles. She had either not noticed us or had ignored us. With autopilots in common use these days the former was probably the case. Anyway she charged right past us at high speed. It was in the mid-forenoon. I remember her name, a year later, but I do not write it.

Our old hand-held VHF radio, with a line-of-sight range of about five miles in good conditions, was useless. Svante had missed a grab—it couldn't be helped—off Cape Gardafui, and dropped it down the after companionway.

We had sighted another ship far to the north of us even as the sun set the same day, but she had been almost hull-down beyond the horizon. Then, late that night Svante had sighted the steaming lights of a ship away ahead of us, in the east, and she had been heading north, probably for the Gulf of Iran. She, too, had been much too far away for us to signal without a radio. We were now well into the central part of the Arabian Sea. To the south of us stretched the vast emptiness of the Indian Ocean as far as the mind could imagine. Far, far to the north of us the wild desert coast of the Arabian Peninsula fell back to the Gulf of Iran and the strife-torn Strait of Hormuz. There, about eight hundred miles from us, lay our nearest possible haven where we might replenish our fresh water: Muscat. But with only a hundred liters of fuel remaining and a consumption rate of half a liter an hour, and an economical speed of two knots, the mathematics were simple; there was no way we could possibly reach Muscat under power. To do that we would need at least another hundred liters of diesel and even that, if we met with any contrary currents, would be cutting fine our chances.

We might head due north, directly for Muscat, which was then, if things had not changed overnight, very pro-Western, at least in the top echelons of "government," but unless we picked up a wind as we neared Oman, we might lay ourselves wide open to the attentions of any small-craft marauders who might be lurking off the Omani coast. Some of the South Arabian fishermen were, we knew, not at all averse to a spot of piracy to liven up their hot, wearisome days. With neither wind nor fuel to try to outrun them we would be as vulnerable as a skittle in a bowling alley.

In cooler, kinder, politically more moderate climes small craft sighted could usually be counted as a passing friend (unless it was a French fisherman). There the big shipping was the potential foe; close to it, for a small craft, lay the jeopardy of the arrogant wash of a swift wake, with its commensurate breakages or damage to gear—or the ever-present menace to the unwary of a collision.

In the Gulf of Aden or the Arabian Sea the contrary was the case: These hazards from big shipping still existed, of course, and aplenty the closer to the straits of Bab el Mandeb, but the greater peril by far lay perhaps in the sighting of any small native craft, the crew of which might, or might not, be armed, and might or might not be religiously motivated thugs. There was simply no means of knowing if any crew were murderously inclined and thirsting for infidel blood; or lusting for infidel gold or women. An attack on *Outward Leg*, unarmed, except for our bows and arrows, had to happen *only once*, unless we were very, very lucky. We took no chances. That was another, unspoken, reason why we had made our course so well to the south of Socotra, into the open, empty reaches of the Arabian Sea, and why I had been reluctant to shape a course north, toward the coast of South Arabia.

A further reason for not heading toward Oman was that, now we were east of Socotra, the port of Muscat was, at eight hundred miles, slightly farther from us than the nearest atoll in the Lacca- dives: Suheli. The chances were that one of the fingers of ocean current that wandered, between monsoons, willy-nilly, but more generally eastward, across the Arabian Sea, might pick up *Outward Leg* and drift her slowly but steadily east toward Suheli or another of the Laccadive Islands or Minicoy, a lone island in the Eight Degree Channel, between the Maldives and the Laccadives, where we knew, from our charts, there was fresh water.

On 3 May as soon as I had sighted the discoloration on the horizon that I knew in my bones was a ship, I checked its direction on the main compass. It was west-northwest of us. If she were heading west toward the Red Sea our luck would be out; she would soon disappear. If she were heading north toward Oman, or south from the Gulf to the Cape of Good Hope, likewise. There would be no possibility of *Outward Leg*, even at full speed under power of seven knots (watch the fuel!) catching up with her or getting within signaling range. The speed of a merchant ship in the open reaches of the ocean is around eighteen knots, give or take six knots either way. But if she were heading *east* then there was a good possibility—and with great care in shaping our course—a probability, of getting close enough to the ship to attract the attention of her bridge—*if* the ship's crew were keeping lookout. That was another joker in the pack; in these days of autopilots many ships' bridge watches spent their time at anything else but keeping watch, and especially on the bright, sunny, deadly dull, empty ocean reaches, and even more so to the east of them, as we were, under the sun, against its cruel morning reflection on the face of the waters. Only an innocent, naïve novice could expect to be noticed by this ship, even if she came within a mile of us; it was up to us to get in her way.

There was no sense in doing anything right away except let the lads catch up on their sleep and keep plodding northeast at two knots. I held the wheel with my hip, broke out the binoculars, and studied the shadow. At first it was a mere blob, gracile, filamentous, slightly lighter in colorlessness than the morning horizon-mist before it.

Slowly, gradually, as I sweatily peered through our glasses, the shadow took on an infinitesimally lighter color. I lowered the glasses to wipe the perspiration from the sights. "It might be," I told myself, "merely the sun reflecting on a low cloud." My urge was to grab the throttle lever and shove it down, and head *Outward Leg* directly for the shadow. It would have done little good. By the time we reached a quarter of the way to where the ship was (if it *was* a ship), she would no longer be there but somewhere else, and, if her speed was average, she would be getting quickly away east of us, leaving us to wallow in our own wake, grieving at our hastiness and our waste of precious fuel.

Again I held up the glasses before my eyes. One thing the gods did bless me with was good eyesight. I'd told the boys, more jokingly than not, that I could read an average ship's name and port of registry at three miles in clear weather, and it was true. I could understand their doubt, for I always wore spectacles to read or write, and was for ever misplacing them, unless I tied them around my neck. Even as I stared, a sudden low beam of sunlight caught—not gold—a xanthic glitter that could only be cast by the yellow paint on a ship's upperworks!

In *Outward Leg* there was fitted, in the fore cabin, where the crew lived, a large bronze alarm bell. Against the bell lay a small brass hammer, held fast by a tight stainless-steel spring against an iron lever. On the lever was tied a length of cord, which ran back aft belowdecks the whole length of the boat, to the after cabin. Where it passed through the engine compartment the cord ran immediately beside a watertight window which gave out into the cockpit, from whence was steered the boat. This was rigged by me in San Diego, for use in case of emergency, to rouse the crew in case of catastrophe when I might not be able to move fast enough.

As soon as I was sure that what I was looking at in the vast blue-gray void of the Arabian Sea was a ship, I scrabbled open the cockpit window, grabbed the cord, and hefted it. It was the first and only time that the alarm had been used since the voyage commenced in San Diego two years and six months, and twenty-seven countries, before.

CLANG . . . G . . . G . . . G . . . G!

The noise of the firehouse bell shattered the deadly peace of the between-monsoons Indian Ocean. Inside ten seconds both our crew were piling through the galley companionway out into the cockpit. "Wha—whe—?"

The throttle had been shoved hard down, the boat had leaped ahead. Light smoke was pouring from her exhaust; in her sudden rush *Outward Leg* created a breeze. I was bent over the compass calculating in my head the course to steer so that we might get within hailing distance of the ship. I hardly noticed the crew. I said it in one word: "*Wegottaship!*"

They knew what to do and sprang into action. To improve our

visibility, the mainsail was hoisted within a minute, and six of our most colorful flags and ensigns were hoisted on both signal halyards port and starboard, and flailing in the breeze as our boat charged northeast, at an apparent angle, then, of forty-five degrees or so from the ship, but actually and with luck, converging with her future course—if she held her course straight.

Then Thomas dived into the starboard ama (outrigger) deck hatch and dragged out a sheet of mirrorlike plastic, about six feet long and two feet wide. In *Outward Leg*'s other life, when she had, for a short while, before she became her real self, been cruised about the California islands, this plastic mirror had been affixed over the (then) double berth in the after cabin. I could never understand why anyone should want to look at themselves *sleeping*, or even *how* they could do it; so I had ripped out the mirror. But I had saved it, for just such an occasion as this. It was too early to use it while we were between the sun and the ship, but if she should get to the east of us before she noticed *Outward Leg* then we would be able to reflect from our late looking-glass a sunbeam right onto the ship's bridge.

We shoved ahead to the northeast for a full half hour at full speed, the engine roaring away and exhaust fumes pouring out from under the port wing-deck. As Svante took over the wheel, with strict instructions to hold the course, Thomas plonked a mug of hot tea for me on the cockpit seat; it was the finest coolant in that kind of heat, but now we were rationed to two cups a day. Not to hoard tea—we had plenty—but to save fresh water.

Then I carefully watched the ship. She was closer to us now by a few miles, but nowhere near as close as she should be, nor at the foreseen angle, if her speed was anything like average. I could see her quite plainly now without binoculars. She was almost bows-on to us, and slowly heading east, toward us. I slowed down the engine; then, when I was sure of what I thought at first I had imagined, I stopped it. Over the mirror-flat depths the ship was making for us very slowly; there was no doubt about it, but she was not making more speed than were we—in fact if anything she was slower.

As she crept closer and closer—five miles, four miles, three miles—we saw that she was a general freighter, with a black hull, salt- and rust-stained, and white upperworks, also streaked with rust. Her design was old-fashioned. She was what sailors know as a "three island" ship. That is, she had a high bow, where the crew lived, a superstructure raised amidships with her bridge atop, and her poop, aft, was another raised section.

Suddenly, as I stared and stared at the ship, something stirred in some memory box at the back of my head. I said nothing to the lads at first, in case I might be wrong. Now someone was waving from the ship's bow. I told the lads, but they could not see the waving figure. I grabbed the glasses. There was no error in my eyesight, nor in my imagination. A man was standing by the ship's capstan waving something blue at us. It might be his cap, I thought. Then, as I waved back at the ship (someone on her bridge must be inspecting us through binoculars for sure), it dawned on me: Both Thomas and I knew that ship. . . .

"It couldn't be . . ." I told myself as I grabbed the wheel from Svante and stepped up the engine revs. "I just do not bloodywell believe it. . . ." Then I broke out speaking aloud to our crew, who had been watching me move around like a lunatic mumbling to myself. "Out here in the back of beyond, in the middle of the bloody Indian Ocean . . . eight hundred miles from anywhere . . . I mean it just cannot be true . . . for Chrissake we're . . . Thomas!"

Thomas was all ears. "What . . . what is it?" We were approaching the ship fast now, about a mile from her starboard side. I intended to go close to her under her stern, so I could watch her propeller, which was, I could clearly see by now, half out of the water.

"Do you recognize that ship?" I asked him.

Thomas screwed up his eyes and stared at the ever-growing chunk of steel only a half mile away now.

"I'm . . . I'm not sure . . . but it looks like the . . . the . . . *Phileree . . . Philomena?*"

"Filigree be buggered!" I exclaimed excitedly. Thomas had jogged my memory. I recalled the name now all right. "She's the old *Filioara* . . . for Chrissake. I don't believe it! . . . We're six thousand miles from Constantsa! . . . We're right out in the sodding middle of nothing and *nobleedingwhere!* . . . I don't believe this!"

Svante was staring at Thomas, me, and the ship wondering what was going on. "You really think you know the ship?" he asked us. We were bearing down on her stern now, and there she was, looming over us, all oily and rusty at the same time, heaving up and down slowly, almost agonizing as she paused in between great heaves and sags, as clear as day, her name FILIOARA and her port of registry—CONSTANTSA—and over her poop structure hung, lifeless in the hot air, the—you could have feathered both Thomas and me down with a knock—smoke-dirtied but clearly discernible colors, green, white and red, of our erstwhile host-country, before we'd reached Istanbul: the Socialist Republic of Rumania.

Now several men, all dressed casually in long pants, were standing on the signal deck of *Filioara*, outside her bridge-house door, all beckoning us to go alongside their ship with *Outward Leg*. I was having none of that, no matter how calm it was. I knew only too well the damage that can be done to a sailing boat by rising and falling alongside of a freighter. No one but an outright novice, someone in an exhausted, frightened panic, or a lunatic would ever do a thing like that. There's probably been far more yachts wrecked and destroyed by going alongside freighters than ever would have been sunk if they'd stayed clear. Likewise, the number of yachts that have been lost while being towed by merchantmen is legion. The fact of the matter is perfectly clear: Big-ship seamen, while being admirable—even heroic—in many things, have one failing: they do not, generally, understand the fragile nature of a sailing craft. They do not understand that her strength is only for and against the wind and waters, and not against solid objects like the towering steel sides of a ship displacing thousands upon thousands of tons, and so moving in the water with a distinctly different rhythm to a craft weighing perhaps five tons, and often far less than that.

Neither Thomas nor I believe that chance, or the complex, weaving threads of normal, ordinary human intercourse, all the millions and billions of them, and the factors, man-made and natural, that affect them, could possibly have brought about a meeting, in mid-ocean, between old friends, for that is what *Outward Leg* and *Filioara* were. We had been almost neighbors for a week, moored near each other in the port of Constantsa. We had made friends, then, with the crew of *Filioara* and exchanged banter, and a few other bits and pieces, as sailors will the world over. Now here we were, close neighbors again, only now in the open ocean, with nothing around us but water, Oman . . . Somalia . . . India . . . Sri Lanka . . . Antarctica . . . and . . . it didn't bear thinking about. "Coincidences like this," I suggested to Thomas, as our excitement died down, "only happen in novels written by some scribbler with no idea of the vastness of the seas, whose imagination has run out!"

"Do you think your readers will believe you when you write about this one?" he asked me.

"Yes," I replied.

"Why should they?" asked Svante.

"Because the odds against it having happened are too damned long for it not to be true."

"You'll have to go into every detail about it," said Thomas, as he and Svante prepared our dinghy for launching over the stern of the wing deck.

"*Ja*," added Svante. "You must write the longitude and latitude; exactly where we are. Then they will believe you!" He opened his blue eyes wide. "Some of them . . ."

Quick as a flash Thomas got one in on Svante: "Do you really think so?"

So, a year later almost to the day, here is the position: 10°50′ north, 58°53′ east. We were twelve hundred miles out of Aden. There were eleven hundred miles ahead of us to Cochin.

Laughing, as the dinghy splashed into the sea, and Svante handed him our empty fresh-water jerry cans, Thomas took off to visit our Rumanian friends on board *Filioara*, only a hundred yards away. I stared at her. She loomed over us and lay like a gigantic sea-monster, seawater streaming from her nether parts as she moved, seeming to breathe as if in pain, raised herself . . . hesitated . . . and lowered herself, half modestly, on the long, sedate, mysterious swells of the calm ocean. Smaller seas could stop moving, it seemed to me then; but not the ocean. The ocean, the sovereign of the whole world, never stopped moving, not even after hot, parching, apparent eternity (was it only a week?)—seven days and nights, of humid, heavy, breathless, breezeless calm.

We were near enough to *Filioara* for me to shout a greeting in reply to her captain's, and to wave to the rest of the crew, all lined up on her midships deck, in the shade of the bridge superstructure. Not near enough, of course, for any kind of conversation; I left that to Thomas, who was then clambering up a rope netting placed ready over the ship's side for him.

Soon Thomas was back alongside *Outward Leg* with a dozen full five-gallon cans of the ship's water. "They offer to let us have any fuel we need," he replied tersely to my unspoken query. Within a few seconds he was on his way back to *Filioara*, towing our two big hundred-liter fuel barrels. There would be no need to stow them in the dinghy; diesel oil is lighter than water and the barrels, full, would float.

I had glanced up at the sky in reply to Thomas's unspoken

question: "Can I stay on board *Filioara* for a few minutes?" The sky, steel-blue, told me nothing and I had nodded, wordlessly. There was no point in Svante going. We recalled that none of the Rumanians, if it was the same crew, and they looked like it, spoke English, except for the Party official on board, and he, I knew, was a pedantic Marxist bore (but his thumb was on the water tap!). The rest of the crew spoke their own language, of which Thomas knew a few words, and a little German. At least Thomas would be able to make himself understood to a degree. I would not go because I'd never dream of leaving my vessel at sea. I contented myself returning the stares of the Rumanian seamen—mostly in their thirties and forties—curiously grouped around Thomas on the midships deck, and returning hand waves, now and then at the bridge of the ship.

Thomas returned on board, with two hundred liters of ship's diesel oil, after about an hour. I observed the two barrels of diesel fuel come on board and be dragged across the deck and lashed down between the hulls, like a tiger watching two fat gazelles being dragged into its lair. Now I knew that even without any wind at all, if all went well with our Yanmar engine we could easily reach, first, a sea area where fresh water would be within a day's range, and second, if we were careful with our fuel, the port of Cochin, eleven hundred miles ahead, in India, and fresh food supplies. Then, as the Rumanian ship blew her siren time and again, and to the energetic waves of all her crew, in reply to ours, we put our Yanmar into gear, and revved her up (we had fuel enough!). First standing away from *Filioara* for a couple of hundred yards, we reapplied *Outward Leg* to her course—due east—and soon we were left with nothing, again, but the empty, seeming-barren sea, the hot blue sky, and ourselves. But now we had relief. Besides the fresh water and fuel, the Rumanians had given Thomas three bottles of their fizzy soda-water. It wasn't cold, though, because they had no refrigerator working on board. All the same, it was a touching gift, from seamen to seamen, and very welcome. It confirmed my view of the Rumanians as some of the best, most generous and helpful European people.

"How was it, Thomas?" Both Svante and I were eager for talk of something outside our own craft; outside of our own problems. Such is humanity. "Why're they so slow?"

"They've been having some little trouble with their main engines," Thomas explained.

"Did you offer to give 'em a hand?" I asked him, half joking. It reminded me of a time some years before; I'd been off Madagascar after a cyclone had ripped the shit out of the south Indian Ocean for ten days. Clouds had covered the sky and it had been impossible to get a sextant sight. A Soviet ship had appeared from nowhere— an oldish tramp steamer; I had thought she was Lithuanian, but who knows? I'd managed to get close to her in terrific seas and asked if her navigator could confirm my estimated position. They had replied, "No, he got washed over the side; do you have any idea at all where *we* are?"

Now Thomas looked serious and shook his head. "They have a good engineer, and I told them you were anxious to get to India."

"Where's *Filioara* bound?"

"Thailand . . . Bangkok. She left Constantsa a month ago, but it's been a slow passage. They are not allowed to call anywhere because Rumania has no foreign exchange for a proper shipyard repair job, so it's a sort of running refit. We're the first vessel they've seen close up since they passed through the Bab el Mandeb a week ago. The commissar was asking all kinds of things about us, where we've been . . . where we're heading for . . . oh, every-thing. The engineer is a good guy. He strained the fuel for us, but he says we should strain it again, just to make sure. It's Rumanian diesel oil . . . refined there. . . ."

"Good, then strain out one barrel today, when it cools down a bit this evening. Then you can strike that hundred liters down into the tank. . . . Beggars can't be choosers, and at least it may get us to within a few days' sail, even in light zephyrs, to where we can get our grubby hands on a fresh-water supply."

And so we did, but it made no difference. The Rumanian fuel, we found when the lads started to strain it, was pretty near one-fifth petroleum jelly. No matter how many times we strained it through torn-up shirts and sheets, time after time, jelly fibers still remained in suspension in the fuel, and these fibers passed through any barrier we could think of to put in their way to our fuel tank. For the rest of the whole long, hot, weary, slow traipse to Cochin, all eleven hundred miles of it, all in a dead-straight line, day and night, night and day, for two whole weeks, we, like *Filioara*, carried out what was, in effect, a continuously repeated, never-ending, running, oily, greasy, sweaty, engine fuel-pump overhaul.

"What else?" I'd asked Thomas, as the upperworks of the good ship *Filioara* faded below the misty western horizon.

"Their air-conditioning is kaput, also."

The heat was bad enough for us; what it was like in a steel ship was unthinkable.

"The poor buggers," I said.

"But they really appreciate the cigarettes I took for them. They asked for Kents, of course, but I told them that Marlboro was all we had."

"Well, that's true. We didn't know we were going to meet up with Rumanians, did we?" I observed, remembering how Kents were so popular in Rumania.

The day after we parted from *Filioara* we again sighted her hove-to stopped dead in the water. This time she was about two miles to our south, and dusk was falling, so I silently wished everyone on board her (except the commissar), and especially her engineer, luck. As our own engine was then purring away happily enough, we crept past her without stopping, feeling somehow *cheap*, but we gazed at her until she disappeared into the swiftly darkened night astern of us. Then all we saw of her was her riding light, and we looked back in her direction now and again, until that, too, disappeared, and we saw no more of *Filioara*.

The rest of the voyage to Cochin passed without incident, untoward or not. My leg-stump was gradually healing, but my tooth roots were still giving me hell now and then. All across the eastern half of the Arabian Sea we were too busy keeping the fuel flowing properly to notice much, outside of the boat, in an ocean flatter than I had ever seen it, anywhere.

The ocean was so flat that we sighted the half-sunken remains of a dead whale at ten miles, and changed course slightly just to have a look at it, until the stench of it—fetid, reeking, putrid, rancid, and rotten—drove us hurriedly off back south a mile to the line of our original course. We went close enough, though, to see a slow brigade of sharks slowly circling round and round the corpse, round and round, and now and then diverting to tear a bit of mephitic, rank blubber off the stinking carcass. Our rate of progress was so slow that we sighted the whale carcass in the early morning, reached it in the noontime, and the stench of it was still in the air after dusk fell over us, even though we were moving the whole time. That was on the eighth of May, my sixty-second birthday. To celebrate it, at dusk, we opened one bottle of fizzy warm Rumanian soda pop and shared it among the three of us. As we did so I noted the temperature in my cabin; it was 111 degrees Fahrenheit.

Two days before, on the sixth of May, we had celebrated another occasion. In longitude 62°22' east, *Outward Leg* was geographically exactly halfway around the world from San Diego, her home port, where she had departed almost twenty-three thousand miles before. That we had celebrated with a tiny, one-shot-size bottle of schnapps that had been discovered by Svante while he was clearing out his damp rucksack, one early morning after we had departed Cape Gardafui, and guarded by me like the Holy Grail.

Day after day, night after night, our little Yanmar engine labored on to push our three hulls, burning fuel clogged enough to stop a big ship. Hour after hour, day after day, Yanni served us faithfully. Never once did it fail to start at the first oily touch of the button, though we had to stop the engine every hour to clean the filter and clear the fuel pump of what strands of jelly had got through.

On the ninth of May we were halfway across the Indian Ocean between the Horn of Africa and India and a wonderful thing happened; a breeze appeared from nowhere out of the west-northwest. It was very light, no more than eight knots, but with our genniker hoisted it pushed us slowly due east for seventy-two miles in twenty-four hours and, more important, it saved us the fuel for that distance, and gave us respite from cleaning fuel filters every hour, day and night, in the unbearably hot engine compartment. Running before the breeze, of course the wind-speed effect, for us, was reduced to almost nil, but we sweated it out for the sake of the silence and the saving of diesel oil and engine hours.

On the tenth of May the breeze increased slightly; that day it sailed us seventy-eight miles. On the eleventh, eighty miles, but then, on the morning of the twelfth it backed to due west, dropped, and died. By then it was obvious to us that the Tropical Convergence Zone was at last, but still very laggardly, on the move northward. There was much more cloud in the sky, and every now and then rain squalls in the distance. Now we were relieved of the nagging anxiety, which had been with us ever since we had departed Aden, of our fresh water giving out before we could reach another source. Now the source was all around and above us. We avoided the squalls or, wherever we could, used them by sailing on their windward edges. Sometimes we reached six knots in the afternoon, in this manner, but at dusk the wind died. Then it was on engine and plod away, through electric storms so thick and fast and violent, all around us, that we wondered that we were never struck by lightning. Sometimes bolts would hit the ocean only yards away from *Outward Leg*. These electric storms were not as they were in moderate climates; the lightning flashes went on for hours and hours, all the night long. On those pitch-black moonless nights it could have been frightening to see the violent lightning, in sudden shocks, ripping away the night, to reveal heavy cumulus clouds all around our horizon, and, away from the purr of the engine to hear the surprisingly loud hiss of rain falling on the ocean a mile away.

On the late afternoon of the fourteenth we sighted the light structure on Suheli Island, the southeasternmost Laccadive island, three hundred miles west of Cochin. As we passed a half mile south of the reef, I told the lads that I thought that Robin-Knox Johnson had named his vessel, in which he made the first-ever nonstop voyage around the world (I couldn't answer why when they asked me), after this unprepossessing strip of coral and sand. This tiny dot on the chart was, we knew from the *Admiralty Pilot for the Indian Ocean*, supposed to be uninhabited. We had no need of fresh water. I was anxious to reach Cochin before the new monsoon grew to full force. Then the whole of the west coast of India would be a tremendous lee-shore, and navigating into a low port on that coast, with shallow approaches, would be hazardous.

That evening, as we passed near Suheli the wind piped up to a good breeze, and again we hoisted the genniker and let her go until midnight, when the breeze dropped as suddenly as it had risen, and we were again back to plodding on the plonker.

For days the sail-changing and handing, hoisting, and stowing went on, day and night. In between we cleaned the engine oil filters every hour. On the sixteenth of May we sighted Kalpeni Island, the closest Laccadive island to Cochin, only a hundred miles from that port; on the mid-afternoon of the seventeenth we sighted, gleaming red and white in the sun, over a dark line that we knew was palm trees, Cochin lighthouse bearing due east ten miles off.

We had, however, known clearly the previous night that we were approaching the end of our month-long, twenty-three-hundred-mile passage from Aden; to show *Outward Leg* that she was only a score of miles off the coast of India, a host of flies had swarmed on board, and had plagued out of us any thought of sleep.

16

The Temple Bells Are Callin'

There was another way in which we had known that *Outward Leg* was close to the Indian shore, even before the flies found us; the whole eastern night horizon, just after dark, had been a band of golden glow, and I knew that this was caused by the gas lamps of the fishing craft that crowd the waters of Kerala State whenever the southwest monsoon is not blowing its head off. We had slowed the boat down when we came closer to the fishing fleets, and waited until pale dawn before wending our way among hundreds of small craft and closing the coast.

The fishing craft were all shapes and sizes. The larger ones, in the far offing of Cochin, rushed about at high speed, much faster than Western boats would ever dream of doing, even Frenchmen. As soon as we were among the Kerala craft we were aware of a recklessness of life or limb and that the fish they sought were evidently of far more value to the skippers than any human could be. The larger craft tended to be similar to small Western trawlers, except that they were—not crowded—they were *jammed* with people, men, women and kids, waving and shouting at us as their craft roared by, often only two feet clear of us, and usually belching thick black smoke from its exhaust. The smoke would hang in the windless air for a few seconds, then descend on the flat sea, and leave a trail of black soot on the blue waters, so that the whole

offing of Cochin, as we neared the port, was an incrementally
expanding mass of heaving black-soot streaks on the sea, gaudy
fishing flags, and shouting natives on jam-packed boats rushing
around the big ships at anchor in the roadstead off the narrow
gullet in the low shore that is the entrance to Cochin harbor.

As soon as we had passed the first fishing craft, and had them
to seaward of us, we were back in the busy thrall of the world. All
the morning and forenoon, we cleaned ourselves, sloshing our
remaining twenty gallons of fresh water around as if it had fallen
out of the sky, wondering at our wastefulness, delighting in squan-
dering, then, what for weeks had been more precious to us than
all the gold in Fort Knox.

All at once it was as if some celestial scene-shifter had pushed
up from below the sea a curtain of color. The sight of thousands
of palm trees, all lined up, lush dark-green, swaying over the
dazzling golden beaches, was almost as novel for me, even though
I'd seen India years before, as it was for the lads. Apart from the
poor trees on Aden waterfront and the one, single, gnarled growth
we had sighted in Somalia, those were the first trees of any con-
sequence that we had seen since Port Sudan's market square. They
were to us so strange a sight that they seemed almost unreal,
artificial, and as we wove our way through the harbor entrance,
dodging flotillas of darting, dashing, shouting Keralan fishers, I
had to remind myself that what was around us was not a painted
backdrop, that this was *India*.

Somehow, we were immediately aware that from that surprisingly tidy-looking tropical parkland that seemed to float each side
of us on the sea, a whole world, entire unto itself, a vast continent,
teeming with life, hundreds of millions of people, reached all the
way to the far-off roof of the world, the Himalayas.

Most continental landfalls in small craft were gradual. Normally
at the end of a long ocean passage, for a host of reasons, you were
already part of the scene before the first glimpse of land. A degree
of foreknowledge of what was there usually blunted, to some degree, the shock of arrival. Not India.

For days—weeks—there had seemed to be a void. Of a sudden,
like magic, southern India spread herself before us, and as we
passed the outer buoy to enter the narrow Vypin Channel, off Fort
Cochin, I knew, as I sniffed the cloves in the air, that if we had
not had a fixed purpose in our voyage it would be very easy to get
lost in India for a long, long time.

One side of the boat-cluttered port entrance was taken up by the old town of Fort Cochin, on Mattancheri Island, to the south of the entrance channel, still looking very Portuguese. Cool, shaded parkland and ancient but elegant wooden villas lined the waterfront in gaps between moss-grown fortress walls and seedy looking go-downs (warehouses). On the other, northern, side of the channel, on the shores of the low island of Vypin, crowds of passengers on ferryboat landings, many of the men in turbans, bearing black umbrellas, and most of the women in colorful saris, shimmered in the heat. Both shores were lined with squads of loinclothed men and boys hauling on rickety-looking contraptions of long, bent, shorn tree-branches and huge nets, which, even as we warily glanced around to shear off from rushing craft, slowly, gracefully, dipped into the brown waters, then were raised again, their nets gleaming with fish fry.

That evening, almost six thousand miles from Istanbul, we dropped our hook into the choppy waters off the northern point of Willingdon Island, and looked around to fix our bearings. Down one channel big ships lay to anchor, working barges huddled close to their clifflike sides. All down the eastern waterfront of Cochin, as far as we could see, small fishing boats crowded the jetties. To our north lay a vast expanse of calm, light brown water, with islands dotted here and there. Close by us, all around the Customs Office, carefully manicured lawns bore pristinely painted white colonial bungalows almost into the harbor.

On sighting our yellow jack flag at our starboard signal halyard, a harbor launch hailed us. The helmsman, a thin, sallow Indian, in his thirties perhaps, smartly dressed in the best traditions of the old Raj, in white cap, shirt, socks, shoes and shorts, asked us where we had come from. His English was very good. "Aden!" I called back. I had to shout hard against the noise of passing ferries, which missed us by only feet, their passengers all staring. "Aden!" I repeated, feeling as though I were telling him we were from the moon.

He smiled, welcomed us to India, then told us not to go ashore. It was Saturday. There were no offices open until Monday morning. We settled down, the lights of several towns shining all around us, and made ourselves another meal of canned food.

All the next day we sat at anchor amid rushing ferry craft and barges, watching coolies, men and women (no weekend for them!), working in the cool of the morning and sleeping in the shade of casuarina trees in the heat of the afternoon. Well-dressed brown sahibs, all Gucci shoes and sunglasses, in turn watched us from the shelter of poinciana trees in front of what turned out to be a hotel nearby. We wondered what would happen if airline passengers, on arrival in a country, were made to sit on the tarmac for two days because it was the weekend. We had just made a painfully slow crossing of the Indian ocean, one month at the rate of seventy-two miles a day. But we were happy enough; the boat harbor official, after reflecting for a moment, had allowed the lads to land at the nearest jetty, right before the Customs Office (holier, it seemed, than the Taj Mahal in India) and collect fresh water. When I had told him about my tooth problems, he passed to me a tiny bottle of oil of cloves.

Our crew, with the light of curious wonder in their eyes, returned from their fresh-water forage talking excitedly of trishaws and turbaned Sikh guards, huge in their resplendent uniforms, who guarded the jetty. Thomas wanted to return there with his camera. Svante seemed a little nonplussed to have cast eyes on "third-worlders" to whom he need not feel he owed something. It seemed to have put him off-balance.

"We're in the East, now," I told the lads, over supper (rice, boiled carrots, and corned beef). "No need to rush. It won't do any good. Learn to go with the flow and always remember whenever you see something that's strange to you, that there's plenty more, of whatever it is, about. The East has waited for you for thousands of years. A few hours more won't hurt." As I turned in an hour later, though, I hoped to myself that I could hold my patience to get ashore half as well as they seemed to be doing. A small craft, after several months of continuous cruising, can be very confining, and even more so in a hot climate.

Because of my sore stump, on Monday morning Thomas, having wangled a temporary landing permit from the jetty guards, took off, with our passports, and a polite note from me, for the port Immigration Office. Anyone would naturally assume that this establishment would be close to the port Customs Office. But this was India. Immigration was about two miles inland, he was told.

Soon—by Indian bureaucratic standards, which meant four hours later—he was back on board. He had seen the Immigration chief. We were not allowed to land. We had no visas. The chief had almost thrown him out of the office.

Anger is good therapy. In four seconds after Thomas returned

on board I had my leg on, pain or no pain. In six seconds my
sunhat was rammed on my head and in eight seconds I was lowering myself into the dinghy. Svante, silent but alert now, over-
towered by a Sikh giant, guarded the dinghy at the jetty. Thomas
and I clambered into a tatty trishaw which looked as if it must have
once waited for Clive to step ashore to conquer India. It was pe-
daled so slowly along a dusty dockside highway by a man so
ancient that, about two hundred yards from the Immigration Office, both Thomas and I alighted. I paid the man off, but he would
not leave us, so we walked alongside the trishaw with the ancient
mumbling at us. Whether he was thanking us for giving him twice
the fare, or begging for more, was impossible to tell. Even I, in
pain at every step, could manage to hobble faster than the old man
could pedal.

The road to hell, it is said, is paved with good intentions. The
way up to the Immigration chief's office in Cochin was paved with
cowshit from two sacred Brahma beasts who occupied the straw-
strewn open space below the arches on which sat the offices.

On clambering clumsily up the narrow stairway and entering
the Immigration Office we were shown to an inner sanctum by a
thin, effeminate man who looked like a professional sycophant.
The Immigration chief was a chubby chap wearing thick-lensed
glasses, a sparkling white shirt and a wart on one of his chins. His
desk was two feet thick with papers. He smoked like a chimney
the whole while we were there. He wore five rings on his fingers.
He was a high-caste Brahmin, at the opposite end of the Indian
social system from the trishaw peddler. As soon as I clapped eyes
on him I knew that Thomas and I, on our first trip ashore in India,
were certainly cutting the cake down the middle.

"Please sit down, Captain," the chief said, waving his arm
loftily toward the single chair. "This is a temporary office, but you
are wery velcome."

No sooner was I sat down (no chair for the younger) than the
chief started into a long, involved rigmarole about our not having
"wisas." He was, at first, adamant about it. "No wisas, I'm wery
certain, no landing." His English was not easy to understand unless
I listened very intently. It was a bit like hearing *Tipperary* sung in
Spanish.

"But we were in the Red Sea," I explained, "and before we got
to the Indian Ocean we didn't know if we'd be calling in India or

not . . . we've been months on this passage . . . and all we want to do is buy food and fuel. . . ."

That wasn't exactly true. We wanted to stay for a few days to rest and look around, and the southwest monsoon was even yet absent, but I thought I'd get the thin end of the wedge in.

"They wend wittels in Aden?" the chief asked.

It took me a moment to realize that he was asking me if "victuals" were "vended."

"Some, but that wasn't the prob—"

"Then you should have vent to the wittel purweyors and purchased more wittels and fuel you knew you vanted before you vent avay from Aden," was the chief's reply. "It vas wery foolish to not have sufficient wittels and vater ven you vent avay ven you knew you vould vant them, eh?" His gold teeth gleamed in the hot, sticky gloom.

A noisy fan whirled above the chief's head. I stared at a heap of loose files of documents, all of five feet high and ten feet long, which, thick with dust, tied up with scarlet ribbon, were piled drunkenly against the peeling paint of the wall. Those documents, probably going back fifty years by the look of them, were obviously the overflow from a dozen ancient wooden cabinets which lined the other walls of the room. My eye fell to the base of the heap of paper. The floor was actually bowed under the weight of the red-ribboned mass. The floor was sagging; there was a dip of at least six inches in its center. It might give way under the red tape at any minute, and propel everything—the chief, his desk, his filing cabinets, his stacks of ancient records—down into the shit-strewn stable below. Something had to be done, and quickly.

Inside my head thoughts of all the complex ramifications of making a safe voyage across a wide ocean in a small sailing craft —the weight ratios, the time-spatial problem, the uncertainty of weather, the doubt about havens, the million and one calculations—they all flashed before me. None of it would serve to make one iota of sense to this educated, high-caste landlubber sitting poker-faced behind his desk.

My mind spun—and then inspiration hit me. On the chief's wall was a Roman-lettered calendar. On it dates and times were scribbled. I suspected, after studying them for a few minutes as the chief lectured me, that I knew what they marked.

For want of anything more entertaining to do on the long, slow

Indian ocean passage (most of my library having been ditched), I'd tuned in the radio, now and again, to listen for a few minutes to the BBC overseas service cricket commentary from London. I liked cricket; I'd played plenty of it in my youth, but I wasn't too enthusiastic about radio commentaries on the game. But apart from BBC cricket everything else on the air had seemed either political claptrap or like shouts, groans, bangs, and mutters from over a lunatic-asylum wall. In my after cabin I'd shut it all out, except the cricket, very soon after we'd left Aden.

I broke the lengthy silence between me and the expressionless Brahmin.

"India did quite well at Lord's," I said.

You would have thought that Everest itself had been transmuted to solid gold; that the Ganges at Benares had changed to a flow of pure silver; that the Mahatma himself in all his simple glory had returned to comfort and advise his beloved, sorrowing people, complete with walking stick and spinning wheel. In other words, the Brahmin chief's face *glowed*. I knew, of course, that India had won the cricket Test Match, though I cracked on I wasn't sure about the eventual result, as radio reception, I said, had been impossible.

I was right. The calendar marked the matches in the recent cricket Test series in London. I felt like Sherlock Holmes. I kept my face as innocent as I could.

Chiefy right away offered me a cigarette, then as we lit up, he went into an hour-long account of every bowl, every "over," every run, in the series of games just ended.

I glanced at Thomas, standing beside me, now and then as the Brahmin rambled on. My mate looked like he thought we had both gone stark-raving mad, as I nodded and smiled at the chief's enthusiasm. By then we both willingly smoked his best English cigarettes one after the other, and drank tea brought into the sanctum subserviently by the bobbing, swishing minion.

Time was drawing on. Evening was closing. Through the cobwebbed office window we saw the sun lowering over the roofs of nearby houses. As the chief rambled on, the floor creaked. Nervously I glanced at the pile of old dusty forms, thousands of them, as they settled down another zillimeter, on their gravitational way toward the center of the earth, pressing down on the worm-eaten floor beams below us. . . .

The chief stood up, patting his pockets as all chiefs do the world over. It was always a good sign. He looked round as though he had forgotten something and couldn't quite remember. Then he smiled at me, his gold teeth gleaming in the gloaming of the dark office: "Oh yes, that wisa thing . . . no problem, old chap" (It was "old chap" now). "Of course I can't give you anything in viting, stamps and all that. You just anchor over by the Bolgatty Hotel. It's closer to the main town . . . so you can purchase wittels easily and there's vater close by . . . the boatmen vill assist you . . . stay as long as you vish." Smiling, flushed, he snatched up his rolled umbrella and made for the door.

Elated, silently nudging each other in the ribs, Thomas and I followed him, hardly able to prevent ourselves from bursting out laughing. "Come ower to my office venewer you vant, Captain," he chortled kindly as we descended the creaking stairs to the cow stable below ". . . and ve'll talk cricket again, vat?"

"He speaks strange English, *hein*?" observed Thomas, as we navigated our way past the cow droppings and out into the street.

A walleyed beggar shoved a filthy claw too rapidly at me. His fist hit my plastic leg. He withdrew the claw and hid it in filthy rags. I didn't mind one bit; we were free, and that's all that counted.

"That's how you used to pronounce your *v*'s and *w*'s," I told him. Thomas seemed surprised.

Despite the chief's protestations of "nothing in writing," we were back at the Customs Office the next morning and were soon (only six hours) through the procedure of officially checking in *Outward Leg*. While we waited interminably for yet another stamp on yet another piece of paper, we could watch long lines of coolie women, heavy baskets of earth on their heads, walk gracefully over the garden of the Malabar Hotel. Brown sahibs—guests at the hotel or overseers, it was hard to tell which—lounged under the shade of the trees and ignored utterly the coolies passing only feet away from their cool-drink-laden tables. The brown sahibs glanced at the coolies, if they looked at them at all, as if they were the piled dust in their baskets.

While I waited and waited for stamps with Svante in the limbo of the Customs House, Thomas, now back on board, made an Indian courtesy flag. This he did by drawing, with a laundry marker, a black sun or wheel of life in the middle of our old Hungarian flag. It served very well, and raised no complaints at all from the white-uniformed officials who, almost hourly from then until we left Cochin, passed *Outward Leg* in fast harbor launches, on what seemed to be tours of inspection. There was no fuss over flags in

India, though. In great countries there generally isn't. It's usually only in insecure little tin-pot dictatorships that the native officials are paranoid about their particular bit of cloth hanging up, and slap huge fines, or even imprisonment, on transgressors of their rules.

The Bolgatty Island anchorage off Ernakulam, the main town of the huge Cochin complex, was a couple of miles from Willingdon Island, through a channel so shallow that, even at high water, *Outward Leg* kissed the mud a few times.

As soon as we dropped the hook off the Bolgatty Hotel, several bumboats crowded round *Outward Leg*. The rowers shouted at us, all at once: "Ice?-you-vant-ice?" "Fuel-I-get-fuel-Johnny!" "Vater-Johnny-you-vant-vater?". After a few minutes of haggling, I engaged an older man—"My name-Charlie-sah"—as our boatman, and for the whole of our stay in Cochin My-name-Charlie hardly ever left the side of *Outward Leg* unless it was to fetch some supplies or row us to and from the shore. He would wait alongside *Outward Leg* for us to return to the jetty, and would be at the end of the landing stage in his boat before we reached it. At first Svante pulled a face when My-name-Charlie started hauling us around. We had our own dinghy, but My-name-Charlie only charged a dollar for a whole day; why should we deprive a good man of his means of livelihood? What else did he have? Svante saw the light and from then on rode around quietly like a good sahib, and paid up, along with the rest of us.

"This is the East," I told Svante and Thomas, back on board. "Don't be shy of wanting someone to do something for you. Don't forget it's their living. Service for you may even be, to them, a matter of surviving or not. You ask for it and you get it, if you can pay for it! If you can't God help you!"

I went ashore with the crew to the Bolgatty Hotel, which turned out to be a huge, run-down, cool old Dutch mansion sitting among shady trees. We arranged to have showers there. The crew were puzzled when the hotel staff, in the Lascar way, wagged their heads from side to side quickly as they talked, and smiled broadly and said, "Yes, you may have showers, but there's no hot water, and only water for one hour, in the early morning." Their head movements were strange. It was somehow like a tulip shivering in a breeze.

When Thomas and Svante returned on board, they tried to emulate the smiling wag, but it took them some time to do it

anything like the Indians, and even then they could never quite
get that blossom-quiver right.

"Is the kerosene stove empty of fuel, Svante?" Thomas would
ask. Svante would shake his head, smile, and say, "Yes!" Then
the two would break into howls of laughter. It reminded me of
Bulgaria, which was another country where people shook their
heads instead of nodding when they meant "Yes."

The landing stage on the Ernakulam side of the Bolgatty Channel was always a lively scene, but the first time we landed there
the panoramic gush of humanity flowing along the jetty, from
ferries arriving every few seconds, was almost too much of a shock
for us, freshly arrived from our Indian Ocean void. The most surprising thing was the quietness of everybody. They were all talking,
laughing, crying, arguing, yet there seemed to be no more noise
than there might have been if the jetty had been empty.

As we stood and gawped on the landing stage, it was as if the
whole of south India was passing us in waves. Women of all ages,
graceful yet strong in silken saris of a thousand bright colors, gold
bangles on their wrists, gold slippers on their feet, gold clips on
their ears and in their noses, hennaed eyes and cast marks on their
foreheads; little girls, skin like a puppy's belly, eyes like oil wells,
almost exact replicas of their mothers; small serious boys in white
trousers and knee-length coats tightly fastened at the neck, with
little forage caps, looking like six-year-old Pandit Nehrus; intently
hurrying businessmen, many in turbans and long white gowns,
toting briefcases and black umbrellas; thin wiry coolies bearing
loads on their backs that would stop a truck; citified youths in
("they think," said Thomas and Svante) the latest Western style
preening gear; students by the hundred who looked as if they
actually *studied*; naval officers in their British-looking uniforms; and
peasants from a thousand tribes, all of them the color and with the
dry strength and even the consistency, it seemed, of the very earth
they labored—all of India seemed to pass us by, and all without
undue *noise*. It was one of the few times in my life I'd ever had an
ear-warp. It was as though I'd gone deaf.

"All this place needs is Gungha Din," I joked to the lads. Scarcely
had I spoken than an ancient, parchment-faced man, naked but
for a ragged, dirty loincloth, carrying a goatskin water bag, was at
my side, offering me an almost-rusted-through tin mug.

"You ask for it—you get it—if you can pay for it!" laughed
Thomas.

I gave the old man a coin, but turned down his proffered mug of water. I noticed one of his big toes was missing. I wondered if it had been shot off on some Afghan rampart. I winked at him. With a one-yellowed-tooth grin he took off into the dust under the casuarina trees.

On the main street between the landing and the town, the traffic roared. Great juggernautlike trucks, buses, cars, taxis, gharries, little three-wheelers, trishaws, and bicycles by the thousand speeded and rumbled past sidewalks jammed with people. Over everything, in this windless, between-monsoon heat, hovered a thick pall of exhaust fumes. The stone and concrete buildings on both sides of the street were grubby and begrimed. Here was another shock for voyagers fresh from the clean ocean.

Once safely across the highway though, and into the more or less traffic-free shopping streets of the town we were back again in old India, with all its marvels.

There was a Christian church, St. Mary's Basilica, in one of the back streets, and we went to look at it. Cochin was where the first Christian to reach India, Saint Thomas, had landed. He'd later been killed in a brawl in Madras, but not before he'd converted a lot of Indians. Cochin was still the biggest Christian community in India. That was, the sexton, an interesting little man in a black frock-coat, told us, why Kerala State had been the only Communist-governed state in the subcontinent, but, he said, the local communism had been based more on Christian compassion than on Marxism. I asked him if he did not think it was because the Kremlin wanted to control the sea-lanes across the Indian Ocean, and they'd given up on Kerala and were now supporting instead the Tamils of Sri Lanka, with the aim of grabbing the huge natural harbor at Trincomalee, to gain another Aden, another Can Ranh Bay. Confused, he thought for a moment, then he politely admitted I might have a point.

Many of the shops in Ernakulam had pictures of Pope John Paul on their walls. He had visited the area recently is his bullet-proof Popemobile. I told the lads the Pope was no dummy. He might be a stick-in-the-mud when it came to regulating the social mores of his flock, but he sure knew the score when it came to Russian ambitions on the sea-lanes and Moscow's growing empire of naval bases. "You watch—he's been in Ireland—he'll be in Chile next," I told them, "and good luck to him!" In some of the shops, although they had the Pope in the window or by the door, in the gloomy interiors, on the back wall, images of Krishna or Kali lurked in the shadows.

In the streets of Ernakulam, religion was evident at every corner. There were mosques and minarets, ear-splitting muezzin calls from their loudspeakers, and holy cows wandering everywhere. In Fort Cochin, which we later visited for a day by harbor ferry, there were even synagogues for the oldest Jewish community in India, there before Saint Thomas cast away his doubts and took his new, burning faith across the Indian Ocean, probably by the very same route that we had come from Israel.

In the India that we saw there were still many signs of the British Raj. The street signs were exactly the same as those in London; so were the red pillar (mail) boxes, and all the official notices had the unmistakable touch of Whitehall about them. The policemen looked even more British than had those in Cyprus, Israel, and Aden.

The British veneer was punctuated with reminders of the Indian core. Near the ferry landing was a sign saying WOMEN'S POLICE STATION. It was full of women, jam-packed at the windows, in uniform and in saris. Clearly the separation of the sexes in India reached even unto the administration of the law.

We entered a bank to change dollars into rupees. It took forty minutes. Each one of the eighty-two clerks in the bank, all at their separate desks, had his or her own ceiling fan whirring away. The walls were lined with solid ranks of filing cabinets, all jammed, packed full of brown files. Every chair in the place, every table, every desk, every fan, had a letter and a number painted neatly in white on it. I studied the labeling system. Sure enough, "C" and a number was on the chairs . . . "T" and a number on the tables . . . "D" and a number on the desks.

To break the boredom I asked Thomas, "Guess what letter is on the fans?"

Thomas pointed out a notice on the wall of the bank:

CUSTOMERS ARE REQUESTED KINDLY NOT TO BRING FIREARMS INTO THE BANK, BUT THIS DOES NOT EXCLUDE SIKHS FROM CARRYING THEIR KIRTIPANS.

As we left the bank clutching our rupees, I explained that a kirtipan was a small dagger that each Sikh, to conform with his religion, must carry at all times.

At the local boatyard there were skilled workmen and resources enough to refit a yacht properly, without doubt. Holy cows wandered around on the slipway, and got in the way of hauling up a fishing boat. Everyone waited patiently for the cows to move away in their own good time, which we thought was very good of them.

That first evening we intended to visit a cinema. *Fifty-five Days in Peking* was showing. But when we arrived, even a half hour before the show was due to start, the crowd of men and boys outside was so thick, and so *violent*, that we gave up all hope of ever getting inside. One man in the squeeze at the narrow gate was pushing his open hand hard, I mean *shoving*, right into a small boy's face for a good five minutes, to hold the urchin back from getting in before him. Clear of the pushing mass, standing to one side, I watched silently the microcosmic demonstration of Third World attitudes, as the boy finally was hurled to the ground, rolled himself over in the dust, picked himself up, and barged back again at the mass of pressing, squeezing, shoving males.

Then we gave up and sought a Moslem restaurant, which had, for us, the best food and the cleanest tables. They were generally the cheapest, too.

On the way back to the landing stage, at around ten in the evening, no more, the town was almost deserted. Trishaws and three-wheeled scooters were secured by the hundreds behind the padlocked cinema gates. All along the street pavements and sidewalks all the mile to the landing jetty, people slept. The majority were men; fewer were women. Many more were boys, of any age from two upward. They, we were told, fed themselves by sweeping the food droppings at the markets, and lugging loads when they could find them.

The air was heavy as we tramped along the silent streets in the night. "I hope the monsoon changes, soon," observed Svante. "Then we get some rain, eh?"

I nodded at the sleeping bodies lying on the roadside. (Were they all sleeping?) "Pity those poor buggers when it does," I said.

On the waterfront, hundreds and hundreds of Indians poorer by far than the dirt they lived in, the *harijans*, the untouchables— those innocent victims of an apartheid far more ancient, entrenched, and rigid than even South Africa's—slept, many under a huge, brilliantly lit billboard: RUN FOR THE HUNGRY OF AFRICA! it shouted over the prone bodies of the harijans, at the upper-caste joggers of India. With us in his boat, My-name-Charlie shoved off.

17

Where the Flying Fishes Play

We stayed in Cochin for ten days, with still few signs of the new monsoon's approach. It was now almost a month overdue, and was reported to be slowly creeping northward toward the southern tip of Sri Lanka, four hundred miles away. By the twenty-ninth of May the crowded life, the heat, the dust, the flies, even the busy, curious friendliness of the townspeople in Ernakulam were beginning to pall. We had almost two thousand miles, and the notorious Bay of Bengal, ahead of us on our way to Thailand, and the monsoon's lateness had already delayed our ordained arrival there by six weeks.

On *Outward Leg* we had been busy. We had risen every day to catch an hour or two of congenial coolness before the sun bore down too hard on us. Splashing in the muddy waters of the Bolgatty Channel, the lads had scraped the growth off the three hulls; three inches of brilliant green grass, collected over half the way from Aden. They had suffered the consequences—festering cuts, which took weeks to heal. My-name-Charlie had ferried the old Rumanian fuel ashore, burned it (or sold it), and rowed barrels of replacement fuel back to the boat. I, having been in India before, had drawn off a sample of each consignment, to see its purity. I'd had to return, with threats and imprecations, only the first barrel,

219

which was one-fifth water. Then we were ready to sail again, to hunt the wind.

Outward Leg was so reluctant to leave the vividness of Indian life that she grabbed on and clung to the mud of the harbor channel *six times* on the way to the Customs Office on Willingdon Island. There, again Thomas and I waded our patient way through battalions of bureaucrats, a maze of dark, fanned offices, a veritable blizzard of paper, a stampede of stamps, a plethora of platitudes, and, the crowning glory of Cochin, a four-hour lecture by the chief Immigration officer on the comparative virtues of every fast bowler —Indian, Sri Lankan, South African, Pakistani, West Indian, British, New Zealander, or Australian—over the past forty years of Test cricket. But no one, at least no Briton, could ever, surely, leave India angry, even though we did miss the tide and were delayed yet another four hours, so that we had to negotiate our departure by the wan light of a fading moon over Mattancheri Island.

There's always some saving grace about getting back to sea, and in this instance, as we wended our way out through the boat-choked channel, the setting moon was ahead of us. Her light raised before us the black, ghostly silhouettes of a score of unlit fishing craft bobbing about, and so allowed me to avoid them. But one low open boat we missed by a mere foot or two, and knew it was there only when the gleam of our starboard light reflected at us suddenly from a piled heap of sleeping bodies all brilliant emerald, shining in the blackness under the crescent moon. We slid past them silently, after my first mumbled curse, and wished them well.

The first thing we did when we got out into the offing in the Indian Ocean was put the ship's clock one hour forward, so as to put ourselves onto Sri Lankan time. West India had been somehow out of phase with our ideas of natural time. The sun had risen, it had seemed to me, in the middle of the night and set just after teatime. India had been five hours ahead of Greenwich—now *Outward Leg* was six, and as dawn crept toward us from the Malabar Coast we already felt divorced from all the hot-breathed rumble that is India.

The second thing we did was check the echo-sounder anode, on the bottom of the main hull. Our sounder had shown no reading on the way out of Cochin. Thomas went over the side as soon as it was light, and gently, three feet under the water, rubbed off any growth that might still have clung to it. But to no avail. The sounder anode was dead. Now, whenever we entered shoal waters, we

would need to sound with a lead and line, in the "good old fash-
ioned" way. (We finally got hold of replacement anodes *eleven
months* later!)

Again we went into our sea routine. We kept our watches and
we kept out of each other's way as much as we could. Cochin had
well refreshed us, and we had fresh food (the first day—on ice!)
on board and plenty of fuel should the breeze fail us.

At sunrise a northeast breeze, easing down the coast of India,
gave us a good, but for us slow, at three knots, quarter-reach for
that night and the following, but in the day it died, and so, as the
heat of the sun beat down on us, and we motored along, almost,
did we. Then, 123 miles south of Cochin, just before dawn, we
sighted the loom of the light on Cape Cormorin, the southernmost
point of India.

"Better keep your eyes skinned," I told the lads over breakfast.
I swept my arm over to the east. "This is the Gulf of Mannar. Sri
Lanka's over there, too, beyond the horizon. This is where the
Tamil rebels smuggle their arms over to northern Sri Lanka. There
are probably government gunboats about, too. If you see—even if
you only suspect you see—anything at all, I want to know!"

That morning we got the first decent wind we'd had since we
had been off Cape Gardafui, almost two thousand miles astern. It
was still a northeaster, and so not the new monsoon's herald; but
it blew at a good twenty-eight knots by mid-afternoon, and with
our twin headsails winged out on the poles, so as to give a total
sail-spread of forty feet, from tack to tack, *Outward Leg* zoomed
along, even loaded as she was, and leaped, slithering, sliding and
crashing, from sea to sea, as did thousands of flying fish in her
van. By teatime we were making over six knots steady and at times
surfing at ten.

Then, as dusk promised a fine breezy night, we changed course
to the southeast, and brought the wind more onto our beam. This
gave us a fine broad-reach; but the sea was very heavy and short,
so for the first time since *Outward Leg* had been in the Caribbean,
we reefed down the mainsail, but only to ease her motion. There
was no fear of a sudden capsize; with the cooltubes standing by
to press the bottom of the keel downward toward the earth's center
with a two-ton force, she was always safe enough and stiff as a
church.

The northeast breeze was squally toward midnight, and kept
us busy all the middle watch, with violent rain and gusty blasts.

I stayed in the cockpit all night. The nervousness of the weather was affecting my bones. Something was up. It was far too dark to see anything, and the periodical rain didn't help. Then the wind eased off and finally almost died; but at false dawn, all of a sudden what was left of it veered right round 180 degrees, just like that. Now it was blowing from the *southwest!*

Bleary-eyed in the pale light of dawn I stared at the horizon to the southwest. It was nothing but thick, high, heavy cumulus cloud, pregnant with rain, black with the promise of squalls and shifting toward us like a vast army marching over the rim of the world.

"?" Thomas looked at me.

I nodded. "Yes, that's it all right," I said.

The new monsoon was with us. It was a month late. "You and Svante stand by. Course southeast. Let her go!"

I clambered down the after companionway, (*Oh, Lord, let her go!*), shut the hatch, closed the door, lay down on my berth, and quietly rejoiced as the wind and rain, and Thomas, and Svante, sang their songs overhead, and I felt the boat lurch forward. In ten minutes the temperature must have dropped by as many degrees. The relief of coolness in the air was like taking off a sweaty, hairy shirt.

Then I remembered something, I rose again, lurched toward the hatch, opened it as rain streamed in at me, and tugged on Thomas's foot. He bent to hear me.

"I think we can ditch all but five cans of fresh water, Thomas! We might as well lighten her by a ton or more!"

I turned to rest again, but the thought of helping to dump the weight of all that water, which had been so very precious to us until now, was too much. Out into the cockpit I hoisted myself, to hand up the cans from the galley, where Svante was stacking them as he brought them from their stowages in the big, roomy midships engine compartment. In a kind of mad wet celebration, as the boat tasted the wind and jerked away, we just dumped the water in our self-draining cockpit and let it all gush merrily down the plughole into the ocean. Now we knew we were really free.

Then we could, if we had wanted to, make directly for Thailand, all of fifteen hundred miles away, except for two things: Svante and mail. Our Swedish crewman, having tasted and seen a few of the delights of India on his daily rambles in and around Ernakulam and Cochin, had been avid to leave *Outward Leg* there, so as to travel overland for a while in India. He had, he told us, only a month more remaining of his leave from the Stockholm Post Office. At the time, with little sign of the monsoon in view, I had been concerned about long, weary hours for Thomas and me hand-steering the boat to Galle. So I had persuaded Svante, with glowing accounts (remembered from visits to what had then been Ceylon decades before) of the wonders of Sri Lanka, to stay with us until Galle. As I told him, he could have a quick hike around that lovely, lush island, and then fly up to anywhere he wanted to go in India.

Svante, now being a good, sensible, and fair seaman, had agreed. Now, with the monsoon wind and the *Aries* wind-vane steering gear to do the chore of keeping a course, all the time, any time we needed relief, Svante was even more free to go, although we'd miss him. The reduction of his weight on board, and the food to nourish it (although he wasn't a big lad) would be welcome too, I told myself, to get us more quickly over the fourteen hundred rough miles of the Bay of Bengal. So must work a skipper's mind.

The second, and to us, out at sea, more important reason for heading in to Galle was to collect our mail from the past three months. On a long voyage meeting up with mail is a constant headache. For the lack of a better, more certain prospect, months before, when we had left 'Akko, I had arranged for all our mail to be forwarded to Galle, on the southwestern tip of Sri Lanka. At the time it had been a wise choice of destination, rather than Cochin. If the southwest monsoon had been blowing in full strength, Cochin might have been very hazardous to enter, being on a dead-lee shore. Galle might be fetched in either monsoon. Whichever sensible course we had taken when we headed past Cape Gardafui, to reach Thailand we would have, in some way, to pass Galle.

Over the cruising grapevine it was notorious that there was no other place that a sailing yacht could call in at Sri Lanka without risk of severe trouble from the authorities, or of being attacked even, by government forces or the Tamil rebels. Colombo, the main port and the capital, did not want us; it was too busy collecting fat harbor dues from big shipping. There was no other haven on the west coast. The north and the east of Sri Lanka were being consumed in the flames of the Tamil rebellion. We could only call at Galle.

It was plain from the chart that the entrance to Galle would be a tricky business, and especially with our electronic depth-sounder out of action. We hove to for the night eight miles off the entrance, amid, it seemed, a thousand fishing boats, keeping our eye on our bearings in case the strong currents thereabouts should drift us closer to the rocky shore. In the morning light, against a handsome backdrop of majestic mountains in the distance, and alluring golden beaches overhung with palms on which the ocean seas broke with an almost shattering roar, we shaped our winding course over a shallow, narrow channel, heavy with broken seas, between the breakwater heads, and so into a recently built, tiny, crowded, but monsoon-safe port on the eastern side of Galle Bay, a few miles from the old Dutch-built town.

No sooner had our hook dropped onto the mud of Galle harbor than a noisy harbor launch, crowded with soldiers, all carrying rifles, looking like a gang of brigands in dirty rags, and white-uniformed harbor officials, roared alongside. They made to come right up against *Outward Leg*'s side, but I hopped up onto the cockpit seat, grabbed a lower shroud with one fist, and with the other hand shooed them away. They obviously had no idea that two minutes of being banged by a heavy, rusting-iron, slab-sided vessel, with jagged metal poking out of its side at intervals, could do more damage to a sailing boat than a stormy ocean-crossing. A thin brigand, toothless, in the bow of the launch screamed something at me, louder, over the roar of the engine, than the rest of the launch's complement, who were all waving their arms and shouting at me, all at once. All I understood was "harbormaster!"

I grinned broadly and nodded. This seemed to send everyone on the launch into a frenzy. By the way the helmsman, another brigand, was maneuvering his wheel, his throttle, and his gear lever—ahead, astern, ahead—you would have thought that there was a full gale blowing.

"What . . . ?" shouted Thomas. Svante was already below, sorting out his gear into his rucksack, getting ready to head for the hills. I gestured him down to the cockpit. Breathlessly he asked, "What's the problem?"

"No idea," I replied. "But when in danger or in doubt, hold your counsel and do not shout."

Then, as suddenly as the launch had arrived, it roared off, in a cloud of thick black smoke, for the harbor entrance, and so out to sea, and that was the last we saw of it or its crew that day.

That was about seven in the morning. After breakfast—a cup of coffee—I stared through our binoculars around the harbor, at soldiers guarding a row of drab warehouses on one side, and a sleepy fishing haven on the other; at men, dressed for the most part in sarongs, moving around slowly, as if in a trance, and at others prone under the trees, while Brahma cows, their ribs showing, tick-picking birds on their shoulders, grazed around them.

Close to us, at anchor also, there were two or three other cruising boats, mainly Australian, on their way, I guessed, westward somewhere. But, by the growth on their waterlines, they looked as though they had not moved for months. On their decks, in their cockpits, nothing stirred.

By eleven o'clock it was plain that nothing would stir until we stirred it ourselves. Svante was by now anxious about catching his train to Colombo, from whence he hoped he would travel up to the beautiful hill-capital of Candy. Our yellow jack still flapped in the high wind at the signal halyard, showing that we had arrived from another land and were awaiting inspection.

Our entry into Sri Lanka, we were to find, was governed, as in much of the ex-colonial Third World, even in 1986 (after men had reached the moon and probed the planets, after huge masses of people, for decades, had been moving about the globe by air, with the minimum or paperwork or entry problems), by rules and regulations for visitors-by-sea that had been formed in the days of big sailing ships, back in some cases as early as the seventeenth century. In those days, when a ship arrived after a long voyage at sea, the dangers of plague and disease arriving with the ship had been a real concern. Trade, and the movement in and out of ports, had been, as the years passed, more and more rigidly controlled by an ever-growing bureaucracy. In the old days, when the system was started by the colonial powers, the clerks and officials must have had some idea of the problems and difficulties encountered on such long, arduous voyages, because they themselves had traveled to the colonies in sailing ships. But then a second, and a third generation of clerks and officials, born in the colony and more removed from the knowledge of voyaging, had taken over the port administration of shipping agents had been appointed, to go between the ships' captains, and the authorities and merchants on land, to "husband" the ship, to make sure that everything was properly done and that no excessive payments were gouged out of the mariners. For this the agents charged their fee, which was usually 10 percent. The same system still prevailed, we knew, in Galle.

In the old days the ships' agents' runners would wait offshore for the arriving craft and find out its state of health. If there had been no fever on board, by the time the captain had tied up or anchored all his shoreside arrangements would have been made for him by an agent. If on the other hand fever had been raging in the ship, it was anchored in the harbor and left in quarantine for days, or even weeks, until the plague had done its worst.

We knew who the Galle ships' agent was—his name was legend among cruising folk leaving or bound for the Indian Ocean. How could it not be remembered, when one of his names meant "Lord" in Spanish and the other was very nearly the same as the British royal family's?

My leg was still too sore and the heat far too great for me to walk comfortably. Thomas ferried himself ashore, argued for an hour to pass through the police control at the gate and headed off to find our agent.

The agent invited us to supper in his palatial mansion (for which we were charged well over the going rate in the local chophouses). The agent, a small, neat bronze-skinned Singhalese of about my age—perhaps a little older, although he later told me he was younger—rose to greet me from a thronelike chair on his porch, where he had been holding court with his cronies. He was dressed in a pure-white shirt secured with gold cuff-links at his wrists, and a silken embroidered sarong; a sensible mode of dress in the clammy heat of the Sri Lankan coast. On his feet he wore real hand-tooled leather sandals and gold rings. His animated fingers were asparkle with gems, which flashed as he talked brooking no interruption. As he rose, and we stood at a lower level on the stoop, I noticed that his beautifully carved chair was decorated, where his head had been, with what looked to me very like an attempted replica of the British crown. Above his front door hung photographs of Queen Elizabeth and Prince Philip; to one side was a picture of Prince Charles and Lady Di taken at their wedding; all around the walls of his veranda were various sayings framed and hung like pictures: "England Expects Every Man to Do His Duty —Horatio Nelson"; "You Can Fool Some of the People All of the Time, You Can Fool All of the People Some of the Time—but You Can't Fool All of the People All of the Time —Abraham Lincoln": that kind of thing.

It looked to me as though his house had been decorated, at least the veranda, by the editors of the old *Boy's Own* magazine.

Something was missing—I looked around for it—sure enough, there it was, hidden behind the open front door, also neatly framed in carved teak: "There is No One Depressed in This House; We Are Not Interested in the Possibilities of Defeat —Queen Victoria."

After supper, served by innumerable female servants, dressed in beautiful saris draped around their graceful shoulders and over their sinuous hips, the agent tried to sell us gems; but who needs diamonds or pearls when they have the ocean? Pleading weariness after a long day's wait, we left the agent's mansion gemless; but as I told the lads: "If the state of my wallet is anything to go by, and if lack of excess weight is the criterion of speed in a multihull, then *Outward Leg* should sail across the Bay of Bengal like shit off a shovel!"

The agent offered us a lift to the Galle post office next day, and charged for the ride. The Galle post office was a fine old stable of a building crowded with people coming and going. In front of it, with the monogram *"ER VII"* (King Edward VII) emblazoned a foot square on its cast-iron solidity, was the biggest mailbox I'd ever seen in my life. It was almost as big as a London taxi, and must have weighed as much as a tank. I wondered if the Sri Lankans had kept it there out of sentimentality for British rule, or simply not bothered to remove it because it was too heavy!

The public seemed to wander everywhere in the post office, and so did Thomas and I. In the back sorting offices there were heaped piles of loose letters seemingly dumped willy-nilly on the floor. In the parcels office there were small cooking stoves, asteam with the aroma of boiling rice, set on the desks among the glue pots and brown paper, cardboard boxes of opened parcels.

There were only three letters waiting for us: one for Thomas, from his family in Munich; an engraved invitation (which had already been opened) to me to attend a gallery show of hunting paintings in Upper East Side Manhattan two months previously; and a letter from a British publisher to say that he was sorry, he didn't think there would be any demand for our *Danube Pilot* in "the foreseeable future" but he wished us luck with it.

I leaned on the *"ER VII"* mailbox, amid a mass of pushing, shoving men in bright sarongs, and envisaged the thousands and thousands of yacht masts in northern Europe, from Helsinki to Brest, and the great deep ditch we'd seen almost completed in the hills of Bavaria, and the publisher's office high in a London tower-

block with, I hoped, cold rain bucketing onto its windows, shook
my head, rammed the letter into my back pocket, and hobbled
down through the ramparts, headed for the town.

The agent never did bother to get out to see *Outward Leg*. Apart
from having him arrange our entry and exit from Sri Lanka, and
being charged the dues for those services, we did not see much of
him, nor have much to do with him, after the mail lift. If there
was ever money earned for old rope, the hundred dollars or so
that he received from us was a case in point. I suppose that seeing
the agent and his veranda was worth the money we had paid.
There was so little of that kind of ultramundane, colorfully extrinsic
experience left in this world. I did not, then, know how Thailand
would be, of course. I reflected that the agent would have excelled
on Broadway in any capacity.

The harbor fees in Galle were stiff particularly in view of its
amenities. During the day the southwest monsoon wind blew straight
into the harbor, raising a steep chop, and making any dinghy work
a wet job. The soft mud on the harbor bottom was not good
holding—*Outward Leg* dragged three times. Twice we had to shift
at no notice (once in the dead of night) to make way for ships
arriving to offload at the warehouse jetty. (We later found that the
godowns were main ammunition stores for the Sri Lankan Army!)
Apart from a water well near the bouncing old-iron landing pontoons at the top of a dangerously rickety ladder on the seawall,
there were no amenities for us at all inside the port of Galle. All
the same, the charge was a flat sixty dollars, whether a boat stayed
for a day or a month. There was a bright side, though: There had
been so few multihulls visiting Galle that no one had yet slapped
a double charge on them, for which we thought ourselves lucky.

Svante managed to get away from *Outward Leg* on the second
day of negotiation with the Immigration police at the gate for permission to travel overland. At the police station, he said, they were
holding four Tamils, "on suspicion."

"Suspicion of what?" I asked him.

"They just said 'suspicion,'" replied Svante.

Both Thomas and I were sorry to see Svante leave. He'd been,
in time, good, cheerful company and a willing hand. He'd learned
slowly but thoroughly. He'd saved us many, many, long, weary
hot hours at the wheel, and he had kept his night watches well.
But he felt the call of India, her hot, damp plains, her mountains
and all the wonders among them, and beyond them the cold of

Sweden, the snow and Stockholm Post Office. Svante, with shy grins and handshakes all round, hefted his rucksack onto his shoulders and left us. He'd even learned to say good-bye like a sailor, without turning his head once as he strode off.

Ashore, our reception in Galle, and the impressions it left us with, were entirely antithetic to our fond memories of Cochin. The place was full of beggars. They were everywhere and of all ages and sexes. From the start of a run ashore until its end we were under a barrage of whining pleas for "monee" unless or until we could find refuge in some café or hotel. Those who did not whine as they begged demanded money or cigarettes as if we owed them. The more aggressive types, when they were waved away or ignored, shouted loudly after us, until they turned away to find some other paler-skinned foreigner to bug and badger.

Some of the beggars appeared to be deserving cases: old, old men and women, thin and in rags so shredded it seemed they would disintegrate at the slightest puff of breeze. To these we handed a few coins or a cigarette or two; not out of charity, but out of recognition, because we ourselves, both Thomas and I, knew very well what it was like to be without comfort. But others, and especially the youngsters, were quite obviously begging for the sake of "something for nothing." Very few of the begging children showed any sign of hunger (we knew the signs full well), and most of them were clean, sturdy, even fat, and well dressed by Third World standards anywhere.

On one occasion in Galle, as I waited outside the town railway station for Thomas to return from Colombo, where he had gone to get the VHF radio repaired, a woman, very well dressed indeed, wearing a small fortune in gold ornaments on her fingers, ears and in her nose, leaned to speak to her two equally well dressed daughters, aged about six and eight. As she spoke to them she kept glancing and pointing her chin at me. Sure enough, even though I could hardly believe it was happening, a minute later the two little girls trooped over to me, held out their palms, and whined "Monee?" I gently refused. A minute later the woman and the two girls were picked up by a smartly dressed man driving a car which looked almost new to my unpracticed eye. Once inside the car and moving, the woman and both girls pulled faces at me. I laughed, but I was still astonished.

One refuge in Galle from the unceasing begging or the arrogant disdain of the better-off local Singhalese toward strangers was the

Oriental Hotel. It was in the middle of an old Dutch town which was surrounded completely by fortifications in a good state of repair. There, if we could manage to dodge around the cow droppings of sacred Brahma beasts and a flotilla of shouting, persistent, gaudily dressed women outside, selling "souvenirs," we were safe. Inside the otherwise customerless Oriental, Thomas and I could sit coolly under silent fans on the high ceilings, listening to quiet, good music, surrounded by dark old Dutch marine paintings, and, for a matter of cents, be served tea by a squad of gliding waiters decked out in white sarongs and jackets, red collars tightly buttoned at the necks. After the hot, close confines of *Outward Leg*, it was nirvana to relax for an hour in the Oriental.

A little river ran through the town of Galle, and, where it debouched into the ocean, there was what would have been a pleasant park, shaded by huge trees spreading their branches over green grass. But the whole area was plagued by arrogant beggars, buggers, and drug pushers, separately or all three at once. One of the riverbanks was the town dump as we discovered in one visit there, in mid-afternoon, when we had thought to cool ourselves. At night, one old beggar told us, there was danger of death in that park for any unwary stranger.

Closer to the port was another glorious old hotel, the Closenburg. Over three centuries before, this had been built for a retired Dutch sea captain, and it was a thing of legends. Stately, cool, replete with fine old teak, mahogany furniture and draperies of the best Chinese silk, it sat on a headland overlooking Galle Bay and the fortified Old Town.

Inside the Closenburg the public rooms had floors of cool marble. A terrace encircled it with lovely views over waving palms to the surf breaking on the coast to the eastward. There again, as in the Oriental, the silent, watchful, efficient staff, dressed in white sarongs and jackets, outnumbered the customers at least two to one. And Thomas and I were two, and there were two more patrons in the place. There was no doubt in my mind as I sat on the terrace in the cool monsoon breeze, above the sea pounding on the rocks below, that this was the kind of place I could stay in very contentedly for the rest of my life, or at least for a long time, except for the thought of all those importunate beggars outside. It was as if we were under continual siege.

Outside the port gates, close by, was a Muslim village strung along the shore. After our experiences in the town, Thomas and I spent more time there than in Galle. We found the Muslim villagers, fishermen in the main, with their strong admixture of Arab blood (or an unnameable race, old before Muhammad—or even Buddha—was born), much more open and honest and easy to deal with than the townspeople. We got to know the villagers better because of our curiosity about their fishing craft. These were praus very similar to those of Polynesia, with narrow dugout hulls built up to add freeboard, and with simple, lashed, tree-branch outriggers. The men all looked like Sinbad in their flowing robes. The youths (Thomas observed) resembled budding Michael Jacksons. We would walk there to eat a cheap meal at about fifty cents each in the flyblown little Hotel Hameeb, dirty but friendly, and with one of the finest greasy-kitchen ocean views I ever saw outside of a boat. It was by no means a well-off village, but very rarely did anyone beg from us. Once a monsoon shower caught us in its full downpour. A little old woman, as poor and as bent as a rusty nail, invited us with gestures to shelter in her dirt-floored hovel. We gave her all we had with us—a packet of biscuits.

When the downpour ceased we found that there had been that other bane of tropical life: a general power failure. We ate (rice and lamb) with our right hands by candlelight in our favorite dive, which wasn't much darker than it normally had been. Then, after grave and polite handshakes all round with our Sri Lankan fishermen friends, we set off back for the boat. A few of the houses and cottages, tin-roofed and unpainted, mostly open to the weather but out of the mud, were now lit fitfully by flickering candles. As we sloshed along the dark street we saw a group of men huddling by an open window. We approached the men and silently peered over their shoulders. There, inside another hovel, an old man lay dead in his simple boxwood coffin, all washed clean and laid out in his best djellaba on pure-white bedsheets which reflected the eerie candle-glow.

I shivered with the dampness of my shirt and tugged Thomas's arm. "Come on, mate, we're sailing tomorrow, and it's going to be blowing its fu— hard in the Bay of Bengal," I said, remembering to respect the dead, and my vow to the old sea god back in Jebel Zuquair.

Thomas nodded in the dim glow of the vigil candle. He knew that more often than not I was right.

18

The Wind Is in the Palm Trees

We hadn't idled in Galle, except during the heat of the afternoon hours. After midday, as *Outward Leg* had jerked and bridled in the chop, it was uncomfortably sweaty belowdecks and anything up to a full gale topside. Thomas would ferry me then to the broken ladder on the harbor wall, I would clamber onto the jetty and hobble off to do errands and later to find cool haven somewhere out of the heat and away from the ubiquitous street solicitors.

From the son of the English owner of *Passat*, a burned-out yawl in the port, we bought a good, solid, British-built, many-pronged, fiberglass-encased satnav antenna. He wouldn't need it, he thought. He was stripping everything out of *Passat* and replacing it with new gear being shipped from England. I admired him for his faith in the safe arrival of his ordered equipment, for his willingness to let us have the old antenna, and for the low price he was asking for it.

For weeks—ever since we had emerged from the Red Sea, with our jury antenna made from an old wire coathanger—our satnav passes had been erratic and infrequent. On some days we might get one or two indications of our position, but we could never trust them. This real antenna, which we had been able to acquire so far off the beaten yacht-tracks, was one prize; our other prize for patience was even better.

Months before we had arrived in Galle, a yacht built locally by a Danish commercial aircraft pilot who worked for a Sri Lankan airline had struck a "submerged object" at speed and been sunk on her maiden voyage. Word was that the "object" had been either a submarine lurking just below the surface of the sea, or a shipping container which had been washed overboard. Either one of these was a likely possibility close to a busy international shipping lane.

Before the vessel sank entirely, the owner and crew had managed to salvage several of her most valuable bits of gear. One of these, gossip had it, was a good, solid, British-built electric autopilot, an Autohelm 5000. It was in fact for sale, at a very reasonable price. But the airline pilot was on leave in Denmark, and would not be back in Galle for two weeks.

Two minutes after I heard that I made up my mind; we would wait for Svante's replacement. I knew very well the excellence of the Autohelm—it was legend among ocean sailors. It would take a good half of our ready money, but in the coming passages it would save that over and over again. This was the type of unit I had always wanted for *Outward Leg* but never been able to afford. We had not had time to wait for one in Israel for fear of missing the monsoon. Never again would we need a third crewman, with all the problems that involves. With an autopilot we would be free ourselves—once and for all—of the tyranny of the tiller in potentially deadly calms.

Four hours after we met the airline pilot and paid him for his autopilot, we had fitted it, in *Outward Leg*, cleared the authorities, and departed from Sri Lanka. Anyone who knows anything at all about autopilots and how they are custom-fitted to each individual vessel, will know what drilling and hammering and screwing and sawing, and cursing, and mumbling, and running after esoteric tools and bits and pieces, was involved in our task and how speedily we accomplished it.

Time and tide wait for no man. We had to hurry, it was Friday; besides the high tide, due at early evening, the Immigration port control police chief's office would close at five o'clock, and he, an ambitious, professional imprisoner, who kept an ever-sharp lookout for likely candidates for hospitality of his dank, concrete, iron-barred cells, held our ship's papers. We had to get to his office before he shot off home to his wife, family, and fanside comforts. We had to have those scraps of vital paper before we headed out into the full monsoon to tackle the Bay of Bengal, one of the most fluky-weathered, stormiest areas of ocean in the world. Without that natty nabob's nod we would be condemned to a whole week-end more in Sri Lanka, and any effort was worth avoiding that. As it was we cleared his gun-bedecked office with five minutes to spare before his office closed and the tide, taking its cue, it seemed, from the pistol-toting lord of the port, started to recede.

The four Tamil prisoners whom Svante had seen were still in their cell, all packed together in the heat (although there were empty cells all around them). They were open to public view, sitting on the floor, heavy chains around their black-gray ankles. A grin-ning, pension-serving elderly copper told us they had been there for six months without any charges being filed against them. He seemed proud of that, and looked as if yet another medal-ribbon might be due to him, to join the World War II British Defense and Victory medals, already displayed on his tunic.

As I studied the old rozzer, in his neatly pressed, British-style uniform, I felt angry and sick at heart. Mountains bore down on my soul. I stared for a full minute, silently, at that time-serving, uniformed groveler in his false colors, who had spent his life wait-ing for orders to bully. I gripped my stick, held my breath and my tongue, aching to lash him. Then, without a word I stomped out of that sinister place; *Outward Leg* and Atlantis needed me still. An empty cell was available; this was no time for an angry outburst.

Defense of what? Victory for what? I wondered bitterly as, without a word, Thomas shot off ahead to ready the dinghy. Carefully avoiding sacred Brahma cows, I hobbled painfully back over hundreds of yards of searing hot, dazzling-white gravel to the teetering ladder on the broken-down dockside wall torn between anger and relief. Five minutes later, as a downpour of monsoon rain sluiced us, we were under way.

It was the twenty-first of June. With our delay in Sri Lanka awaiting the return of the Danish airline pilot and the acquisition of our prized autopilot, we were now two months late on our voyage schedule, as we had laid it down in Istanbul ten months before. Now the southwest monsoon was well set in and blowing its head, and everyone else's hat, off.

Getting out of Galle harbor before dark, and clear of the shallows where heavy seas were breaking was nerve-wrenching. We hoisted the main, free-sheeted, even before we weighed the anchor. Thomas had also "stopped" the yankee jib onto the forestay, with very light thread, so that one mighty heave by me on the jib sheet would break all the "stops" and let the jib fly, ready to be trimmed immediately.

All of these preparations meant that if our engine for any reason failed us as we bashed and crashed our way out of Galle, we could, in a matter of two seconds, have the boat under working sail. It would be a very risky business. On all sides of the narrow navigation-channel were rocky shoal banks on which the full force of the mighty monsoon seas, unhindered all the way from Africa, fumed and roared. It had all looked picturesque enough on the postcards sold ashore by shouting touts; from the cockpit, as we shoved into the gloaming through the breakwater heads, it looked and sounded terrifying.

It wasn't that we mistrusted our Yannie. Ever since *Outward Leg* had left San Diego, even in the deep freeze of the German rivers, our little engine had served us loyally and well. It was a tiny machine, only twenty-two horsepower, but each and every one of those seas crashing into Galle Bay would have smashed a thousand London brewery cart-horses into quivering meat in seconds. Our main concern was not for the engine, as slow as it was, but for sand, stirred up from the bottom by the heavy breakers, which might block gallant Yannie's cooling system.

I'd kept my promise to the old sea god, I recalled as, wet with perspiration, I wrestled with the water tugging on the rudder. I'd moderated my language in places and at times, in Sri Lanka, when surely even the angels would have cursed. . . . My attention focused back on the fighting, heaving, pushing waves demanding careful concentration. Yet another huge sea broke over the bow, sending Thomas, secured by his safety harness, sliding in a welter of water, right aft, from the pulpit to the mast.

"All right, Mate!?" But I was drenched myself, up to my knees in surprisingly, shockingly cold seawater. The strange thing, as always with cold, was that I could feel it in my *leg that wasn't there.*

"Sshhpplltt!" And Thomas grinned at me.

The old sea god kept his word, and, after half an hour of relentless violence, *Outward Leg* found herself being bounced around in deep water at last.

As I heaved the wheel over and eased the mainsheet our main filled joyfully. I grabbed the jib sheet, hauled with all my might, broke every stop on the forestay and the yankee whipped out wing-and-wing with the main, like the shadow of a vast, huge, flailing rabbit jerking noisily out of some thin, sinister conjurer's hat.

I felt the wheel steady as the boat picked up speed . . . three knots . . . four . . . five . . . six . . . seven . . . eight. For ten glorious minutes, as Galle slid steadily out of sight in the lowering dusk, I steered the boat, glorying to be free. Then I remembered our newly acquired autopilot.

By now Thomas had slid down into the waddling cockpit. Under sail, at speed, running free and surfing, with the wind astern, *Outward Leg*'s movement was like a series of ever-faster exhilarating glides. The seas were high; even only a mile offshore in those parts, there were full ocean rollers.

We didn't say much. Thomas and I never did converse uselessly.

"?" He asked the unspoken question: "Shall we try out the autopilot?" I could see he was dying to switch it on. He was still wet through and dripping. His hair looked like a drowned hedgehog's.

I spoke out loud against the screeching of the wind on the stay wires. "Might as well. We haven't tried it yet. This is as good a place as any for a trial, Mate!"

Thomas opened the cockpit window to the engine compartment, behind which we'd fitted the autopilot's control panel. In the weird reflection of the subdued red light of the compass I could see his grimace as he searched blindly with his fingers for the right buttons to push.

There was a sudden unfamiliar noise from somewhere near my false leg. The wheel pulled itself round, while I yet gripped it, and, against my strength, pulled itself back again . . . and I knew that the boat was steering herself, holding a far more perfect course, before those seas, than I, who had been at it for almost fifty years, could ever hope to keep. It was like magic. Even when the log showed twelve knots—fourteen in a sudden surging surf—never, as I stared fascinated at the red glowing compass, did the boat veer more than ten degrees off our course—due east!

I sat back on the cockpit seat as the boat raced before the wind toward the Bay of Bengal, and thought of all the weary hours—days, months, years—of steering I had endured over the years, even after the wind vanes had been developed. But wind vanes had been nowhere near sensitive enough, to the minor changes of wind direction caused by the boats' great speed, to steer fast multihulls.

In *Outward Leg*, all the way around the world, until now, someone, either my crewmen or I, and mostly I, had been by the wheel to make adjustments when the wind vane's steering had erred. The whole way—all 22,500 miles of it. Whether under sail or power, whether with wind or without, whether on the sea or on rivers, the whole slog had been made under hand steering, or as close to it as I could remember.

As I gazed at the wheel moving as if of its own volition, I thought bitterly of the long years of poverty in *Outward Leg*, when I would have given, almost, an arm to have had this gear to ease a tremendous burden. It took an effort of liberality to accept the forces that had made steering so easy—almost painfully so—when previously it had taken from me so much effort, over more than half my life. The men who had invented and developed things like this had made child's play of what had been such a tremendous physical test of endurance. I was tempted to resent the ease with which modern sailors can cross an ocean. I'd known about the wonderful satellite-navigation systems (when the antennas didn't fail), and how they had taken a lot of craft, guile, and plain brainwork out of voyaging, and tempted many people out beyond the beaten, comparatively safer, paths of yachting, but I hadn't experienced ever before in my life this effortless, passengerlike situation where nothing was required except to *watch things*, even in a full gale of wind.

For a few moments I was sad. It was as if all the *humanity* had, somehow, been taken out of voyaging. But then I resolved that even if some of the magic appeared to me to have been taken out of one of the last areas of human endeavor where man is not subject to outside control, he would still be at the mercy of *things*. And the old sea god nodded his head and comforted me, and told me he'd make damned sure that his damp breezes would take care of electronic gadgets all right, and his violent banging would still knock quite a few more electricity-generating power units off their mountings, no fear, and he'd make bloody sure that any compulsive button-pushers who got too big for their boots and trusted *things* too much, and didn't learn the real ways of sail, properly, would get their rightful deserts and pile up on some godforsaken atoll reef in the middle of a watery, drinkless nowhere. Then I strangely felt better. There would always be many hazards for good, skilled men to overcome, and I rejoiced in our newfound ease, even in storm.

Thomas fretted for a few moments, and then was pleased, too.

Youth always did find it easier, I reflected, as I watched him holding on to the binnacle, staring at the red-glowing compass, his eyes half closed, to take for granted that anything they fixed would work—and rightly so, and so they should. But they also, I recalled from my own youth, took as gospel that anything that made effort easier was for the betterment of life; that I wasn't so sure about now. There were more things to a good life than ease, as I was sure that many an armchair- and office- bound landlubber would agree.

For a few minutes Thomas and I talked about this, and I wound up saying that I could see the point of climbing a mountain, but to land on the peak from a helicopter, just to see it, what was there to that?

"Ah . . . first you have to learn to fly your helicopter," said Thomas, and that shut me up. He was right. There's only one Truth, but so many different ways of viewing it, and youth will never see from the same angle as age, I told myself as I swung down into my after cabin.

We were well clear of the worst of the ground swell off southern Sri Lanka by then. There was much ship traffic passing east and west in the night to the south of us, but we could keep well north of it and still head due east. I wedged myself between the companionway ladder and the chart table and studied the rising and falling chart laid out in front of me. By rights and custom and all wise advice, we should first head south, even down as far as latitude 5° north, so as to avoid the worst of the hard blows that are brewed in the middle reaches of the Bay of Bengal. But we were going so fast, and so well, and "Mike"—in keeping with the navigator's tradition we had named our autopilot—was steering so fine, and the island of Phuket was only fourteen hundred miles away, almost due east—and that was our destination—"Why frig around heading south on a broad-reach for sixty or seventy miles?" I asked myself.

I flung down my pencil. I'd never used round ones that would roll about. *Outward Leg* lurched, all glowing red. The pencil jumped right off the chart table and hid itself under my berth lockers which were open to the air at the bottom for ventilation. Forgetting my leg I bent down to scrabble for it. The boat lurched again and over I went, crash on the cabin sole. This time I was lucky. I didn't bang my head on any sharp corner. It was nothing unusual—I must have been thrown a hundred times, for one reason or another, on that voyage. There was no point in calling for help. Thomas would never have heard me over the noise of the water and the wind as the boat was thrust through huge seas. There was even less reason to feel sorry for myself; there was no one else around. As I started to heave myself back "upright" I remembered my word to the old sea god. "Damn!" I muttered. Then, finally back leaning on the drunkenly moving chart-table, I quietly grinned to myself. *Outward Leg*, I reflected, must be wondering what the devil was wrong with me, such mild oaths had never been heard from the after cabin before Jebel Zuquair.

In the after cabin, by the dim red light over the table, the old sea god nodded in approval and observed that I was lucky—I was just the right age to be among the last of the old Victorians and among the first of the new. Now even Mr. Bowdler himself might deign to accompany me on some celestial voyage, he suggested, and disappeared, looking satisfied that he had done what no Bible puncher back home in Wales, no snot-nosed Bloomsbury-bred junior Royal Navy officer, had ever been able to even make me *think* of doing. At last I was choosing my words when I was *in extremis*; and that's a hell of a thing for a Welshman, and a mariner at that. I felt like Saint Paul after he'd picked himself up on his road to Damascus. I have never been habitually foulmouthed, as some critics, without thinking about it or reading my words closely, have assumed. But I have reported words as they truly were spoken by people who were, perhaps, not conscious at the time of the meaning of some of the words they used. And if they spoke in ignorance, *were* they foulmouthed?

Nursing my bruised ribs, I switched on our Zenith radio to wait for the BBC time signals. We were not yet sure that the newly acquired satnav antenna would operate correctly in a jerking vessel (as it turned out, it did).

Somebody in London was interviewing an Indian guru about Western attitudes toward Eastern philosophy. "Oh, yes," said the guru, "there is great and growing interest in our philosophy among modern Westerners, especially the young. The West has lost touch with things like nature, compassion, telepathy . . . and is turning to the East. . . ."

"Telepathy? Western attitudes . . . ?"

I'd forgotten my aching ribs. I very nearly punched the radio. I completely forgot the old sea god or my oath to him. Over the outside roar of water zooming along the ship's sides I shouted aloud at the blank-faced radio: "Telepathy . . . *bullshit!* . . . What in the name of fucking Jehoshaphat does he think bleeding radio *is* . . . but Western sodding telepathy . . . and a zillion times more effic—"

The program ended. The strains of "Lillibulero" issued forth, followed by the pips of the Greenwich time signal. (*Kyrie Eleison!*) I checked the chronometer—three seconds slow—and marked the date and time on the chart margin automatically as was my wont.

Then I switched off the little red chart-light, and listened for a few moments, over the roar and screeches of a trimaran in full progress over the ocean seas, to the odd, but soon to be comforting, sound of Mike laboring away in the night. Leaning back on my berth for my two hours' rest before my watch I excused myself to the old sea god saying "Well, it was only a couple of eggheads burbling in London, after all . . . it was nothing to do with the wind or the sea. . . ."

"All right, in that case . . ." he let me off. "I was going to say the same thing myself, anyway," he went on, kindly. "It's all right this time; you may hold the course and let her go. . . ."

I remembered I hadn't handed the watch over to Thomas properly. Like a reprieved convict creeping out of death row, I imagined, I hoisted myself up again, felt my way over the lurching after cabin, grabbed the companionway door handle, and opened it. A blast of cool air swept down from above. Thomas was sitting quietly, as was his custom, his feet thrust down the galley companionway, staring forward out into the black night. I called him. He turned and grinned at me. "Let her go, Thomas! Hold the course and let her go! East! *Oh Lord let her go!*"

Thomas nodded, and I, at peace with myself, returned, like a groggy drunk, over the bucking cabin-sole, back to my berth, to nurse my stump, still sore and very bruised.

The run east across the thousand miles of the Bay of Bengal was fast. We had, of course, teething problems with the electrical supply to the autopilot. We found that in heavy seas, when its power demand was heaviest, we had to charge the batteries every four hours or so, which meant running the engine at idling speed for an hour. But that used only a couple of liters of fuel each time, and was a small price to pay for the freedom we now had to stay away from the wheel, and yet know that the boat was well and truly on the course we had set her, and ordered from Mike.

Day in, day out, night in, night out, we ran before the wind under a sky covered with thick clouds, between heavy squalls, often soaked by driving rain. But the wind was always in the southwest, astern of us, so with the after dodger window-shield buttoned down in place we could have a comparatively dry cockpit. Of course, with the galley companionway facing aft, and with heavy rain driving through the gaps in our shield, we mostly had to shut the galley opening, but that was daisies in a bull's mouth to us. We could use the engine-room walkway and the after hatch. If Thomas was too hot in the forward cabin, he could always put his head down, while I kept watch, in the after cabin.

On the twenty-third of June we winged out our twin headsails and changed course very slightly, to east-northeast by northeast, as a current was carrying us southerly. Then the motion of *Outward Leg* was much smoother, as we allowed the running seas to overtake us, instead of being carried before the odd one now and again. Still she ran well, and we covered 176 miles, noon to noon.

By the twenty-sixth the wind was west-southwest and we decided it had changed its direction a few degrees because of the lay of the high mountainous island of Sumatra, to the east-southeast of us.

Daytime sailing was now a luxurious progress, with Mike in charge of steering. I read through *The Oxford Book of English Verse* again, to refresh my soul, and through the *Admiralty Pilot for the Malacca Strait*, to refresh myself on what we should expect when we reached Southeast Asian waters. I had brought our copy up to date in Cochin, at an Indian chart-dealer's store in Ernakulam. It's probable, when ocean sailors approach a coast, if they do it properly and read up on it, that they know more about the hazards and havens on any given shore than do the native mariners (away from their immediate home area).

On the twenty-sixth, a fine, dry day, we sighted our first ship since parting from the shipping lanes four days earlier. For want of any steering duties, I decided to test the newly repaired VHF hand-held radio. I hailed the ship, which, I could tell by her funnel marking, was South Korean. I kept, in the radio log, a record of our conversation:

Me: "Do you have any weather forecast?"
Ship: "Oh, weather she very fine, where you from?"
Me: "San Diego, California, by way of London."
Ship: "Oh, California very nice. Where you go?"
Me: "Phuket."

Ship: "Where that?"

Me: "Thailand."

Ship: "You go Thailand? . . . You come across Pacific? . . . You go wrong way!"

Me: "No. We did not come across Pacific. We came across Atlantic."

Ship: (Laugh) "Oh, hokay! Very good. You hokay. You go right way. We change watch. Good-bye!"

Thomas and I, and I do believe, *Outward Leg* too, were still laughing when the Korean's upperworks and mast sank below the horizon.

At noon on the twenty-seventh, after running free for almost a week on twin headsails, we sighted the southernmost island of the Nicobar group, Sambelong, hazy mountains under thick cloud. We knew—it was legend among Indian Ocean voyagers—that there would be no welcome for us in the Nicobars, nor in their sister group to the north, the Andaman Islands. These, like the Laccadive Islands we had passed to the west of India, were that country's fief (colonies, to be precise about it) and were jealously guarded from intruders. There were rumors about the reasons why, but the strongest ones were of Soviet missiles being based on some remote island, or a secret base for the Soviet Imperialist Navy.

I was monitoring the airwaves during my watches (now that I had, with Mike in charge, the opportunity to do it). Even as we lost most of the wind to the north of Sumatra, and started to plod slowly under the genniker alone, eastward across the Andaman Sea, I was picking up ham radio traffic between yachtspeople in Phuket and two yachts which had gone out to the rescue off an American powerboat whose engines had broken down off the Andamans. Now they had been arrested, it seemed, by the Indian Navy, and forced to go in to Port Blair, the chief settlement of the Andaman group. Apart from keeping a radio watch, there was little we could do. We were much too far west to be of any assistance. All we could do was listen in, in case there might be anything we could report when we arrived in Thailand. (As it turned out, India was courting the U.S.A. for a massive loan at that time, and so, a few days later, the yachts were all released with no penalties.)

We sighted the loom of Breueh light, on the northern tip of Sumatra, on the twenty-eighth. It was sixty miles from us, but in that cloudy darkness, it reached us through the rain squalls, as

Mike steered us on and on, in a dead-straight line for our destination.

By late morning on the twenty-ninth of June, with only two
hundred miles to go to Phuket Island, it was clear that the wind,
which had dropped to almost nothing during the night, was not
going to return for quite a while. As it dropped, the sky had cleared
completely of clouds, and the stars in their millions had been revealed, like scattered snow gleaming on an upturned bowl of black
crystal. On we plodded under Yannie and Mike, and occupied
ourselves during the fine day, not too hot, with cleaning up *Outward Leg* for her arrival in Thailand.

All the while our salvaged satnav antenna gave us regular po-
sition-fixes every couple of hours, even as Thomas also took his
morning, noon, and evening sights, as did I. We would have laid
a bet, if there had been any takers, as *Outward Leg* steadily approached Phuket Island, that she was the most tightly navigated
vessel east of Suez and west of Panama. We could have laid a fix
within twenty yards.

There were all kinds of rumors on the ocean grapevine about
western Thai waters and the Strait of Malacca. Rumors of piracy,
drug running, arms smuggling, and general skullduggery—maritime and shoreside—were rife, alongside the reports (accurate, as
it turned out) of the natural hazards of poorly charted waters and
unmarked rocks. In these circumstances, as in any other part of
the world where these problems are rampant, precise navigation
was vital, so that we could run into a Thai haven as directly as
possible, at right angles from seaward, and lessen the risk of en-
counters with small native craft. In hindsight our extreme care was
hardly needed (except for the natural hazards) but how were we
to know? Heading into a strange haven in most Third World countries can often feel like walking, pockets loaded and jewel-be-
decked, into a mugger's paradise. This was no new phenomenon.
It has always been so, except when the ruling navies of the world
were free to put down crime at sea instead of, as nowadays, merely
rattling their rockets at one another.

Our careful plotting might have been needed if the monsoon
had been blowing at full strength. In the southwest monsoon, the
west coast of Thailand was, generally, a very bad lee-shore, replete
with shoals and rocks, and it could be very dangerous for an ill-
navigated craft to approach in heavy weather. As it was, in fair

weather, with clear visibility, we picked up a sighting of a south-bound coaster on the thirtieth, after midnight, and by that we would have known, all other navigation apart, that we were over the one-hundred-fathom mark, and so, from the chart, about thirty miles off Thailand, west of Phuket Island.

That same day, in the late afternoon, we sighted, far away, the mountains of Thailand. It was too late in the day for a safe entering without a depth-sounder. About midnight, when we were five miles off the main island of Phuket we hove to, under no lights but keeping careful watch.

After taking bearings on a couple of known lights and making sure that all was clear around us, I settled back to rest on the cockpit seat. "Twenty-five thousand miles, as near as dammit, from San Diego! . . . Very nearly eleven thousand miles since I sat on this same seat in London! . . ." The thoughts, all the memories, dizzied me. I glanced down into the after cabin where Thomas was study-ing our chart in the red glow of the navigation lamp.

His spoken English was by now excellent, but he sometimes still had problems when reading, especially where consonant or-ders like "ph" and "f" were concerned.

"*Fuket* . . ." he murmured. "Is that how it's pronounced?"

I woke from my reverie. The old sea god nudged me. Next thing you knew we'd be drifting onto some rock . . . I grabbed the companionway hatch and leaned down. I put one finger to my lips: "Ssshii . . . sshh! don't say that, Thomas, for Chri— for crying out loud. It's *Peeeooket!*"

We entered Ao Chalong anchorage the next day, sounding our way through with the hand lead, then, to friendly waves of wel-come from busy native craft passing by, we anchored in ten feet of water, right where, months later, this book was written.

A handsome land before us rose up, up, through the beryl green of palm-tree glades and the bice emerald of plantations; amid the emerald mass the scarlet and gold of a temple glinted and beck-oned, up, up through meadows and pastures of celadon and char-treuse, up, up through the off-white citron and gold, ochers, sables and cobalts of high barren rocks, on up and up to a peak reflecting silver and gold from the morning sun into the cobalt-blue of the sky which hung above all, a silent benediction.

Thomas and I stood taking it all in for a moment or two. "What do we do now, Tristan?" he asked.

I turned away from my dreaming: "Do? . . . Do? We'll get the dinghy organized and get ourselves ashore, Mate. Let's get cleared in . . . the party's over . . . there's work to do!"

I went below to stow the binoculars. My eye caught again our chart of western Thailand. It showed much of the Kra Isthmus. The chart had been donated to us by a defunct shipping firm in London. Their official stamp was still on it. It was dated 1962.

Carefully, as Thomas moved on deck overhead, dragging the collapsed dinghy from its stowage, I studied the chart. I stared at fine, tiny lines, showing river mouths . . . "*River mouths* . . .?"

I reached for our tatty, beaten-up old atlas . . . but that's another story.

Epilogue

Within three months of *Outward Leg's* arrival in Thailand, Thomas Ettenhuber and I obtained and fitted out two native "longtail" boats, both with Yanmar engines. With these we started to train young handicapped natives from poor families to earn their own living fishing.

To do this we flew right around the world, via New York, Texas and Boston, and collected money, contracts and a false arm for one of our pilot trainees.

On the second leg of our flight we stopped off at Vienna to place the original of our *Danube Pilot* where we thought it surely belonged, and was welcome: with the Arts Department at the University of Vienna. From there, they promised, copies would be sent to the proper people all over Central and Eastern Europe. In that way we repaid the Czechoslovak police for their attempt to sink *Outward Leg* in the River Danube the previous year.

By early 1987, Thomas and I had established, in a palm-roofed barn, a shore base for Atlantis while I also wrote this book. In the same time we had explored south Thailand, for a viable route of a, later, successful first-ever crossing of the Kra Isthmus, by river and portage, with handicapped crews, in seagoing vessels.

We completed all this work by the end of April 1987. We were two months behind the deadline I had set in Istanbul . . . eight thousand miles away.

Envoi

Had I the heaven' embroider'd cloths
Enwrought with golden and silver light,
The blue and the dim and the dark cloths
Of night and light and the half light,
I would spread the cloths under your feet:
But I, being poor, have only my dreams;
I have spread my dreams under your feet;
Tread softly because you tread on my dreams.

    —W. B. Yeats,
       "Aed Wishes for the Cloths of Heaven"

List of Havens

Turkey

1. Bebek
2. Moda
3. Fernebache
4. Princes Islands
5. Tuzla
6. Haydarpasa
7. Asmalikoy
8. Gelibolu
9. Çanakkale
10. Bozcaada Island
11. Sivrice
12. Alibey
13. Ayvalik
14. Port Badlemi
15. Saip
16. Chesme
17. Sigasik
18. Teos Bay
19. Kusadashi
20. Karakoyu
21. Gumusluk
22. Bodrum
23. Gumbet Bay
24. Dacha
25. Kadirga Liman
26. Marmarice
27. Sanjit Island

Greece

28. Rhodes
29. Kastellorizon

Turkey

30. Kas

Cyprus

31. Paphos
32. Limassol
33. Larnaca

Israel

34. Haifa (Carmel Yacht Club)

251

35. 'Akko
36. Tel Aviv

Egypt

37. Port Fuad (Port Said)
38. Ismailia
39. Suez
40. Abu Suweira
41. El Sudr
42. Tawila Island
43. Sharm el Naka

Sudan

44. Inkeifal
45. Marsa Fijab
46. Marsa Arakiyai
47. Marsa Arus
48. Port Sudan
49. Suakin
50. Sheik Sa'id
51. Sumar Island
52. Taller-Taller Saghir Island

North Yemen

53. Jebel At Tair Islands
54. Jebel Zuquair ("Rattrap")
55. Zubair Islands, northwest
56. Zubair Islands, south bay
57. Bab el Mandeb, cape

South Yemen

58. Aden (Steamer Point)

Somalia

59. Gardafui, cape

India

60. Cochin
61. Ernakulam

Sri Lanka

62. Galle

Thailand

63. Phuket Island